Shop Design

teNeues

Editor:	Sabina Marreiros
Texts:	Heinfried Tacke
Translations:	SAW Communications, Dr. Sabine A. Werner, Mainz. Dr. Suzanne Kirkbright (English), Brigitte Villaumié (French), Silvia Gómez de Antonio (Spanish), Paola Lonardi (Italian)
Layout:	Kerstin Graf
Imaging:	Jan Hausberg

Produced by fusion publishing GmbH Stuttgart . Los Angeles
www.fusion-publishing.com

Published by teNeues Publishing Group

teNeues Publishing Company
16 West 22nd Street
New York, NY 10010, USA
Tel.: 001-212-627-9090
Fax: 001-212-627-9511

teNeues France S.A.R.L.
4, rue de Valence
75005 Paris, France
Tel: 0033-1-55 76 62 05
Fax: 0033-1-55 76 64 19

teNeues Book Division
Kaistraße 18
40221 Düsseldorf, Germany
Tel.: 0049-(0)211-994597-0
Fax: 0049-(0)211-994597-40

teNeues Ibérica S.L.
c/Velázquez, 57 6.° izda.
28001 Madrid, Spain
Tel.: 0034-(0)-657-13 21 33

teNeues Publishing UK Ltd.
P.O. Box 402
West Byfleet
KT14 7ZF, Great Britain
Tel.: 0044-1932-403509
Fax: 0044-1932-403514

teNeues
Representative Office Italy
Via San Vittore 36/1
20123 Milan
Tel.: 0039-(0)-347-76 40 551

www.teneues.com

ISBN-10:	3-8327-9104-3
ISBN-13:	978-3-8327-9104-9

© 2006 teNeues Verlag GmbH + Co. KG, Kempen

Printed in Italy

Picture and text rights reserved for all countries.
No part of this publication may be reproduced in any
manner whatsoever.

All rights reserved.

While we strive for utmost precision in every detail,
we cannot be held responsible for any inaccuracies,
neither for any subsequent loss or damage arising.

Bibliographic information published by Die Deutsche
Bibliothek. Die Deutsche Bibliothek lists this publication
in the Deutsche Nationalbibliografie; detailed bibliographic
data is available in the Internet at http://dnb.ddb.de

Contents

Introduction 8
Europe

Austria	Graz	Albrecht 7	18
	St. Pölten	Center Apotheke	22
France	Paris	Pierre Hermé Paris	26
	Paris	Louis Vuitton	30
	Paris	Moschino	38
	Paris	LaBulleKenzo	42
	Paris	Frédéric Malle Editions de Parfums	50
	Paris	Mandarina Duck	56
Germany	Berlin	Smart-Travelling Store	62
	Cologne	Apropos Cöln . The Concept Store	68
	Munich	Talbot Runhof	72
	Munich	Lebensart R. Wittgenstein	78
	Munich	Gianfranco Ferré	82
	Stuttgart	sigrun woehr	88

Italy	Milan	Spazio Bisazza	94
	Milan	La Perla Uomo	98
	Milan	Pasquale Bruni Showroom	104
	Milan	Moschino St. Andrea	108
	Milan	Paul Smith	112
	Milan	Gucci	118
	Milan	Viktor & Rolf Boutique	124
	Monza	tearose	132
	Rome	La Perla	136
Russia	Moscow	Byblos	142
	Moscow	Moschino Gum	146
United Kingdom	London	Porsche Design Store London	150
	London	Stella McCartney	154

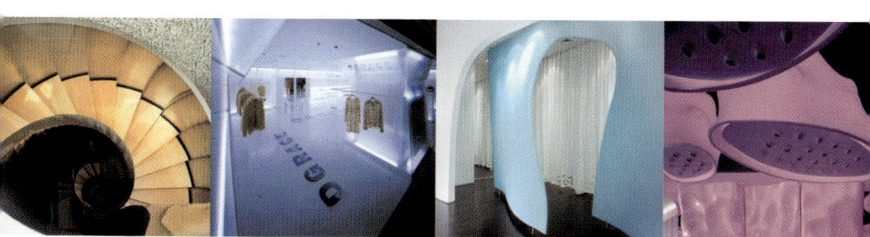

Americas

Brazil	Rio de Janeiro	Forum Rio	158
	São Paulo	Clube Chocolate	166
	São Paulo	Forum SP	174
Canada	Montréal	Holt Renfrew Montréal – Women's Couture Room	184
	Toronto	Holt Renfrew Toronto – Ground Floor	192
USA	Las Vegas	Fornarina	200
	Los Angeles	Snaidero Showroom	210
	Los Angeles	l.a. Eyeworks	218
	Los Angeles	Marni	226
	Los Angeles	Trina Turk LA	232
	New York	Carlos Miele	238
	New York	Fila	246
	New York	Malin + Goetz	254
	New York	Nike iD Studio	260
	New York	Catriona MacKechnie	266
	New York	Stella McCartney	272

Asia / Pacific

China	Hong Kong	Harvey Nichols Store	278
	Hong Kong	Emporio Armani	286
Japan	Fukuoka-ken	D-Grace Hakata	296
	Hiroshima	Stand	302
	Kyogo	Jayro White	308
	Osaka	Apple Store Shinsaibashi	316
	Tokyo	United Bamboo Store	322
	Tokyo	Hussein Chalayan Shop	328
	Tokyo	Le Salon	334
	Tokyo	Advanced Chique	342
	Tokyo	Gomme Laforet Harajuku	348
	Tokyo	Issey Miyake Men	354
	Tokyo	troisO	360
Korea	Seoul	Martine Sitbon	366

Architects & Designers   372

Introduction

Strolling down the shopping boulevards and in malls, everyone has experienced stumbling across a shop and being captured by its magical allure. The art of the discovery is not just down to the seductive power of prettily arranged items, which you had your eye on for a long time. No, the magic emerges from the entire store.
Creativity is applied more and more to the design of a retail outlet as an adventure space. In terms of architecture and design, many shops present themselves as a spatial artwork, giving maximum exposure to the most desirable goods. In this case, shop design means setting the scene in grand style. Internationally, the competition is unleashed to see who can attract top designers to work on their shops. This is by no means restricted to exclusive brands like Porsche, Prada or Paul Smith. Eyeglass shops, drugstores, travel agencies, even book stores are all equally entering in the competition.

This book features more than 50 prominent examples, many of them from international metropolises: innovative and award-winning concepts, created by the stars of the fashion world. The designs are definitely starting to turn the world upside down, such as in the Viktor & Rolf Milan boutique. Internationally renowned design temples feature alongside discoveries that are worth taking a look at. All the shops are beautifully illustrated, with informative captions both about the shops as well as the designers and architects. This book makes an inspiring reference guide: for experts and design connoisseurs, and for everyone who enjoys the simple pleasure of shopping in exclusive stores.

Heinfried Tacke

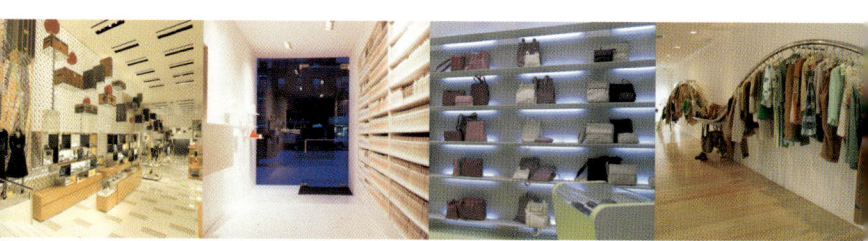

Einleitung

Wer hat nicht schon einmal die Erfahrung gemacht, beim Bummeln durch Einkaufsstraßen und Passagen auf einen Laden zu stoßen, von dem eine magische Anziehungskraft ausgeht? Dabei wirkt nicht nur die Kraft der Verführung durch hübsch dekorierte Auslagen, die man schon lange begehrt. Nein, vom Shop als Ganzes geht diese Magie aus. Immer mehr Kreativität wird darauf verwandt, das Ladenlokal als solches zu einem Erlebnisraum zu gestalten. Viele Läden präsentieren sich als ein Raumkunstwerk aus Architektur und Design und rücken die angepriesenen Waren exponiert ins rechte Licht. Shop Design bedeutet insofern Kulisse im großen Stil. Über den gesamten Globus hinweg hat sich darüber ein Wettbewerb entsponnen, wer wen unter den Großen des Designs für die Gestaltung seiner Geschäfte gewinnen konnte. Dies beschränkt sich keineswegs auf Nobelmarken wie Porsche, Prada oder Paul Smith. Brillenläden, Apotheken, Reisebüros, ja selbst Buchhandlungen treten in diesen Wettbewerb gleichermaßen mit ein.

Dieser Band zeigt mehr als 50 herausragende Beispiele, viele davon aus den Metropolen dieser Welt: innovative Konzepte, von den Stars der Szene gestaltet und mit Preisen ausgezeichnet. Dabei stellen die Entwürfe durchaus schon einmal die Welt auf den Kopf wie etwa in der Mailänder Boutique von Viktor & Rolf. So stehen weltweit bekannte Designertempel neben sehenswerten Entdeckungen. Alle Shops sind reich bebildert und mit informativen Texten sowohl zu den Shops als auch zu Designern und Architekten versehen. Das macht das Buch zu einem inspirierenden Nachschlagewerk: für Experten und Freunde des Designs genauso wie für all jene, die einfach nur Freude am schönen Einkaufen haben.

Heinfried Tacke

Introduction

Qui n'a pas fait l'expérience, en flânant dans les rues commerçantes et les passages, de tomber en arrêt devant un magasin d'où se dégage une force d'attraction magique ? Il ne s'agit pas là seulement de la puissance de la tentation éprouvée face à des objets joliment décorés que l'on convoite depuis longtemps. Non, c'est le magasin en soi qui dégage cette magie.
Une part de créativité de plus en plus grande s'emploie à faire du magasin même un espace événementiel. Les espaces de vente de nombreux magasins se transforment en œuvres d'art alliant architecture et design et fournissent aux objets exposés ainsi mis en valeur l'éclairage adéquat. Aménager un magasin revient à créer un décor de grand style. Tout autour du monde, il s'est engagé une compétition : qui peut débaucher qui parmi les grands noms du design pour la décoration de ses magasins. Ceci ne se limite nullement aux marques de prestige telles que Porsche, Prada ou Paul Smith. Les opticiens, les pharmacies, les agences de voyage, et même les librairies entrent pareillement dans la concurrence.

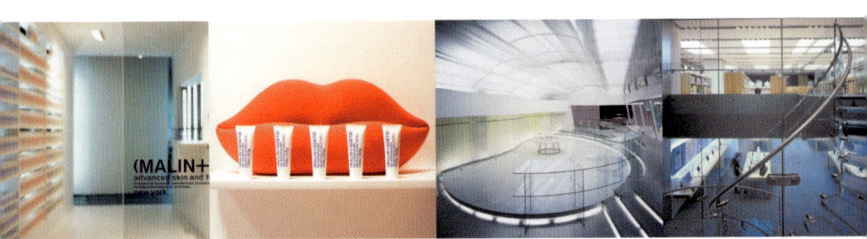

Cet ouvrage présente plus de 50 exemples exceptionnels ; nombre d'entre eux situés dans les grandes métropoles de ce monde : des concepts innovateurs, élaborés par des stars dans ce domaine et récompensés par des prix. A cet égard les projets mettent le monde sens dessus dessous, comme par exemple le magasin milanais de Viktor & Rolf. Des temples du design connus dans le monde entier se trouvent ainsi côte à côte avec de remarquables découvertes. Tous les magasins sont richement illustrés et accompagnés de renseignements tant sur les magasins que sur les concepteurs et les architectes. Ceci en fait un ouvrage de référence, source d'inspiration pour les experts et les amateurs de design mais aussi pour tous ceux qui éprouvent simplement du plaisir à faire de beaux achats.

Heinfried Tacke

Introducción

¿Quién no se ha topado alguna vez con una tienda que irradiaba una mágica atracción mientras paseaba de compras por las calles y los centros comerciales de la ciudad? Esta fuerza no solo proviene de la seducción de unos bonitos escaparates decorados con los objetos deseados. No, la magia proviene de la tienda como unidad.
Cada vez se emplea más la creatividad para que el diseño de estos interiores se convierta en una experiencia. Muchos locales se presentan como obras de arte espaciales de arquitectura y diseño para resaltar los productos expuestos. Por eso shop design significa escenificación a lo grande. Por todo el mundo se ha extendido una especie de rivalidad para ver quién puede atraer a alguno de los más grandes diseñadores para que decore sus tiendas. Y esta carrera no se limita a las primeras marcas como Porsche, Prada o Paul Smith; tiendas de gafas, farmacias, agencias de viaje, incluso librerías participan también en esta competición.

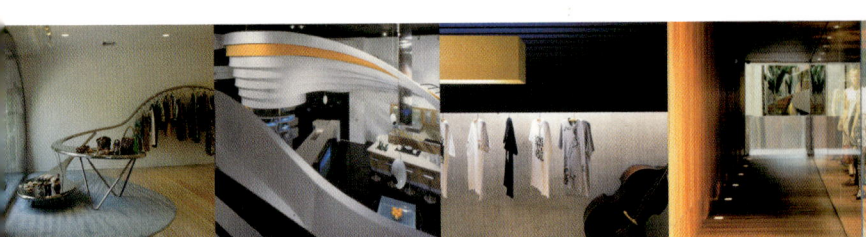

Esta obra muestra más de 50 ejemplos sobresalientes localizados la mayoría de ellos en las metrópolis del mundo: conceptos innovadores creados por las estrellas de la escena del diseño y reconocidos con premios que, como la boutique milanesa de Viktor & Rolf, llegan a poner el mundo del revés. De este modo aparecen por todo el mundo conocidos templos del diseño emparejados a descubrimientos dignos de ver. Todas las tiendas se presentan con un gran número de imágenes y textos informativos referentes tanto a los locales como a sus diseñadores. Esta combinación convierte el libro en una inspiradora obra de consulta, tanto para los expertos y amantes del diseño, como para todos aquellos que disfrutan con las compras.

Heinfried Tacke

Introduzione

A chi non è capitato almeno una volta, passeggiando fra vie e gallerie commerciali, di imbattersi in un negozio dal fascino tutto particolare? Non è solo il potere della seduzione esercitato dagli oggetti del desiderio sapientemente esposti. No, è l'effetto magico che nasce nell'insieme.
Va delineandosi sempre più chiaramente la tendenza a voler trasformare il punto vendita in uno spazio creativo a tutto tondo. Molti negozi si presentano come capolavori di architettura e design nei quali la merce trova la giusta valorizzazione. In questo senso shop design è sempre più sinonimo di contesto in grande stile. A tutte le latitudini e longitudini sembra essere in atto una competizione per conquistare i grandi nomi del design. E questo non si limita affatto ai marchi esclusivi come Porsche, Prada o Paul Smith. Si lanciano in gara anche negozi di ottica, farmacie, agenzie di viaggio e perfino librerie.

In questo volume vengono presentati oltre 50 esempi prestigiosi di shop design, molti dei quali contestualizzati nelle metropoli più importanti del mondo: formule innovative ideate dai protagonisti d'eccellenza del mondo del design ed insignite di premi autorevoli. Soluzioni fuori le righe che non esitano a capovolgere la prospettiva, come la boutique milanese upsidedown di Viktor & Rolf. Accanto a templi del design di fama internazionale trovano posto chicche tutte da scoprire. Immagini numerose e testi esaustivi sulle boutique nonché su architetti e designer impreziosiscono di dettagli il volume fino a farne un'opera di consultazione da cui trarre ispirazione, destinata ad esperti ed appassionati di design tanto quanto a tutti coloro che amano lo shopping di lusso.

Heinfried Tacke

The designers at PURPUR emphasize exclusivity for Albrecht 7 for all items of fashionable footwear. The shop's eye-catching feature looks like an over-sized shoe box. The shelf wall at the rear is reminiscent of a drugstore's interior. As a contrast, the styling of the display area is supposed to look like snowflakes.

Die Designer von PURPUR betonen für Albrecht 7 Exklusivität in Sachen Schuhmode. Wie ein überdimensionierter Schuhkarton erscheint der zentrale Blickfang inmitten des Shops. Die Schrankwand dahinter erinnert an das Interieur einer Apotheke. Das Styling der Auslage soll dagegen wie Schneekristalle wirken.

Les designers de PURPUR soulignent l'exclusivité pour Albrecht 7 dans la mode de la chaussure. Au centre du magasin, un carton à chaussures surdimensionné accroche le regard. A l'arrière, l'armoire murale rappelle l'intérieur d'une pharmacie. Les étalages en revanche sont stylisés en cristaux de neige.

Los diseñadores de PURPUR acentúan para Albrecht 7 la exclusividad de sus zapatos. El elemento del centro de la tienda se asemeja a una caja de zapatos de dimensiones gigantescas. La pared de armarios del fondo recuerda al interior de una farmacia. En cambio, los escaparates parecen, por su diseño, cristales de nieve.

I designer di PURPUR sottolineano per Albrecht 7 l'esclusività delle calzature della griffe. Al centro della boutique un'enorme scatola da scarpe polarizza l'attenzione di chi entra. La parete di elementi componibili ricorda l'interno di una farmacia, mentre lo styling della merce in esposizione vuole suscitare l'effetto dei cristalli di neve.

PURPUR. ARCHITEKTUR Toedtling, Laengauer, Boric und Loebell

Getreidemarkt 14
1010 Wien
Austria

Brockmanngasse 5
8010 Graz
Austria
www.purpur.cc

Photos by Hertha Hurnaus

Albrecht 7

Albrechtgasse 7
8010 Graz
Austria
www.wolfensson.com

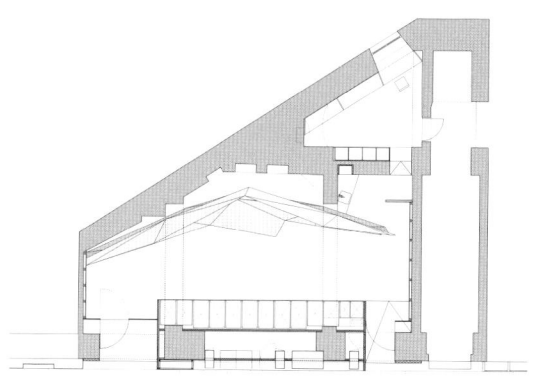

The shelf space is designed to give the drugstore an inviting look. The architects used curved partition walls to achieve this. At the same time, the shelves seem strictly regulated with drawers and containers. The dominant white in the room represents the classic color of a pharmacist's coat.

Die Regale sind so ausgerichtet, dass die Apotheke einladend wirkt. Dazu setzen die Architekten geschwungene Trennwände ein. Gleichzeitig zeigen sich die Regale streng geordnet mit Schubfächern und Behältern. Das dominante Weiß im Raum steht für die klassische Farbe des Apothekerkittels.

Les étagères sont disposées de façon à rendre la pharmacie accueillante. Pour cela, les architectes font appel à des cloisons en courbe. En même temps, les étagères sont bien ordonnées, avec des tiroirs et des récipients. Le blanc, couleur classique de la blouse du pharmacien, domine dans la pièce.

La disposición de las estanterías hace que la farmacia parezca invitar a entrar. Para conseguir este efecto los arquitectos han empleado tabiques curvos. Al mismo tiempo las estanterías presentan un estricto orden con cajones y recipientes. El blanco, color dominante del espacio, evoca el color clásico de las batas de los farmacéuticos.

La disposizione delle scaffalature è un invito ad entrare. L'effetto accattivante è stato potenziato dagli architetti con l'impiego di pareti divisorie dalle linee morbide che fungono da contrasto con l'ordine rigoroso degli elementi espositivi dotati di cassetti e contenitori. Il bianco imperante è una reminiscenza del colore classico del camice del farmacista.

PURPUR. ARCHITEKTUR Toedtling, Laengauer, Boric und Loebell

Getreidemarkt 14　　Brockmanngasse 5
1010 Wien　　8010 Graz
Austria　　Austria
　　www.purpur.cc

Photos by Hertha Hurnaus

Center Apotheke

Daniel-Gran-Straße 13
3100 St. Pölten
Austria

Center Apotheke

If it were not for the strong, fluorescent color and light-plays, then the store would be another example of cool, rectangular architecture. The translucent surfaces of the display cabinets and walls appear to exert a magical power of attraction, diverting the customers' glance to the sweet delicacies in this confectioner's.

Wären nicht die starken, fluoreszierenden Farb- und Lichtspiele, dann wäre der Store ein weiteres Beispiel kühl-rechtwinkliger Architektur. Die transluziden Flächen der Vitrinen und Wände erscheinen jedoch magisch anziehend und lenken den Blick der Kunden auf die süßen Auslagen in dieser Konfiserie.

S'il n'y avait ces intenses jeux de couleurs et de lumières fluorescentes, le magasin ne serait qu'un exemple de plus d'austère architecture à angle droit. Les surfaces translucides des vitrines et des murs attirent comme par enchantement le regard des clients sur les délicieux étalages de cette confiserie.

Si no fuera por los fuertes juegos fluorescentes de luz y color, esta tienda sería otro ejemplo de arquitectura fría de líneas rectangulares. Las superficies translúcidas de las vitrinas y de las paredes parecen ejercer una mágica atracción desviando la vista de los clientes hacia los dulces de esta confitería.

Se non fosse per gli effetti cromatici e di luce fortemente giocati sulle fluorescenze, il Pierre Hermé Paris store non sarebbe altro che un ulteriore esempio di architettura fredda e geometrica. Le superfici traslucide di teche e pareti sprigionano invece un fascino che polarizza magicamente lo sguardo sulle deliziose creazioni di pasticceria.

Christian Biecher & Associes

14 Rue Crespin-du-Gast
75011 Paris
France
www.biecher.com

Photos by Luc Boegly

Pierre Hermé Paris

185 Rue de Vaugirard
75015 Paris
France
www.pierreherme.com

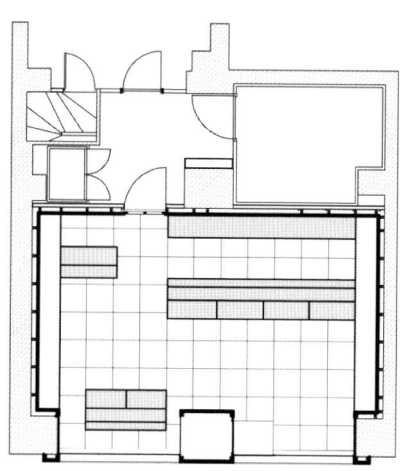

28 | Pierre Hermé Paris

Pierre Hermé Paris | 29

The Champs-Élysées site is Louis Vuitton's largest international store. For architects Peter Marino and Eric Carlson the relaunch was a success. They created a unique luxury landscape, appearing multi-faceted and radiating a sophisticated atmosphere. High value was placed on use of top-quality materials.

Das Objekt auf den Champs-Élysées ist der größte Store weltweit von Louis Vuitton. Mit dem Relaunch gelang den Architekten Peter Marino und Eric Carlson eine einzigartige Luxuslandschaft, die sich facettenreich zeigt und eine mondäne Atmosphäre verströmt. Viel Wert wurde auf die Verwendung hochwertiger Materialien gelegt.

L'établissement sur les Champs-Élysées est le plus grand magasin de Louis Vuitton au monde. Ce remodelage réussi des architectes Peter Marino et Eric Carlson crée un paysage de luxe unique aux multiples facettes irradiant une atmosphère sophistiquée. Ils ont accordé beaucoup d'importance à l'emploi de matériaux de haute qualité.

Esta tienda situada en los Champs-Élysées es la más grande de la firma Louis Vuitton en el mundo. Con su relanzamiento los arquitectos Peter Marino y Eric Carlson han creado un ambiente único de lujo polifacético que irradia una atmósfera mundana. Se ha dado especial importancia al uso de materiales exclusivos.

Il Louis Vuitton store sugli Champs-Élysées è il più grande store monomarca della griffe al mondo. Con la riapertura gli architetti Peter Marino ed Eric Carlson sono riusciti a dar vita ad uno straordinario tempio del lusso, una struttura eclettica dal fascino tutto mondano. Di assoluta priorità: l'uso di materiali esclusivi.

Peter Marino Architects

150 East 58th Street
36th floor
New York, NY 10022
USA

Carbondale, Eric Carlson

54 Rue Etienne Marcel
75002 Paris
France

Photos by Stéphane Muratet / Louis Vuitton
Vincent Knapp / Louis Vuitton

Louis Vuitton

101 Avenue des Champs-Élysées
75008 Paris
France
www.louisvuitton.com

Louis Vuitton | 33

Louis Vuitton | 35

36 | Louis Vuitton

Louis Vuitton | 37

At first sight, what suggests minimalism turns out after a closer look to be a puzzle of many individual parts. In Moschino's Parisian store, Sean Dix turns fashion itself into the central theme: columns are created out of stacks of fabric; chandeliers are made out of blown-glass shoes. A fascinating feature: the sales counter's lace-work.

Was zunächst minimalistisch anmutet, erweist sich bei näherer Betrachtung als ein Puzzle aus vielen Einzelteilen. Sean Dix thematisiert im Pariser Store von Moschino die Mode als solche: Aus Stoffballen entstehen Säulen, aus gläsernen Schuhen werden Kronleuchter. Faszinierend: Die Spitzenarbeit des Verkaufstresen.

Ce qui, tout d'abord, semble minimaliste se révèle être, en y regardant de près, un puzzle composé de nombreuses pièces détachées. Dans le magasin parisien de Moschino conçu par Sean Dix, la mode même est le thème central : des piles de tissus deviennent des colonnes, des chaussures en verres soufflé des lustres. Fascinant : le travail de dentelle des comptoirs.

Una composición en principio minimalista se descubre como un puzzle de numerosas piezas al observarla más detenidamente. En la tienda parisina de Moschino, Sean Dix convierte la moda en el tema central de su diseño: las columnas evocan pilas de tela, zapatos de cristal soplado se convierten en lámparas de araña. Fascinante la obra de encaje de los mostradores.

Ciò che al primo sguardo appare minimalista è in realtà solo il tassello di un puzzle elaborato. Nel Moschino store di Parigi, opera di Sean Dix, ogni singolo dettaglio è un omaggio alla moda: le colonne sono a ben vedere composte di balle di stoffa, i lampadari a corona di scarpe fatte in vetro soffiato. Di gran fascino: i merletti dei banconi di vendita.

Sean Dix

Alzaia Naviglio Grande 14
20144 Milan
Italy
www.seandix.com

Photos by Benoit Teilet

Moschino

32 Rue de Grenelle
75007 Paris
France

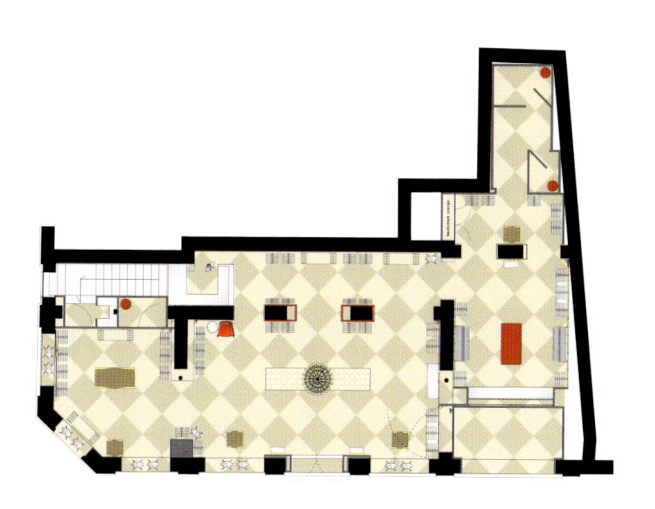

40 | Moschino

Moschino | 41

Allowing yourself some pampering is key at LaBulleKenzo in Paris. The spa also includes a boutique, offering exclusive health-care products. Both facilities are presented in a world full of contrasts: here, artificial and natural fabrics aim to sensitize all five senses.

Sich verwöhnen zu lassen steht im Mittelpunkt von LaBulleKenzo in Paris. Zum Spa gehört auch eine Boutique, die ausgewählte Pflegeprodukte offeriert. Beide Objekte präsentieren sich in einer Welt voller Kontraste: artifizielle und natürliche Stoffe zielen hier auf die Sensibilisierung aller fünf Sinne.

A LaBulleKenzo à Paris, le client peut se relaxer. Le Spa comprend également une boutique proposant des produits de soins corporels exclusifs. Les deux espaces sont présentés dans un monde plein de contrastes : des matières artificielles et naturelles visent à sensibiliser nos cinq sens.

En LaBulleKenzo, París, todo gira en torno al bienestar del cliente. El spa incluye una *boutique* con exclusivos productos para el cuidado. Ambos espacios se presentan en un mundo lleno de contrastes: materiales artificiales y naturales buscan despertar los cinco sentidos.

Farsi coccolare è la parola d'ordine alla spa LaBulleKenzo di Parigi. Alla spa è annessa anche una boutique dove si trovano in vendita esclusivi prodotti per la cura del corpo. L'intero spazio benessere si presenta come un universo pieno di contrasti, in cui artificialità e naturalezza sono sapientemente dosate per stimolare tutti e cinque i sensi.

Emmanuelle Duplay

Photos by Markus Bachmann

LaBulleKenzo

1 rue du Pont Neuf
75001 Paris
France
www.labullekenzo.com

44 | LaBulleKenzo

LaBulleKenzo | 45

LaBulleKenzo

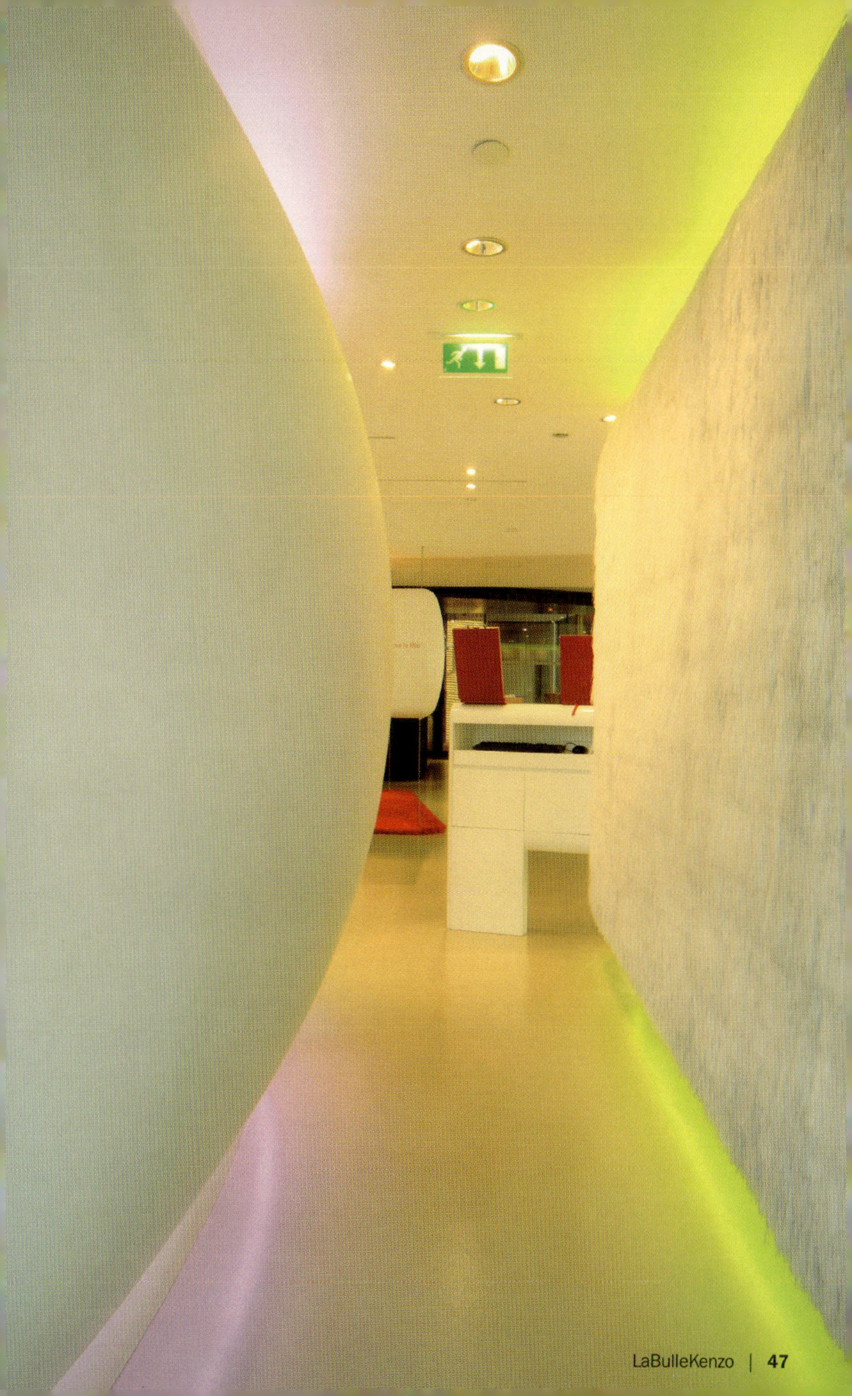

48 | LaBulleKenzo

LaBulleKenzo | 49

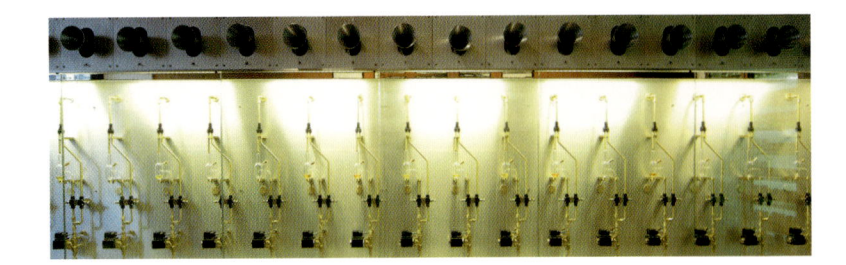

Patrick E. Naggar's inspiration for this store was a laboratory situation, where the special feature is a machine, modeled on designs by Jules Verne, and allowing the fragrant aroma of a perfume to be sprayed about. Overall, the design's impact is as concentrated as the perfume essences.

Patrick E. Naggar nimmt für diesen Store die Situation in einem Labor zum Vorbild. Besonderer Clou darin ist eine Maschine nach den Entwürfen von Jules Verne, mit der sich die Duftnoten eines Parfums versprühen lassen. Insgesamt wirkt das Design so konzentriert wie die Essenzen.

Patrick E. Naggar s'est inspiré pour ce magasin d'un décor de laboratoire. Le clou de cet aménagement est une machine d'après les ébauches de Jules Verne servant à vaporiser la note d'un parfum. L'impact du design dans son ensemble semble aussi concentré que les essences.

Para esta tienda Patrick E. Naggar se ha inspirado en un laboratorio. Especialmente llamativa es la máquina inspirada en los bocetos de Julio Verne con la que se pueden pulverizar las notas aromáticas de un perfume. En conjunto el diseño produce un efecto concentrado, como las esencias.

Per questo store Patrick E. Naggar ha tratto ispirazione da quanto accade in un laboratorio: Clou di particolare effetto è una macchina costruita su modello di Jules Verne con la quale si possono spruzzare le fragranze di un profumo. Nell'insieme stupisce l'analogia di fondo fra la concentrazione del design e delle essenze profumate.

Patrick E. Naggar Architect

189 Rue Saint-Honoré
75001 Paris
France

Photos by Markus Bachmann

Frédéric Malle Editions de Parfums

140 Avenue Victor Hugo
75116 Paris
France
www.editionsdeparfums.com

52 | Frédéric Malle Editions de Parfums

Frédéric Malle Editions de Parfums | 53

54 | Frédéric Malle Editions de Parfums

Frédéric Malle Editions de Parfums | 55

As if it is a single yellow-gray piece—that's the effect of the shop design for the Mandarina Duck brand. Organically shaped displays emerge from the floor, directing your gaze towards the arrangement of bags. The illuminated shelves behind the display add a consistent structure to the design.

Wie aus einem gelb-grauen Guss – so erscheint das Shop-Design für das Label Mandarina Duck. Aus dem Boden wachsen organisch geformte Displays, die den Blick auf das Arrangement der Taschen lenken. Dahinter bringen die beleuchteten Regalborde eine gleichmäßige Struktur in die Gestaltung.

Sorti d'une seule coulée jaune-gris : c'est l'impression que donne le design du magasin pour l'enseigne Mandarina Duck. Des comptoirs aux formes organiques surgissent du sol et guident le regard sur la présentation des sacs. En arrière-plan les étagères illuminées apportent une structure cohérente à l'agencement.

Como una fusión de amarillo y gris, esta es la sensación que transmite el diseño de esta tienda de Mandarina Duck. Los mostradores surgen del suelo con sus formas orgánicas y dirigen la vista del observador hacia la disposición de los bolsos. Detrás, las estanterías iluminadas introducen en el diseño una estructura homogénea.

Come creato da un'unica pennellata giallo-grigia, ecco l'effetto dello shop design della griffe Mandarina Duck. Dal pavimento sembrano spuntare elementi espositivi dalle forme organiche che focalizzano l'attenzione sulla disposizione delle borse. Sullo sfondo la scaffalatura illuminata conferisce all'allestimento una struttura ordinata.

Studio X Design Group

Treviso, Italy
London, England
www.stxdesign.com

Photos by Studio X Design Group

Mandarina Duck

36 Rue Etienne Marcel
75002 Paris
France
www.mandarinaduck.com

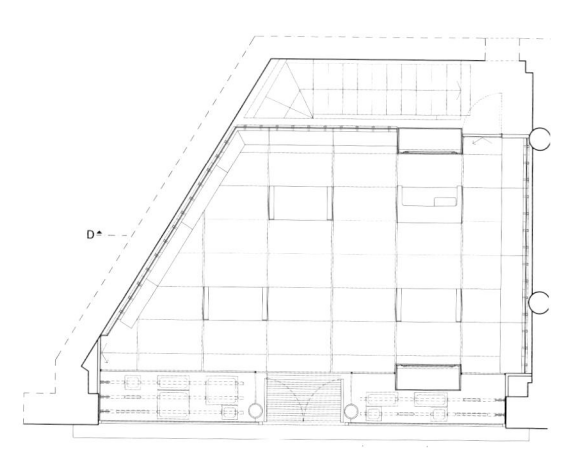

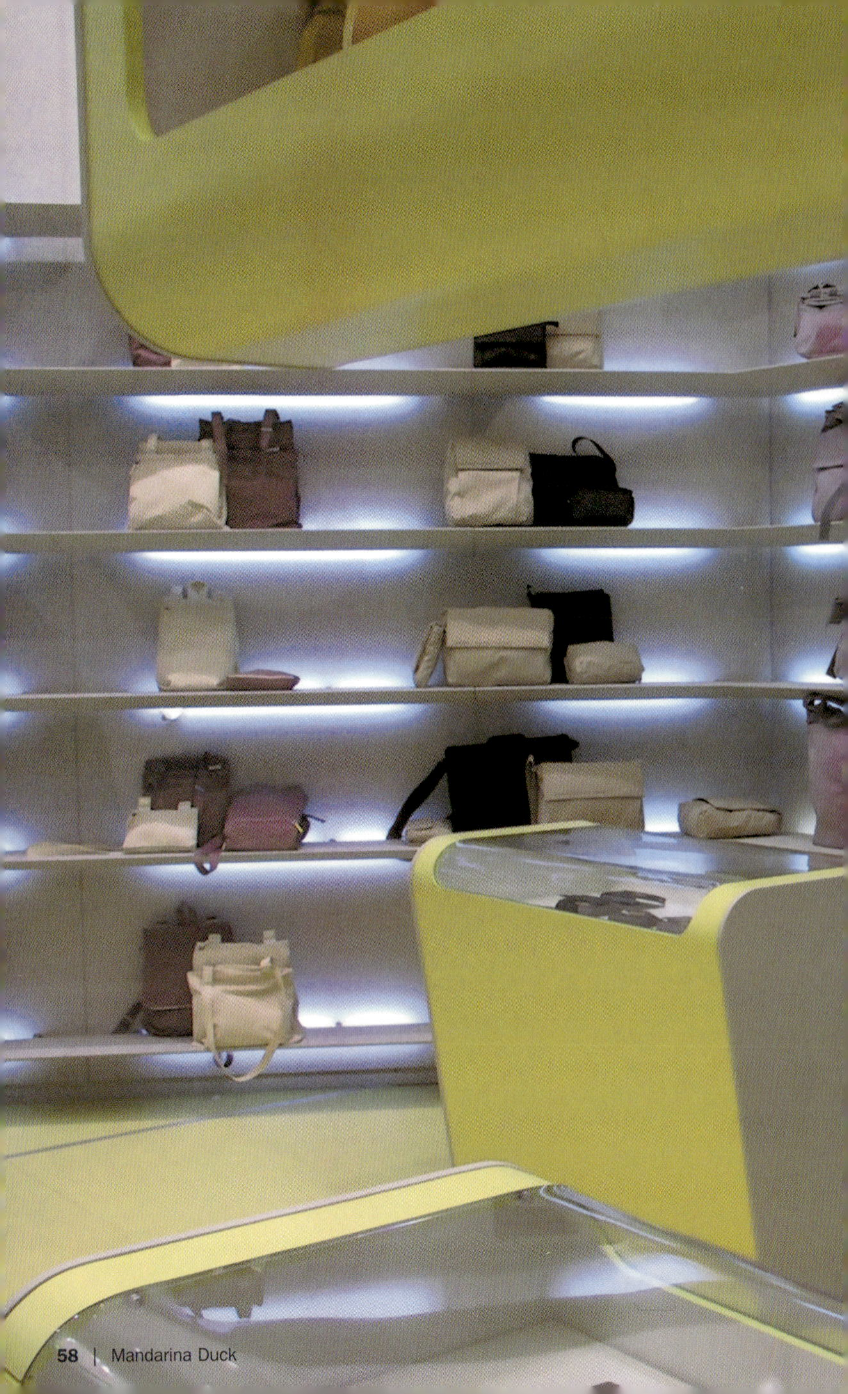

Mandarina Duck | 59

60 | Mandarina Duck

Mandarina Duck | **61**

Products in this Berlin store range from city tours to travel utensils, and deli-products to fashion items. Hybrid figures serve as clothing rails, with a wall highlighting individual products. The special feature is a slate blackboard with an integrated screen.

Das Angebot dieses Stores in Berlin reicht von Städtetouren über Reiseutensilien und Deli-Produkte bis hin zu Modeartikeln. Hybride Figuren dienen als Kleiderständer, eine Wand hebt einzelne Produkte als Highlights hervor. Spezieller Clou ist eine Schiefertafel, in die ein Monitor integriert ist.

La gamme des produits de ce magasin berlinois va des visites guidées aux articles de mode et des ustensiles de voyage aux produits fins. Des figures hybrides servent de portemanteaux, un mur met divers produits individuellement en relief. La grande originalité est un tableau noir en ardoise avec écran intégré.

La oferta de esta tienda de Berlín incluye desde guías de ciudades hasta artículos de moda pasando por utensilios de viaje y *delicatessen*. Figuras híbridas actúan como percheros mientras que una pared resalta productos aislados. Especialmente llamativa es la pizarra, donde se ha integrado una pantalla.

Nello Smart-Travelling Store di Berlino l'offerta spazia dai tour turistici agli articoli di moda passando per gli utensili da viaggio e i prodotti deli. Delle figure ibride fungono da attaccapanni a stelo, singoli prodotti presentati come pezzi forte trovano risalto su una parete. Clou tutto speciale: una lavagna in ardesia con monitor integrato.

studio aisslinger

Oranienplatz 4
10999 Berlin
Germany
www.aisslinger.de

Photos by Steffen Jaenicke, Nicola Bramigk

Smart-Travelling Store

Münzstraße 21hh
10178 Berlin
Germany
www.smart-travelling.net

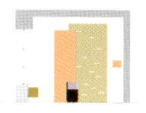

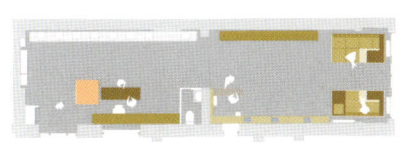

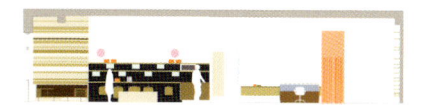

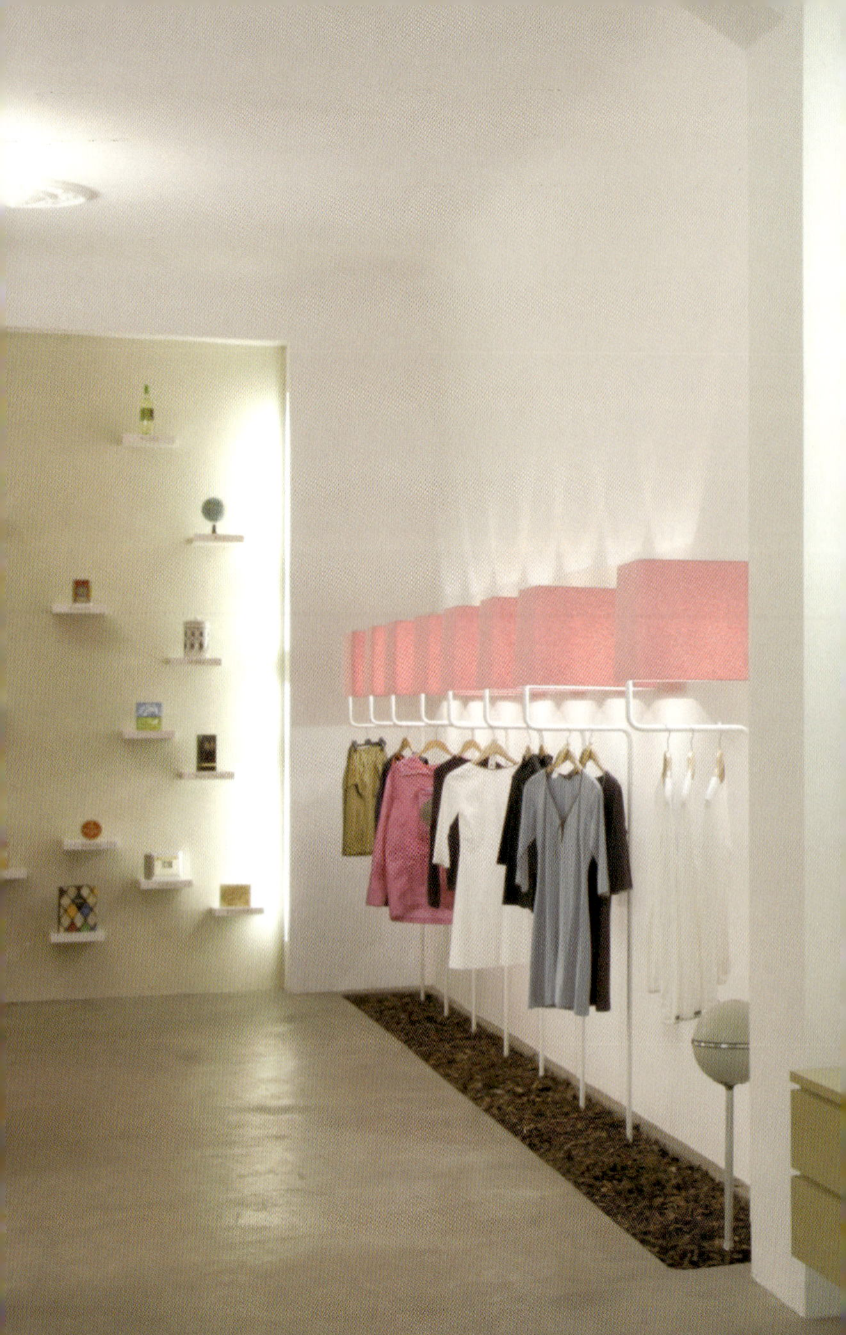

Smart-Travelling Store | **65**

66 | Smart-Travelling Store

Smart-Travelling Store | 67

The Apropos store tantalizes with an exclusive mix from various walks of life: high-quality fashion and trend items are combined with a spa and restaurant. The store design underpins this exclusive aspiration, focusing on clarity and space. Individual shop zones are emphasized by colors.

Der Store von Apropos lockt mit einem exklusiven Mix aus verschiedenen Lebensbereichen: Hochwertige Mode- und Trendartikel verbinden sich mit einem Spa und einem Restaurant. Die Gestaltung des Stores unterstützt diesen exklusiven Anspruch und setzt auf Klarheit und Weite. Durch Farben werden einzelne Ladenzonen hervorgehoben.

Le mélange exclusif de différents domaines de la vie proposé par le magasin Apropos est alléchant : articles de mode et objets tendance de haute qualité se mêlent à un spa et un restaurant. Le design reflète l'exigence d'exclusivité et mise sur la clarté et l'espace. Chaque partie du magasin est mise en valeur par de la couleur.

La atracción de Apropos radica en la exclusiva mezcla de los diferentes ámbitos de la vida: moda de primera calidad y artículos de actualidad se unen con un spa y un restaurante. La decoración de la tienda subraya esta exclusiva pretensión y apuesta por la claridad y la amplitud. Los colores se emplean para resaltar las diferentes zonas de las que se compone la tienda.

La formula vincente del concept store Apropos è il mix esclusivo di spazi espositivi destinati ad usi differenti: all'esposizione di prestigiosi articoli trend e moda, ad una zona spa e ad un ristorante. L'esclusività è sottolineata dal design degli interni che esalta soprattutto spaziosità e linee ben definite. La suddivisione degli spazi è rimarcata cromaticamente.

Enzenauer Architekturmanagement

Königsallee 48
40212 Dusseldorf
Germany
www.enzenauer.com

Photos courtesy Apropos Cöln

Apropos Cöln . The Concept Store

Mittelstraße 12
50672 Cologne
Germany
www.apropos-coeln.de

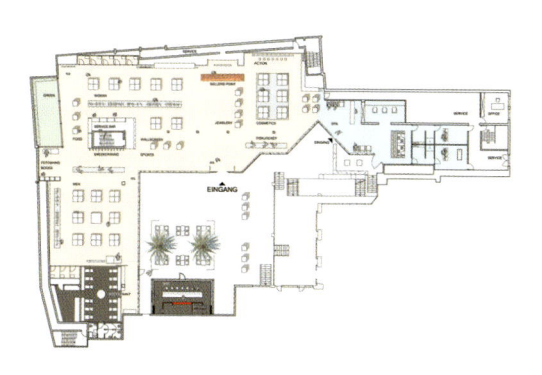

70 | Apropos Cöln . The Concept Store

Apropos Cöln . The Concept Store | 71

The Talbot Runhof brand is defined by cognac and purple tones. Customers at the new Munich store are also greeted by these strong color tones. The white changing cubicles form a contrast. Swing seating in the walkways invites you to relax a while.

Das Branding von Talbot Runhof wird von Cognac- und Lila-Tönen bestimmt. Auch im neuen Münchener Store werden die Kunden von diesen kräftigen Farbtönen empfangen. Einen Kontrast dazu bilden die weißen Umkleiden. In den Gängen laden Sitzschaukeln zum Verweilen ein.

La marque Talbot Runhof se définit par des tons cognac et lilas. Les clients du nouveau magasin de Munich sont également accueillis par ces vigoureux coloris. Le blanc des cabines forme un contraste. Les sièges balançoires des couloirs invitent à la détente.

Los tonos coñac y lila determinan la imagen de la marca Talbot Runhof. En la nueva tienda abierta en Munich los clientes también son recibidos por estos fuertes colores. Las cabinas blancas establecen el contraste. Las hamacas dispuestas en los pasillos invitan a quedarse.

Nel branding della maison Talbot Runhof predominano le tonalità lilla e cognac. E sono proprio queste le tonalità cromatiche d'impatto che accolgono il visitatore all'ingresso del nuovo store di Monaco di Baviera. Forte il contrasto cromatico con le cabine di prova bianche. Le sedute a dondolo dei corridoi invitano a lasciarsi cullare per un momento di relax.

tredup | hamann

Reichenbachstraße 26
80469 Munich
Germany
www.treduphamann.com

Photos by Mickenclever

Talbot Runhof

Klenzestrasse 41
80469 Munich
Germany
www.talbotrunhof.com

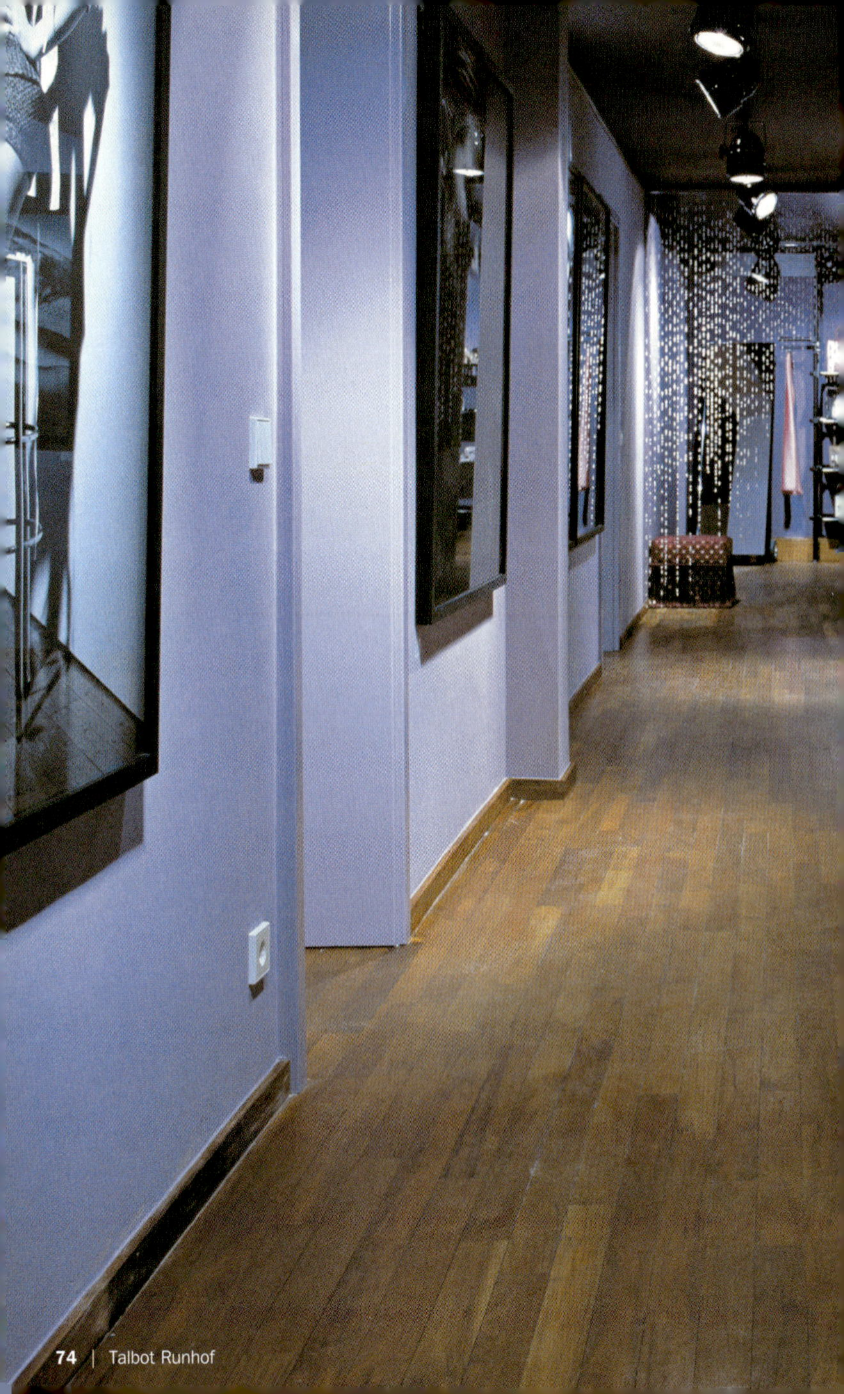

Talbot Runhof | 75

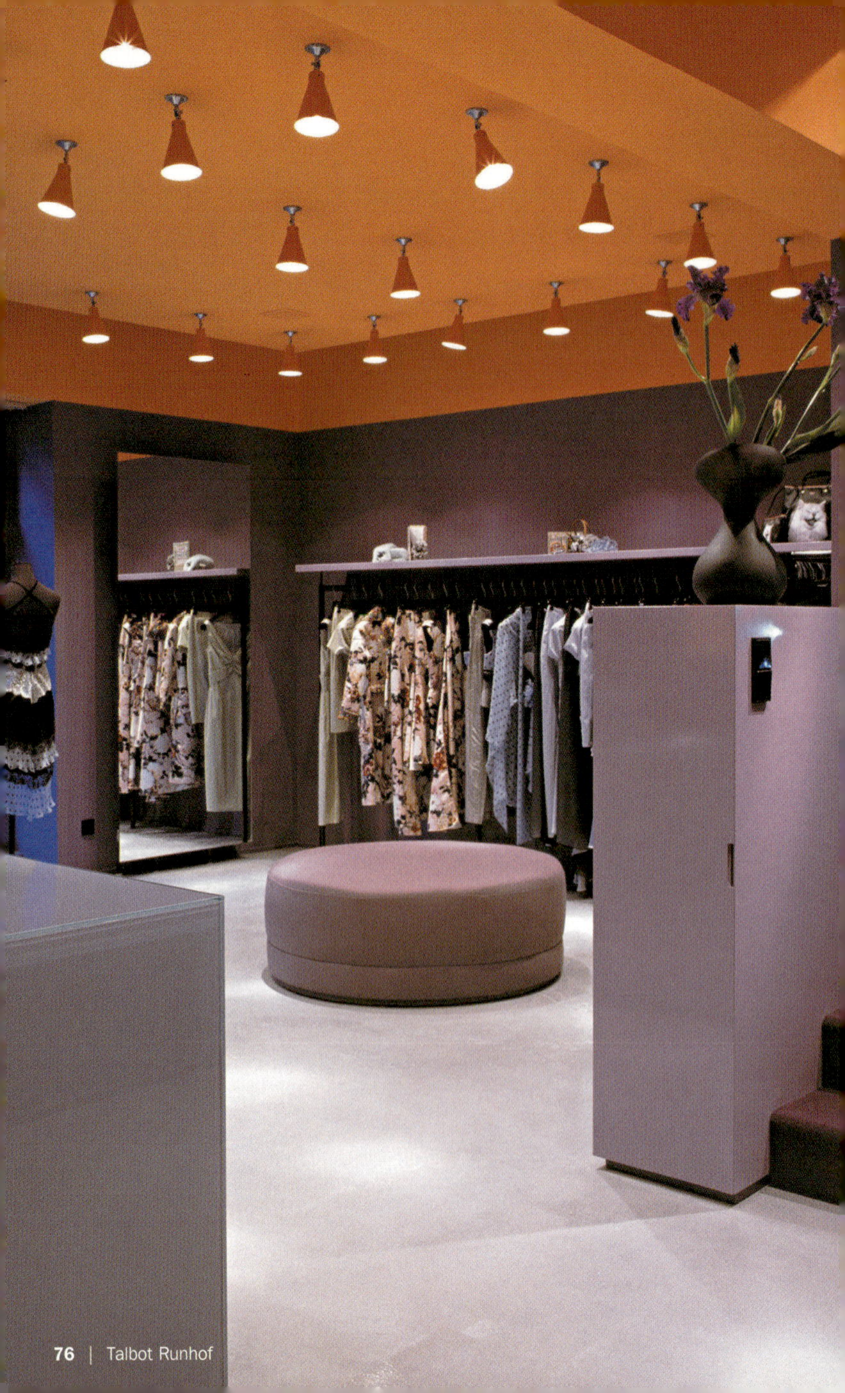

Talbot Runhof | 77

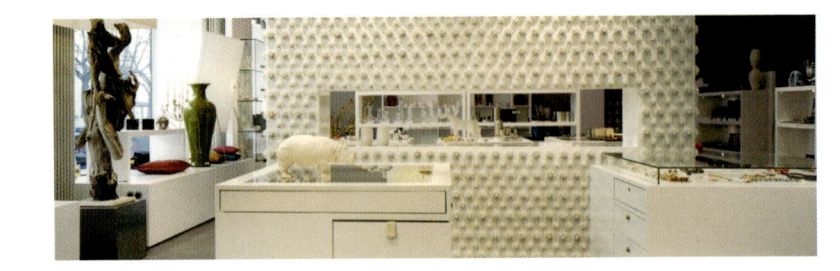

The Munich store's design is conceptionally adapted to the available space. The walls are kept in gray. They contrast with the gleaming white furnishings. The simple design diverts attention to the spring-mounted lighting cubes and the counter's distinctive rear wall with its porcelain roses.

Konzeptionell ordnet sich das Design des Münchner Stores dem vorhandenen Raum unter. Die Wände sind grau gehalten. Sie kontrastieren mit dem glänzend weißen Mobiliar. Die schlichte Gestaltung lenkt die Aufmerksamkeit auf die gefederten Lampenkuben und die markante Tresenrückwand mit ihren Porzellanrosen.

Le design du magasin de Munich est adapté dans sa conception à l'espace disponible. Les murs sont gris et contrastent avec le mobilier d'un blanc brillant. La décoration dépouillée attire l'attention sur les cubes à plumes des éclairages et le mur du fond du comptoir, bien marqué avec ses roses de porcelaine.

La concepción del diseño de esta tienda muniquesa se somete al espacio disponible. Se ha mantenido el color gris de las paredes, que contrastan con el blanco brillante del mobiliario. La sencilla decoración hace que la atención se dirija hacia las lámparas cúbicas revestidas de plumas y hacia la llamativa pared con rosas de porcelana situada detrás del mostrador.

Dal punto di vista della progettazione lo shop design del Lebensart Wittgenstein store di Monaco di Baviera è subordinato alla disponibilità spaziale. Le pareti sono volutamente grigie, in contrasto con il mobilio laccato bianco. L'arredamento sobrio esalta gli elementi luce molleggianti a forma di cubo e la parete posteriore ai banconi di vendita con rose di porcellana in rilievo.

Arno Design GmbH

Friedrichstraße 9
80801 Munich
Germany
www.arno-design.de

Photos by Frank Kotzerke

Lebensart R. Wittgenstein

Blumenstraße 17
80331 Munich
Germany
www.lebensart-rwittgenstein-7.com

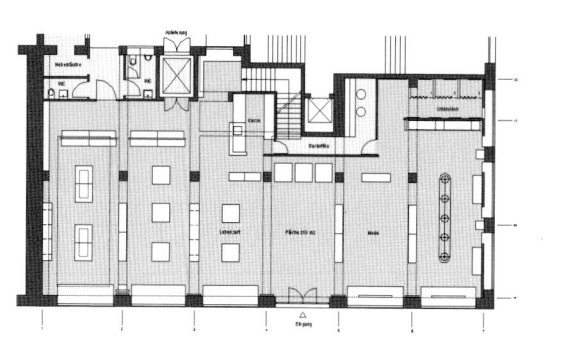

80 | Lebensart R. Wittgenstein

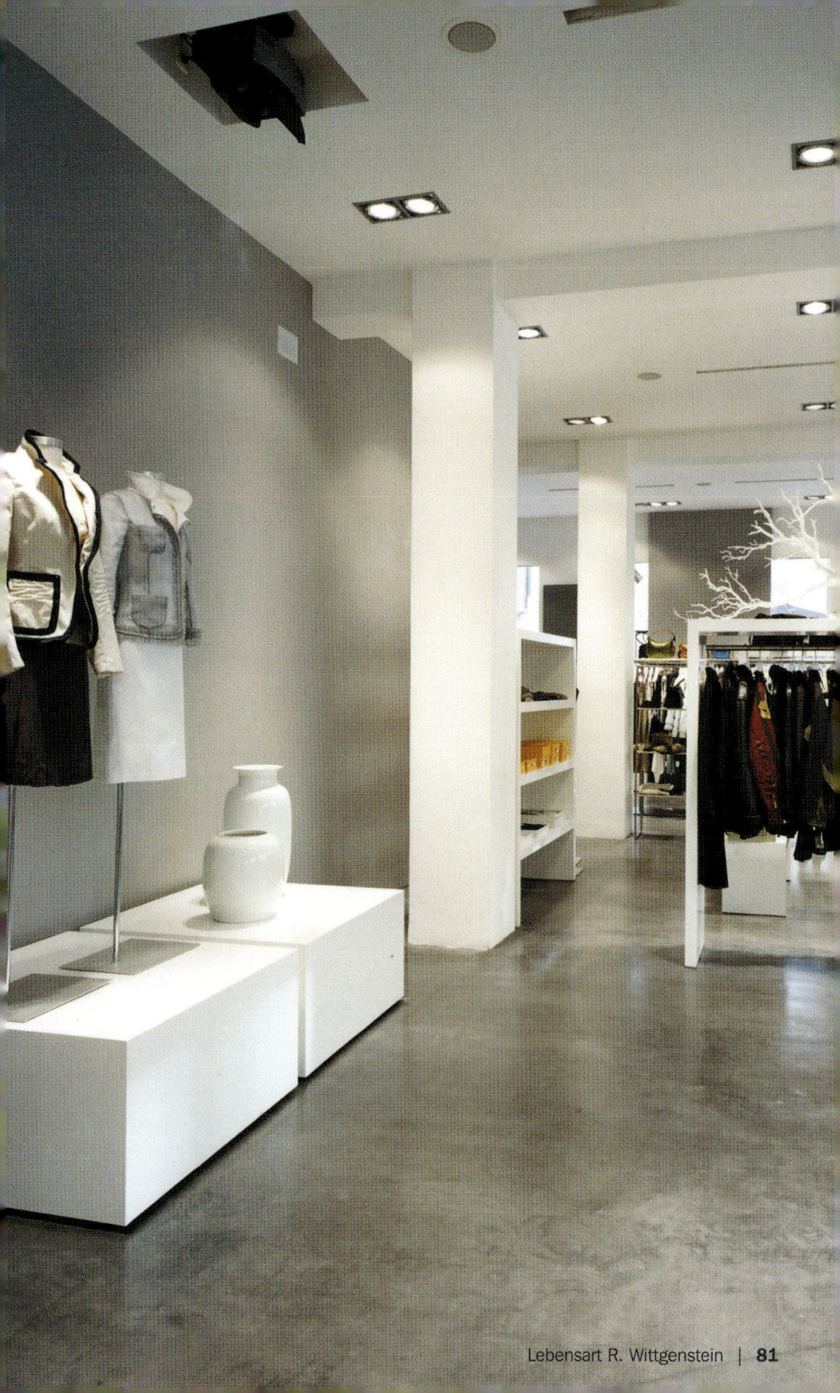

The author of this shop design is the fashion designer himself. In a strong, expressive statement, red influences the ambience—from floor to ceiling. Natural light pleasantly streams into the rooms, where the eye-catching feature is the staircase out of red fiberglass. The dark, refined woods of the interior blend with the strong base tone.

Diese Shop-Gestaltung stammt aus der Feder des Label-Designers. Ausdrucksstark prägt Rot das Ambiente – vom Boden bis zur Decke. Natürliches Licht flutet angenehm durch die Räume, in denen die Treppe aus rotem Fiberglas der Blickfang ist. Zum starken Grundton fügen sich die dunklen Edelhölzer des Interieurs.

L'auteur du design de ce magasin est le designer de mode en personne. Le rouge vif très affirmé crée l'atmosphère – du sol au plafond. Une lumière naturelle inonde agréablement les pièces reliées par un remarquable escalier en fibre de verre rouge. Les sombres bois précieux de l'intérieur s'harmonisent avec l'intense ton dominant.

El interior de esta tienda ha sido creado por el diseñador de la marca. El rojo marca con fuerza el ambiente, desde el suelo hasta el techo. La luz natural fluye agradablemente entre los espacios donde la escalera roja de fibra de vidrio constituye el centro de atención. Al fuerte color básico del interior se le añaden los tonos de las oscuras maderas nobles.

Lo shop design del Gianfranco Ferré store è opera dello stesso brand designer. Mezzo espressivo predominante è il rosso, che pervade tutto lo spazio espositivo, dal pavimento al soffitto. L'ambiente è inondato piacevolmente da luce naturale, in cui spicca la scala rossa in fiber glass di grande richiamo visivo. Alla tonalità di fondo ben si armonizzano i legni pregiati degli interni.

Palazzo Gianfranco Ferré

Via Pontaccio 21
20121 Milan
Italy

Photos by Markus Bachmann

Gianfranco Ferré

Maximilianstraße 11
80539 Munich
Germany
www.gianfrancoferre.com

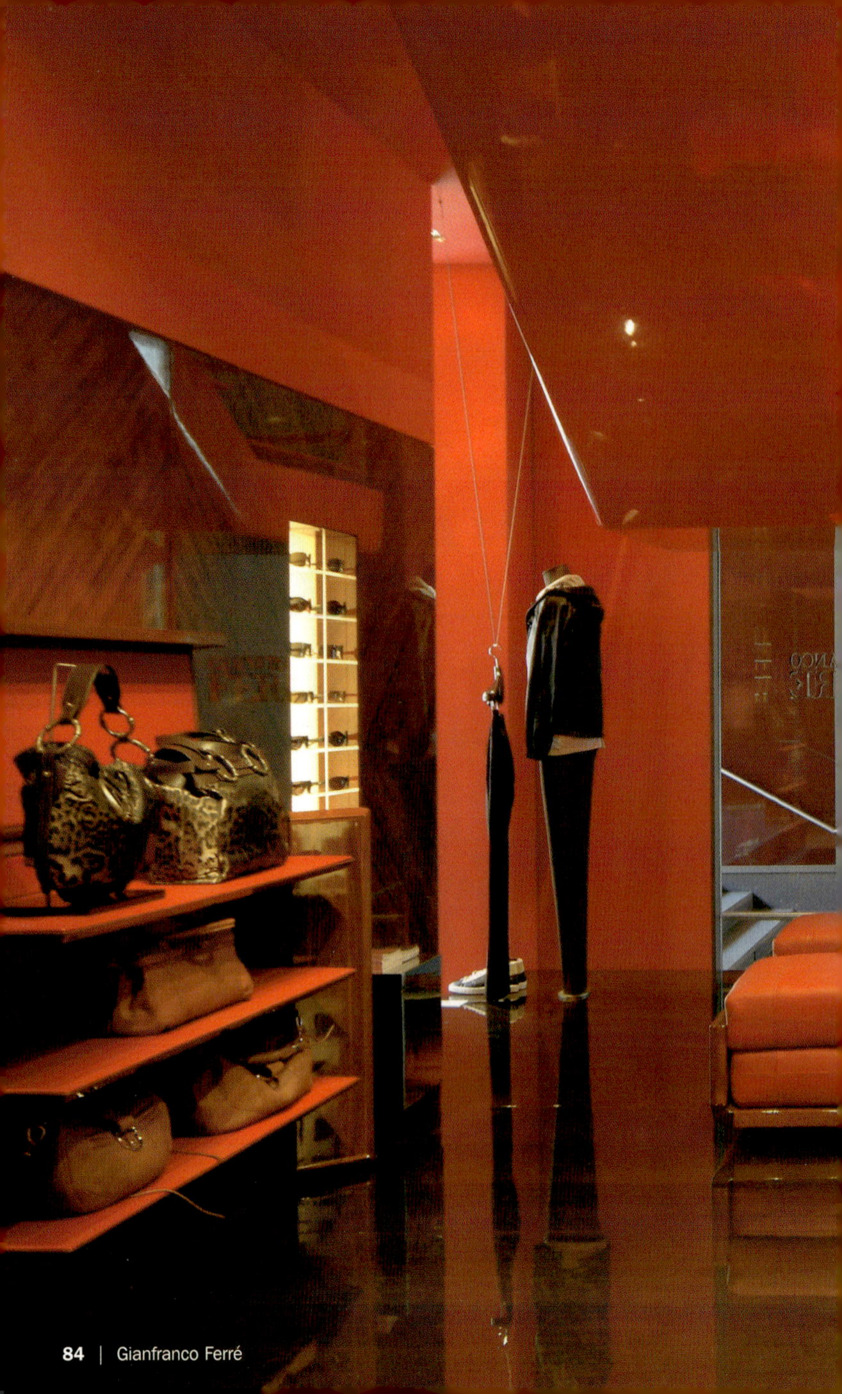

Gianfranco Ferré | 85

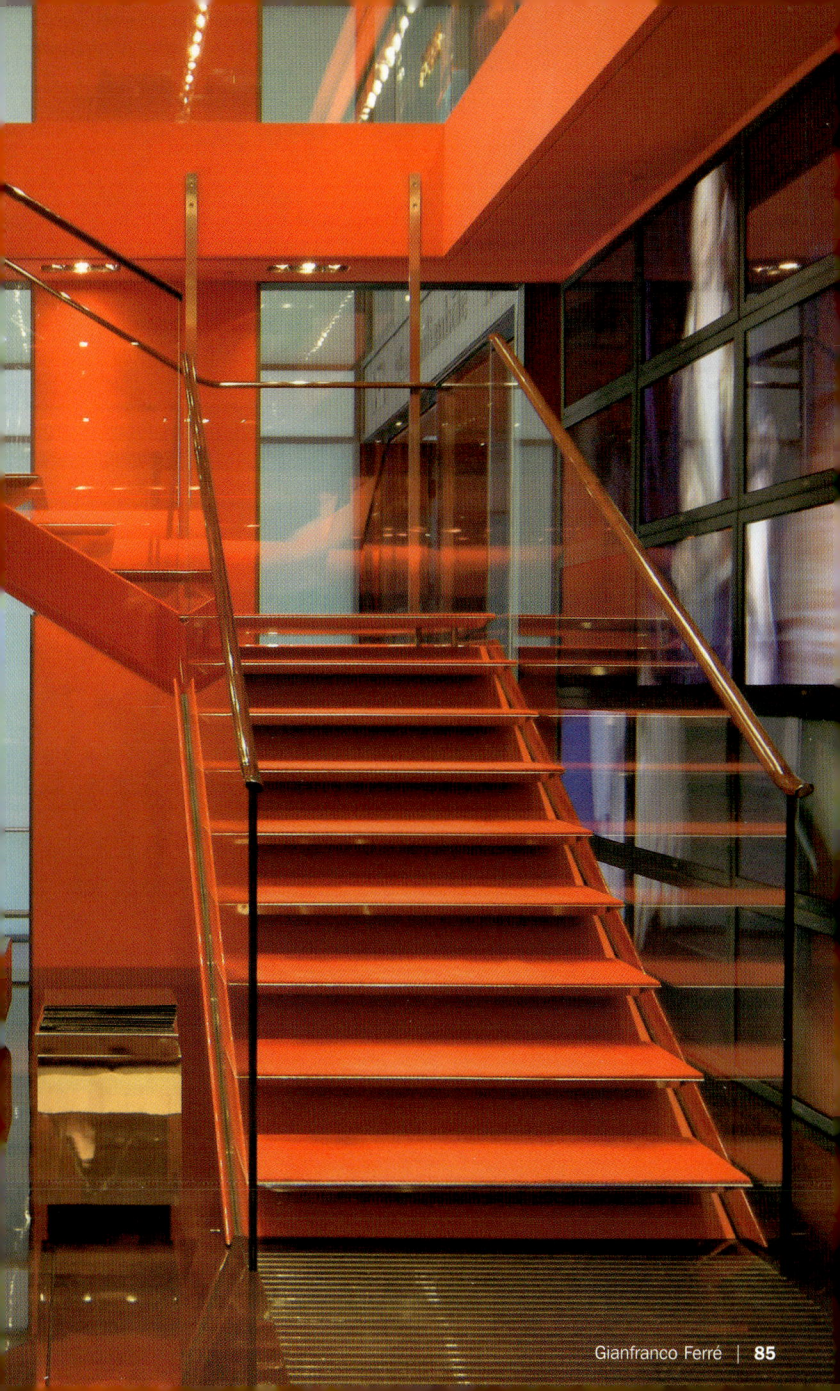

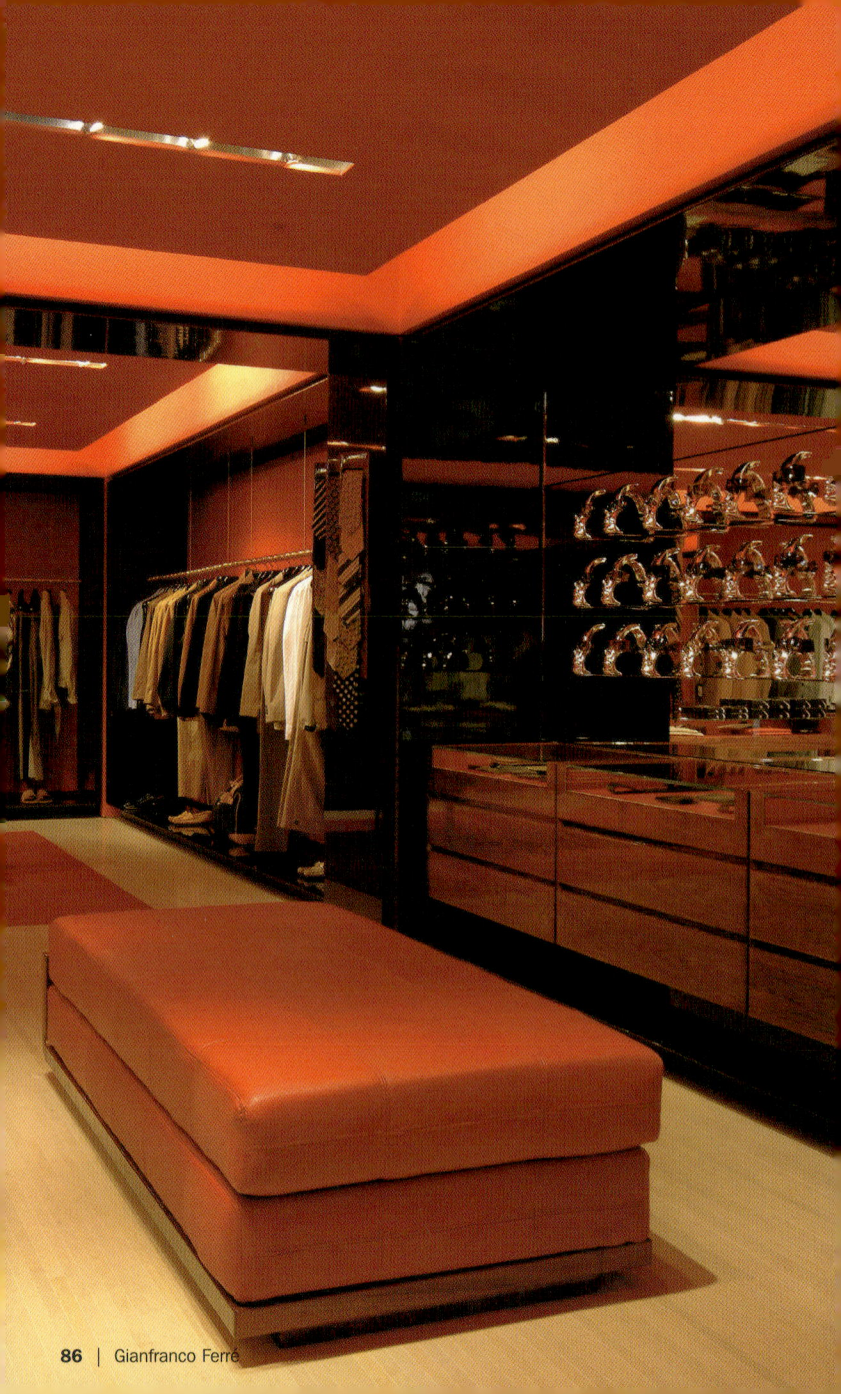

Gianfranco Ferré | **87**

White as a basic color gives a modern touch to the sigrun woehr shoe shop. The petroleum-colored ceiling and delicate tones of the displays introduce colorful accents. A perforated line runs around the room like a seam, which appears to keep together all the parts.

Das Weiß als Grundfarbe gibt dem Schuhladen von sigrun woehr einen modernen Touch. Die petrolfarbene Decke und die zarten Farbtöne der Displays setzen farbliche Akzente. Wie eine Naht durchzieht eine gestrichelte Linie den Raum, die alle Teile zusammenzuhalten scheint.

Le blanc comme couleur de base confère une touche moderne au magasin de chaussures de sigrun woehr. Le bleu pétrole du plafond et les coloris tendres des présentoirs apportent des accents de couleur. Une ligne en pointillé traverse la pièce, telle une couture retenant tous les morceaux.

El color blanco da esta tienda de zapatos de sigrun woehr un toque moderno. El color petróleo del techo y los delicados tonos de los mostradores ponen las notas de color. Una línea discontinua recorre el espacio como un hilo y actúa como elemento de unión entre las divisiones espaciales.

Il bianco come tonalità di fondo conferisce al sigrun woehr store un tocco moderno, cromaticamente in contrasto con il soffitto verde petrolio e i delicati colori degli spazi espositivi dedicati alle calzature. Una linea tratteggiata attraversa il soffitto come una cucitura che sembra imprimere coerenza espressiva all'ambiente.

ippolito fleitz group
identity architects

Bismarckstraße 67 b
70197 Stuttgart
Germany
www.ifgroup.org

Photos by Zooey Braun

sigrun woehr

Kirchstraße 12
70173 Stuttgart
Germany
www.sigrun-woehr.de

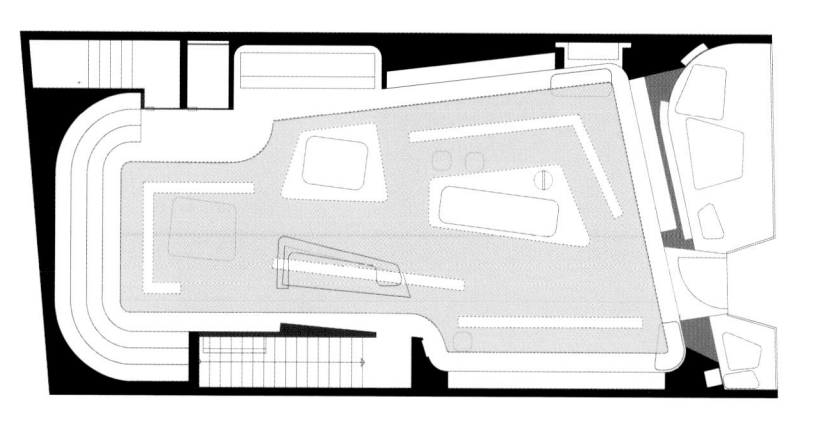

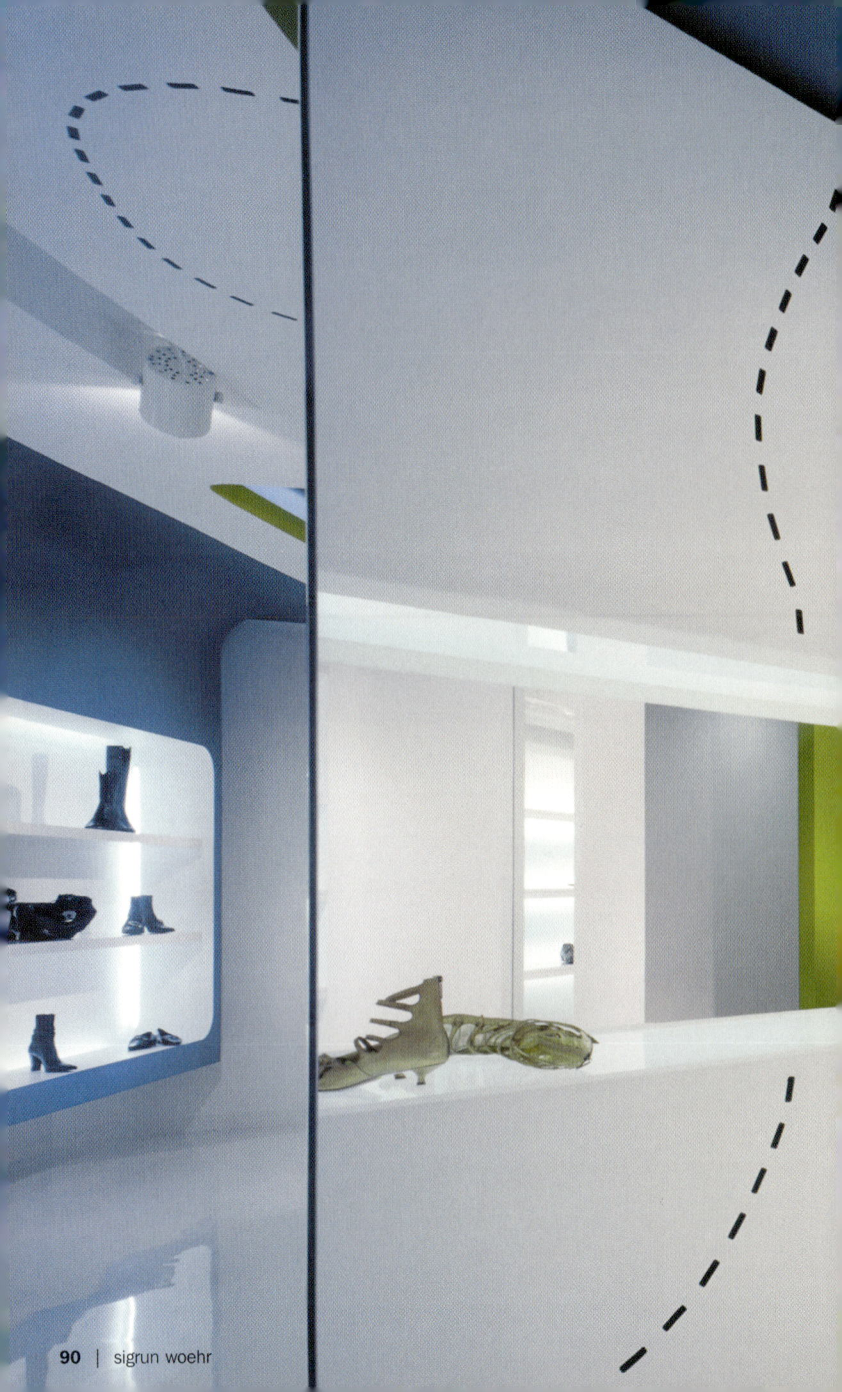

sigrun woehr | 91

92 | sigrun woehr

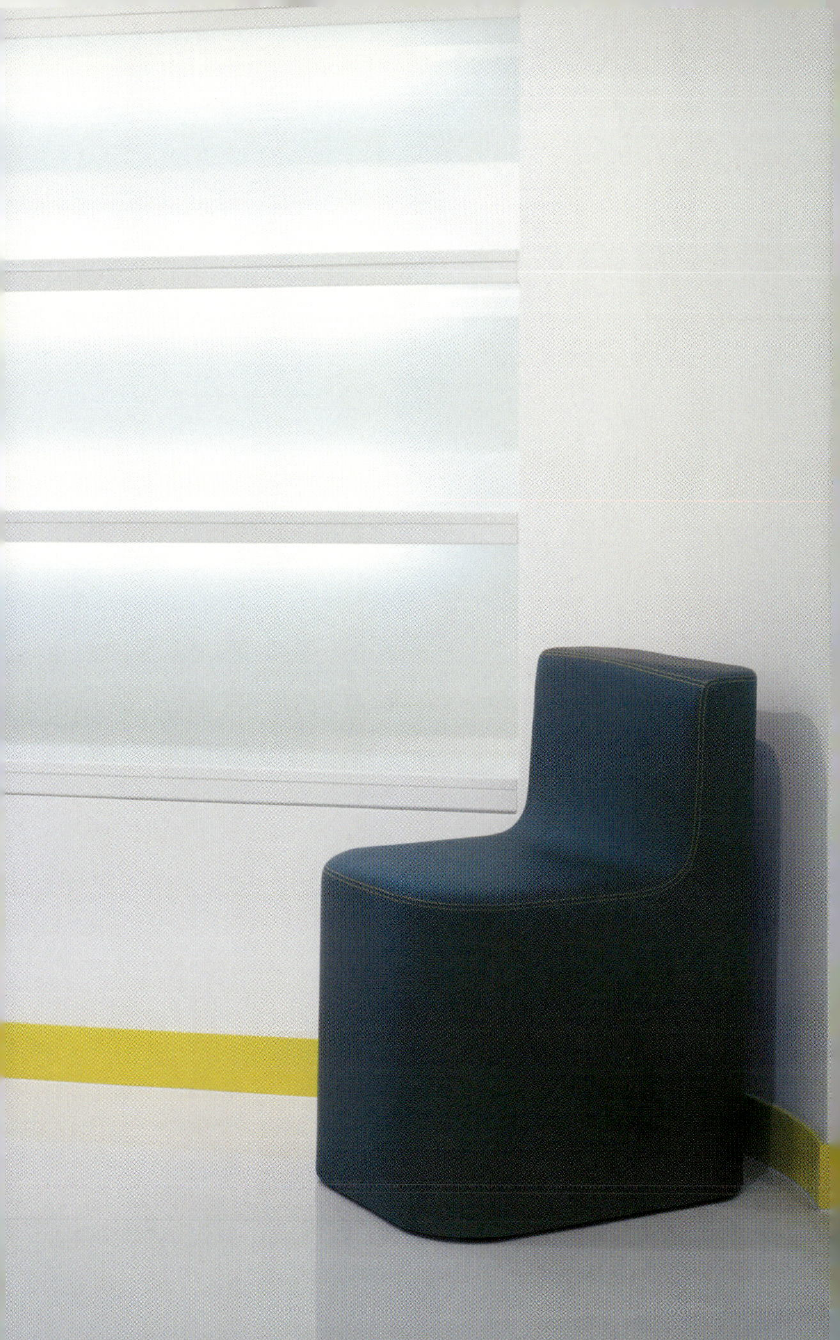

In the Bisazza showroom, not only the in-house product range is on display. The site's beauty also makes it a worthwhile setting for cultural events. All the mosaic artworks originate from famous designers.

Im Showroom von Bisazza kommt nicht nur die eigene Produktlinie zur Geltung. Das Objekt bildet aufgrund seiner Schönheit auch den würdigen Rahmen für kulturelle Events. Die Mosaik-Kunstwerke stammen allesamt von renommierten Designern.

Dans le showroom de Bisazza, la propre ligne de produits n'est pas la seule chose mise en valeur. La beauté du site en fait un cadre magnifique pour des événements culturels. Les mosaïques sont des œuvres d'art signées par de célèbres designers.

En el showroom de Bisazza no sólo se resaltan los productos de la propia línea. Por su belleza, esta tienda es también un excelente marco para eventos culturales. Los mosaicos, verdaderas obras de arte, son creaciones de famosos diseñadores.

Lo showroom Bisazza non esalta solo la propria linea di prodotti. La bellezza intrinseca dell'allestimento lo rende contesto adeguato per eventi culturali d'alto livello. I capolavori-mosaico sono opera di designer rinomati.

Bisazza Design Studio
Carlo Dal Bianco

Viale Milano 56
36041 Alte di Montecchio – Vicenza
Italy
www.bisazza.com

Photos by Ottavio Tommasini, Federico Cedrone

Spazio Bisazza

Via Senato 2
20121 Milan
Italy
www.bisazza.com

Spazio Bisazza

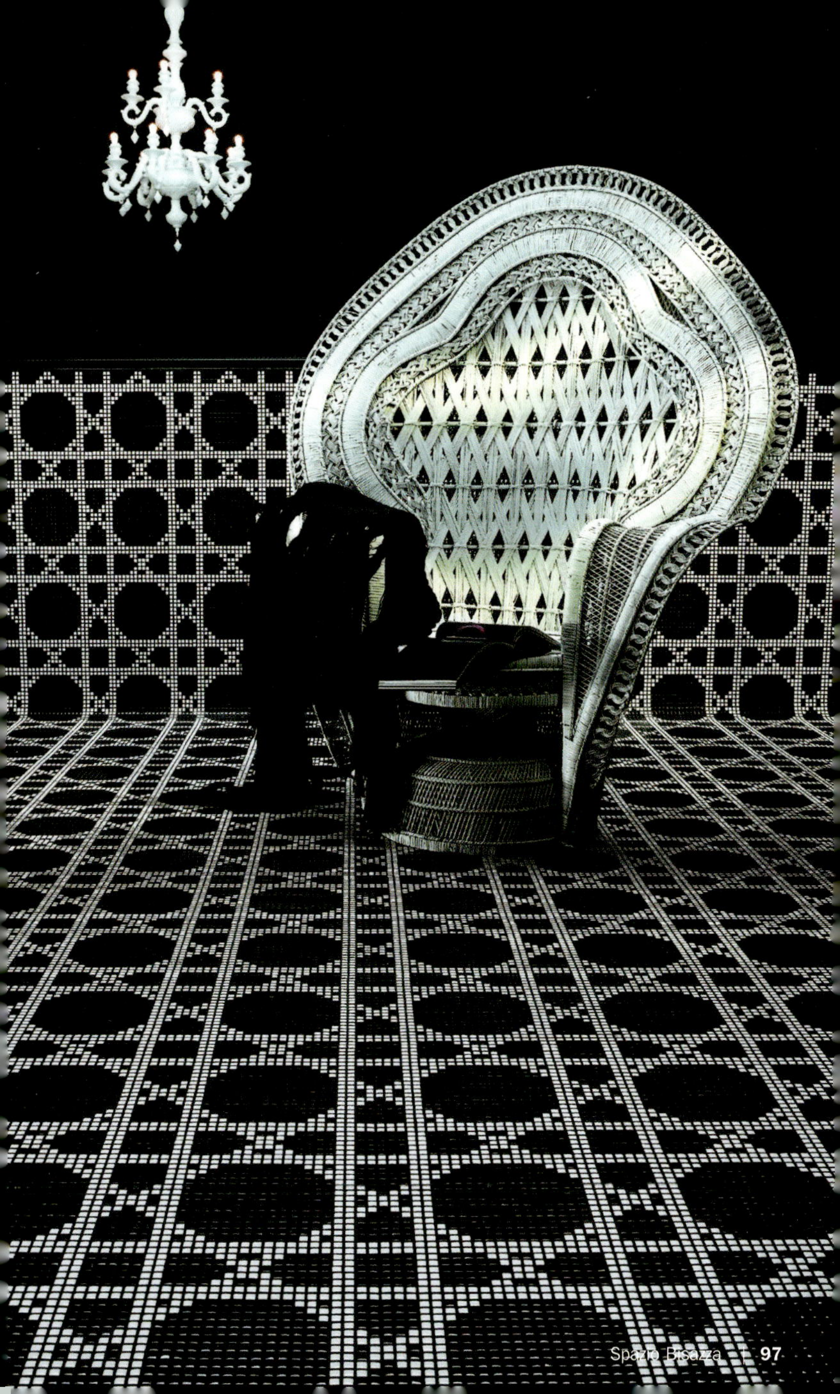

In contrast to its counterpart in Rome, dark color tones are predominant in La Perla Uomo's Milan store. For the shop in their hometown, Buratti + Battiston Architects use mainly woods of elegant appearance, which they combine with black and mirrored surfaces. It is exactly the right tonality for men's fashion.

Im Gegensatz zum römischen Pendant dominieren im Mailänder Store von La Perla Uomo die dunkleren Farbtöne. Buratti + Battiston Architects verwenden bei ihrem Heimspiel vor allem elegant anmutende Hölzer, die sie mit schwarzen Oberflächen und Spiegeln kombinieren. Für Männermode genau die richtige Tonalität.

Contrairement à son pendant romain, les tons sombres dominent dans le magasin milanais de La Perla Uomo. Pour le magasin de leur ville natale, Buratti + Battiston Architects emploient avant tout des bois sobrement élégants qu'ils combinent avec des surfaces noires et des miroirs : une tonalité idéale pour la mode masculine.

Al contrario que su análoga romana, en la tienda milanesa de La Perla Uomo dominan los tonos más oscuros. En su composición, Buratti + Battiston Architects utilizan, sobre todo, elegantes maderas que combinan con las superficies negras y espejadas. Las tonalidades indicadas para la moda de caballero.

Nello store milanese La Perla Uomo predominano, in contrasto con lo store di Roma, le tonalità calde. Per la loro partita tutta giocata in casa, Buratti + Battiston Architects hanno privilegiato soprattutto legni eleganti combinati con superfici nere e specchi: la scelta cromatica giusta per far risaltare le creazioni di moda maschile La Perla.

Buratti + Battiston Architects

Via Cellini 5
20020 Busto Garolfo – Milan
Italy
www.burattibattiston.it

Photos by Andrea Martiradonna, Matteo Piazza (shop front)

La Perla Uomo

Via Manzoni 17
20121 Milan
Italy
www.laperla.com

100 | La Perla Uomo

La Perla Uomo | 101

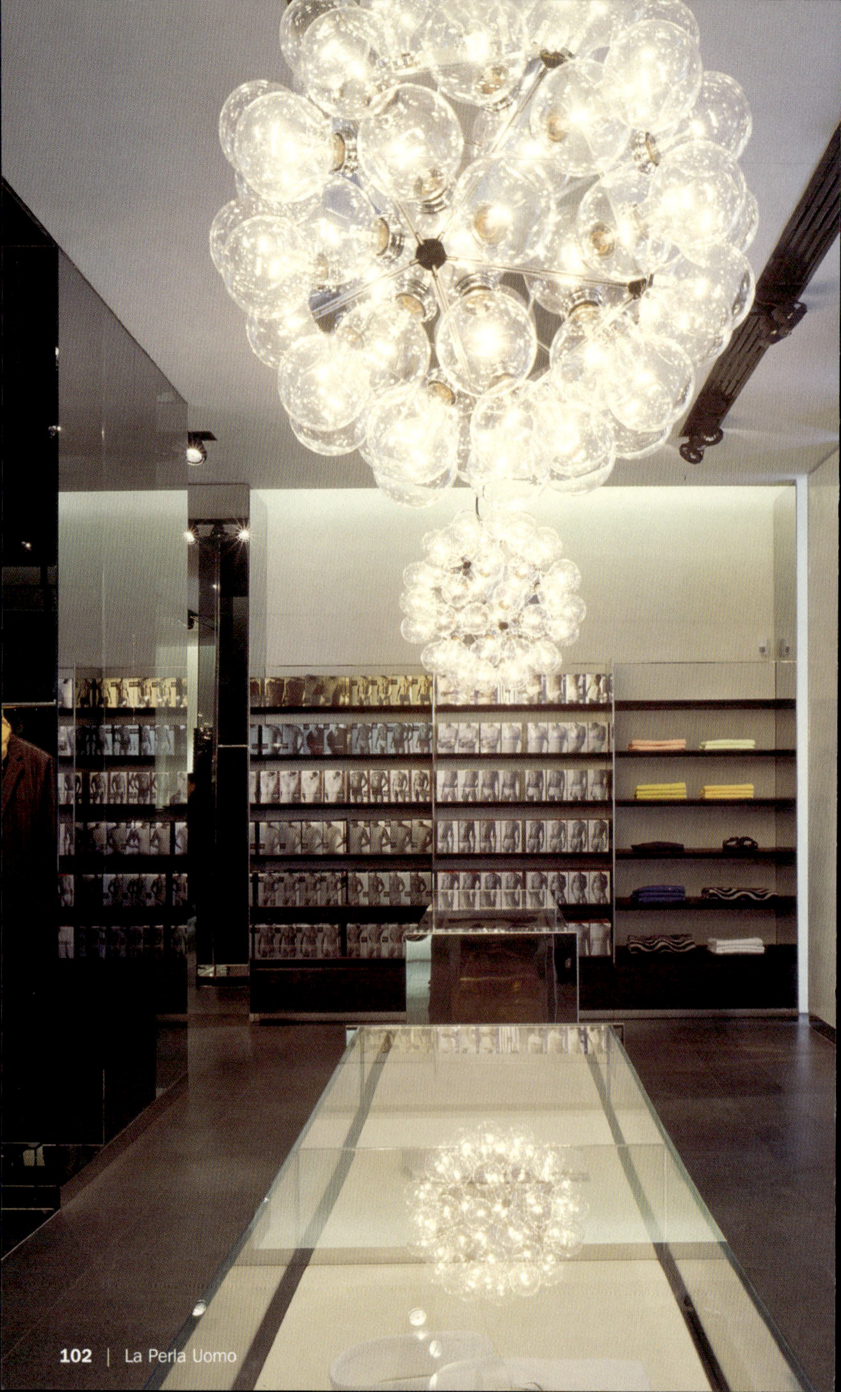

La Perla Uomo | 103

David Chipperfield proves totally unaffected by the store's historic context with its mighty marble columns and stucco ceilings. He creates a showroom that is completely independent of this tradition, using illuminated display cabinets and a backdrop with an intense color harmony of green, yellow and red.

David Chipperfield zeigt sich gänzlich unberührt von der historischen Vorgabe des Stores mit seinen mächtigen Marmorsäulen und Stuckdecken. Er schafft einen davon völlig losgelösten Showroom aus leuchtenden Vitrinen und Kulissen in einem intensiven Farbakkord aus Grün, Gelb und Rot.

David Chipperfield n'est absolument pas impressionné par le contexte historique du magasin avec ses imposantes colonnes de marbre et plafonds en stuc. Il crée un showroom complètement libéré, composé de vitrines et décors lumineux dans une intense harmonie de vert, jaune et rouge.

David Chipperfield no se ha dejado impresionar por las líneas históricas de la tienda, con sus impresionantes columnas de mármol y sus techos estucados. Crea un showroom totalmente desligado con vitrinas iluminadas y un fondo en un acorde de intensos colores: verde, amarillo y rojo.

Ignorando apertamente i dettami storici suggeriti dai dettagli architettonici preesistenti, quali le imponenti colonne in marmo e i soffitti a stucchi, David Chipperfield crea uno showroom innovativo, in cui predominano elementi espositivi e pareti divisorie luminose, giocati sugli accordi cromatici decisi del verde, giallo e rosso.

David Chipperfield Architects

Cobham Mews
Agar Grove
London NW1 9SB
United Kingdom
www.davidchipperfield.com

Photos by Ornella Sancassani

Pasquale Bruni Showroom

Via Manzoni 19
20121 Milan
Italy
www.pasqualebruni.com

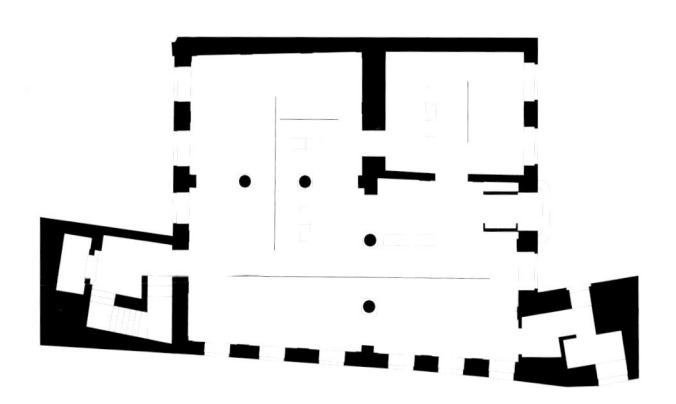

106 | Pasquale Bruni Showroom

Pasquale Bruni Showroom | 107

The philosophy of the Moschino label is reflected in Sean Dix' store design. Majestic red is the predominant color; travertine floors and chandeliers also create a feudal impression. But there is no lack of irony: the outfits on the wall narrate *en passant* the story of "The Emperor's New Clothes."

In Sean Dix' Gestaltung des Stores spiegelt sich die Philosophie der Marke Moschino wider. Herrschaftliches Rot dominiert als Farbe, zudem sorgen Travertin-Böden und Kronleuchter für einen feudalen Eindruck. Dennoch fehlt die Ironie nicht: En passant erzählen die Outfits an der Wand die Geschichte von „Des Kaisers neue Kleider".

Le design de Sean Dix pour ce magasin reflète la philosophie de la marque Moschino. Un rouge impérial y domine; des sols en travertin et des lustres créent également une impression de noblesse. Pourtant l'ironie ne manque pas : les toilettes accrochées au mur racontent en passant l'histoire des « Nouveaux Habits de l'Empereur ».

En el diseño de Sean Dix para el interior de esta tienda se refleja la filosofía de la marca Moschino. Un rojo señorial es el color dominante y los suelos de travertino y las arañas de cristal contribuyen a crear un efecto feudal. Pero no está carente de ironía: *en passant*, las prendas de las paredes cuentan la historia de "El nuevo traje del emperador".

Lo shop design firmato Sean Dix dello store è perfettamente in linea con la filosofia del marchio Moschino. Cromaticamente predominante è il rosso padronale, esaltato dai pavimenti in travertino e dai lampadari a corona che conferiscono all'ambiente un effetto aristocratico. Tuttavia non manca un tocco ironico: come en passant l'allestimento alle pareti racconta stralci della novella "I vestiti nuovi dell'imperatore".

Sean Dix

Alzaia Naviglio Grande 14
20144 Milan
Italy
www.seandix.com

Photos by Santi Caleca

Moschino St. Andrea

Via Sant' Andrea 12
20121 Milan
Italy
www.moschino.it

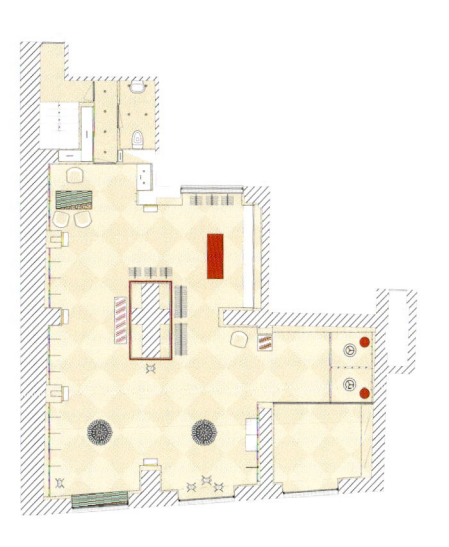

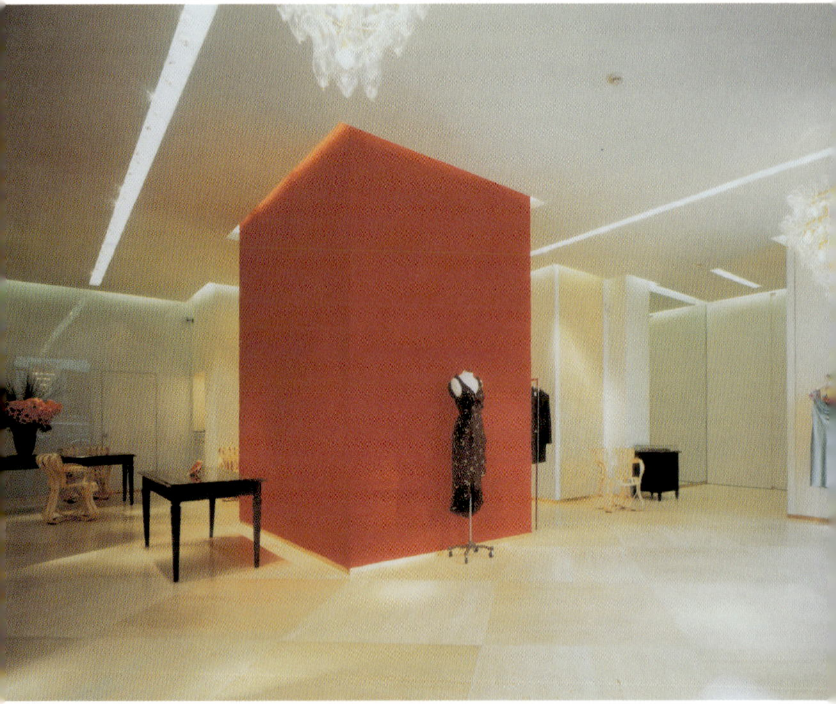

Moschino St. Andrea | 111

Atmospheric arcades in rose-pink colors create the fitting ambience for fashion by Paul Smith. The "tone in tone" principle is valid. The architect, Sophie Hicks, chooses the same color tone for the flooring and floral patterns and the interior also blends in with the monochrome atmosphere that she has created.

Stimmungsvolle Arkaden in Rosarot schaffen das passende Ambiente für die Mode von Paul Smith. Es gilt das Prinzip „Ton in Ton". Die Architektin Sophie Hicks gibt Boden und Blumenmustern den gleichen Farbklang, und auch das Interieur fügt sich in die von ihr erzeugte monochrome Atmosphäre ein.

Des arcades rouge-rosé pleines de charme créent l'ambiance idéale pour la mode de Paul Smith où s'applique le principe du « ton sur ton ». L'architecte Sophie Hicks choisit le même coloris pour le sol et les motifs de fleurs ; l'aménagement intérieur s'intègre également dans l'atmosphère monochrome qu'elle a créée.

El efectismo de los arcos de color rosa crea el marco perfecto para la moda de Paul Smith, que sigue el principio de la armonía de los colores. La arquitecta Sophie Hicks da al suelo y a los estampados de flores el mismo tono de color, y también el interior se adapta a la atmósfera monocroma creada por ella.

Suggestivi archi rosa evocano la giusta atmosfera per le collezioni di Paul Smith. Fedele in tutto per tutto al "tono su tono", l'architetto Sophie Hicks sceglie pavimenti e motivi floreali nella stessa tonalità, creando un ambiente monocromatico a cui sembra subordinarsi ogni dettaglio dell'arredamento.

S. H. Architects Limited

17 Powis Mews
London W11 1JN
United Kingdom
www.sophiehicks.com

Photos courtesy Paul Smith

Paul Smith

Via Manzoni 30
20121 Milan
Italy
www.paulsmith.co.uk

114 | Paul Smith

Paul Smith | 115

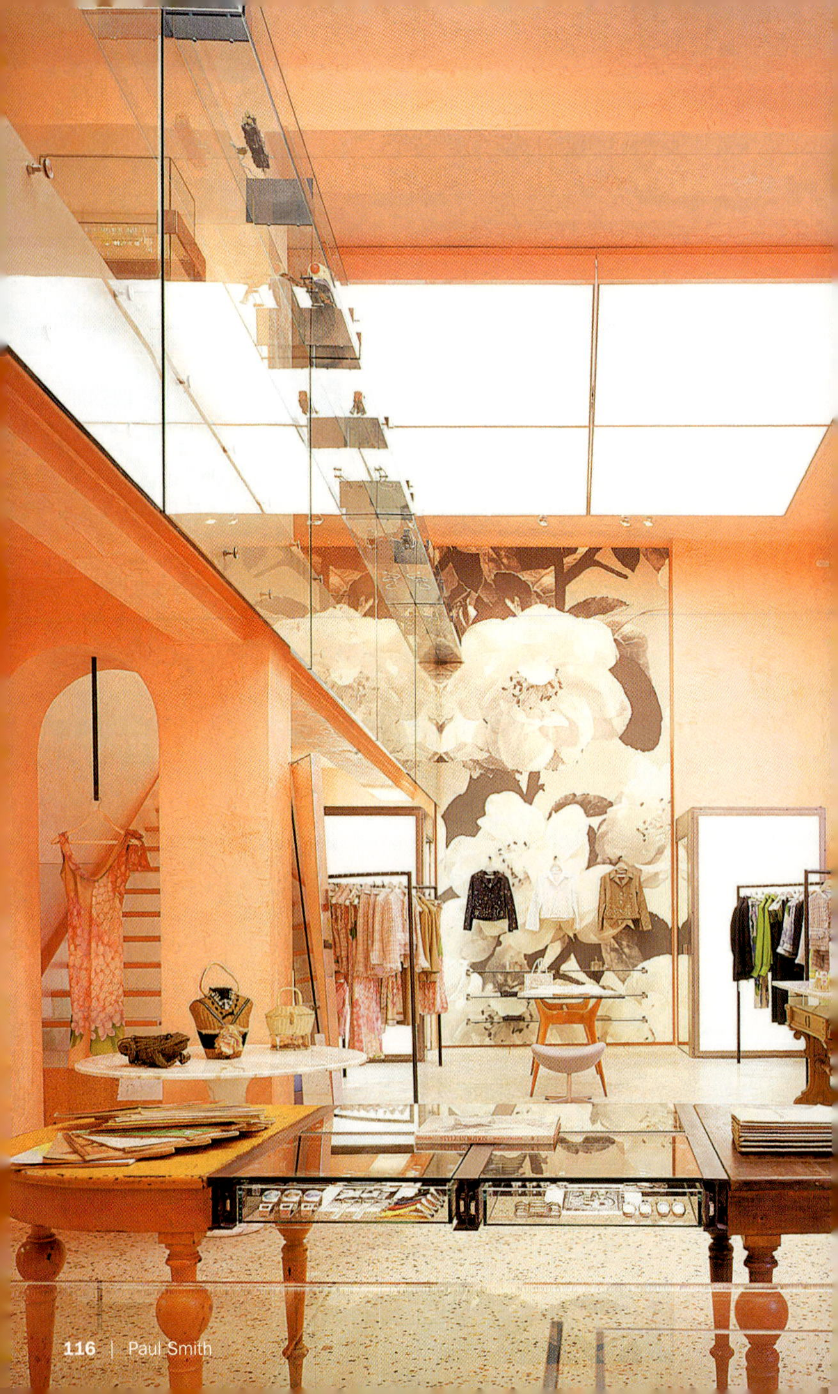

Paul Smith | 117

"An ambience, which says Gucci, without mentioning the name"—this is how Tom Ford sees the design of his New York flagship store. The rooms are dominated by a shimmering, silver gleam. The inspiration was Richard Neutra's classical-modern style, newly interpreted for the contemporary period.

„Ein Ambiente, das Gucci sagt, ohne den Namen zu nennen" – so versteht Tom Ford das Design seines New Yorker Flagship-Stores. Die Räume werden von einem schimmernden, silbernen Glanz dominiert. Vor allem der klassisch-moderne Stil von Richard Neutra stand dabei Pate – für die heutige Zeit neu interpretiert.

« Une atmosphère qui dit Gucci sans en prononcer le nom » – c'est ainsi que Tom Ford conçoit le design de son magasin étendard new-yorkais. L'espace est dominé par un éclat argenté brillant. L'inspiration vient du style classico-moderne de Richard Neutra – dans une nouvelle interprétation contemporaine.

"Un ambiente que habla de Gucci sin citar su nombre"; así entiende Tom Ford el diseño de su tienda insignia en Nueva York. Los espacios están dominados por un brillante color plateado. La gran influencia fue, sobre todo, el estilo clásico moderno de Richard Neutra reinterpretado para adaptarlo al tiempo actual.

"Un'atmosfera in cui il nome Gucci viene evocato ma non menzionato esplicitamente", questa la chiave di lettura dello shop design firmato Tom Ford del Gucci flagship store di New York. Nello spazio espositivo predomina un fulgore argenteo luccicante. Forti le reminiscenze dello stile classico-moderno di Richard Neutra reinterpretato per l'epoca contemporanea.

Studio Sofield Inc.

380 Lafayette Street
New York, NY 10003
USA

Photos courtesy Gucci

Gucci

Via Montenapoleone 5
20121 Milan
Italy
www.gucci.com

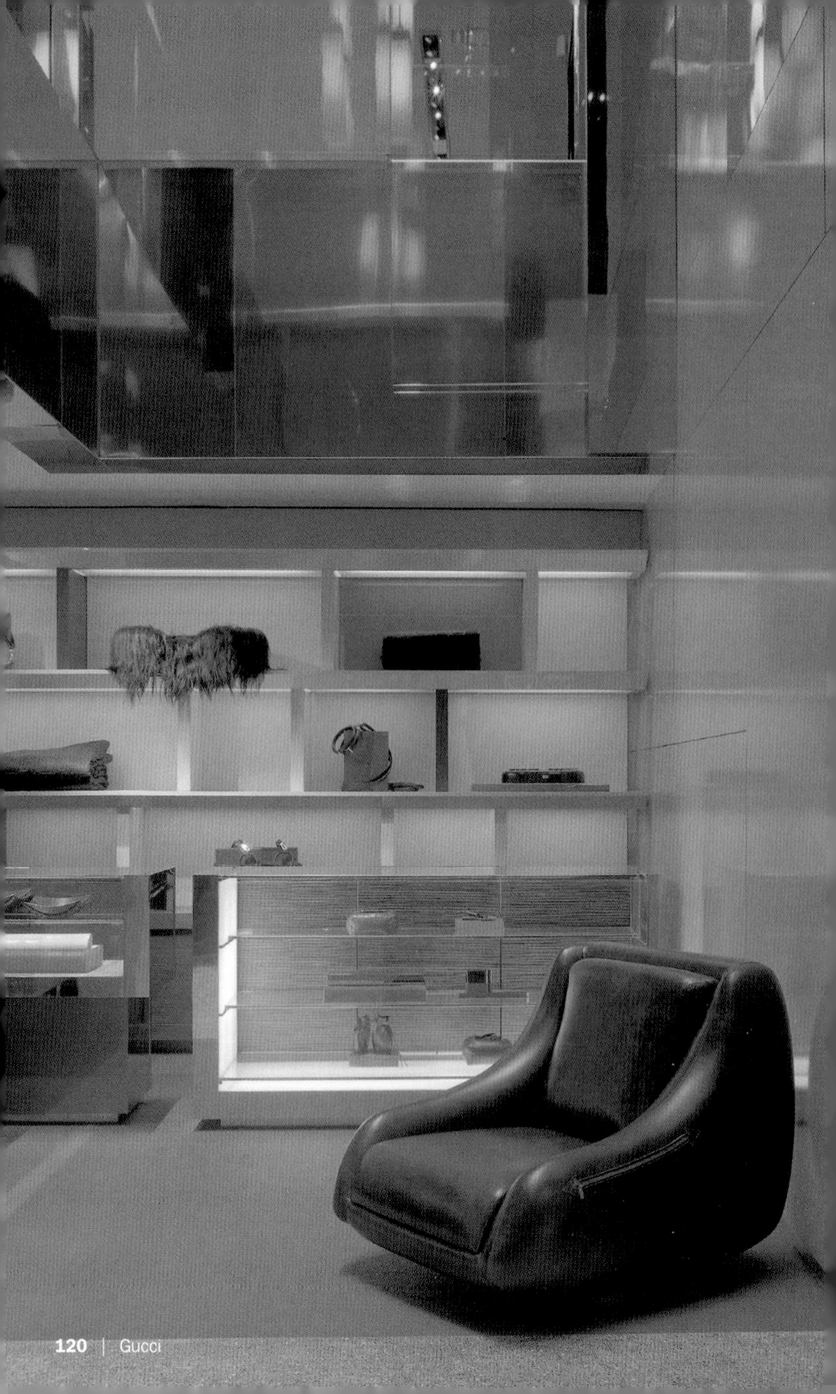

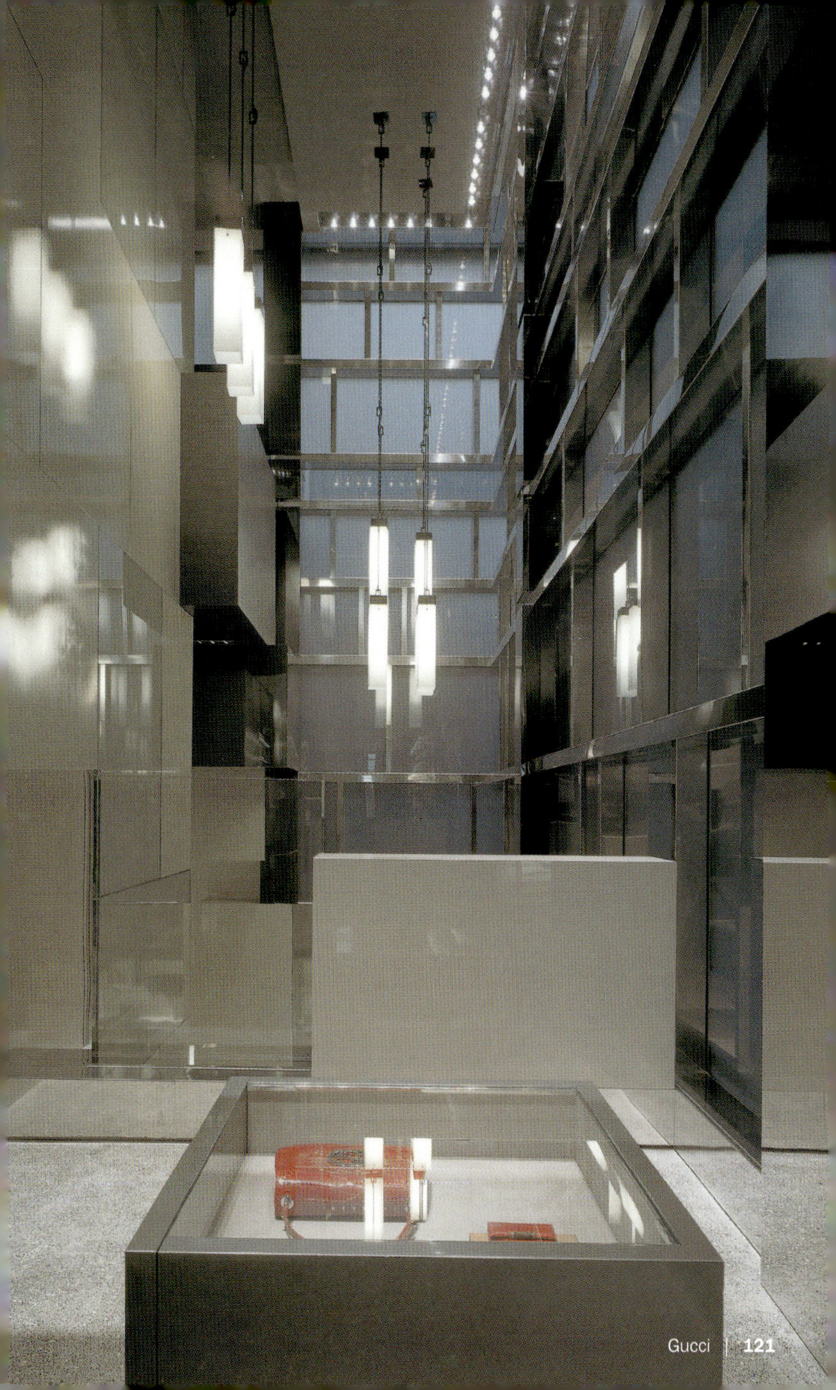

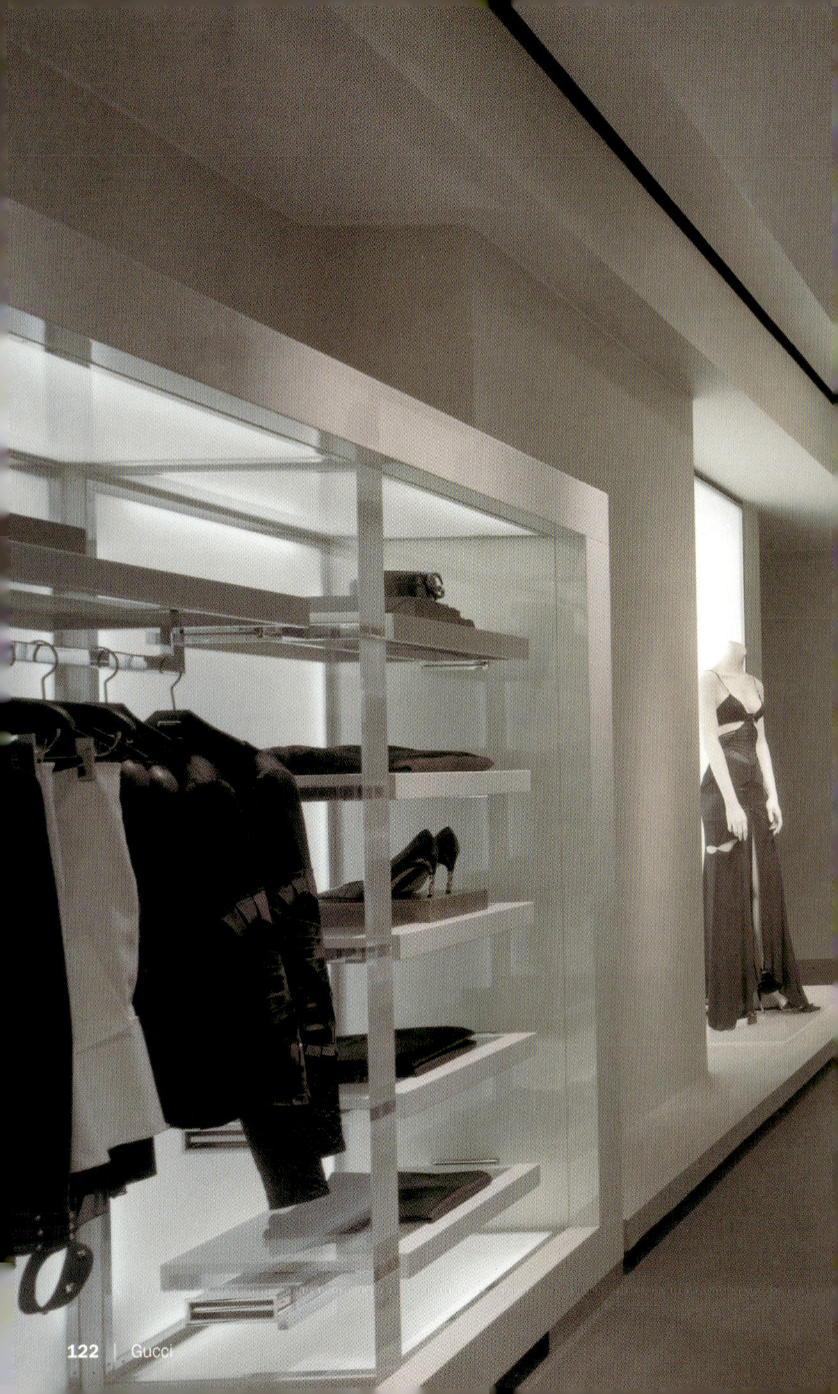

Gucci | 123

The world is topsy-turvy—and all that for fashion. There could hardly be a more fitting characterization for the room design by Viktor & Rolf. In a location like Milan, it surely provides a neat reference. Neo-classicism serves as the inspiration for this upside-down world, with its arches, columns and furnishings.

Die Welt steht Kopf – und das alles für die Mode. Kaum prägnanter ließe sich das Raum-Design von Viktor & Rolf auf den Punkt bringen. An einem Ort wie Mailand sicher eine hübsche Anspielung. Für die verdrehte Welt dient der Neoklassizismus mit seinen Bögen, Säulen und Möbeln als Vorlage.

Le monde à l'envers – tout ça pour la mode. On ne saurait mieux décrire l'aménagement de l'espace imaginé par Viktor & Rolf. Dans une ville comme Milan, assurément un joli clin d'œil. Le néoclassicisme avec ses arches, colonnes et meubles sert d'inspiration à cette inversion du monde.

El mundo del revés, y todo por la moda. Es la forma más precisa de describir el diseño de este espacio de Viktor & Rolf. En un lugar como Milán ésta es una bonita alusión. El neoclasicismo, con sus arcos, columnas y mobiliario, ha sido el modelo para el mundo al revés.

Sottosopra – per amore della moda. Non c'è definizione più incisiva che possa descrivere la filosofia che ha ispirato lo shop design della boutique milanese upsidedown di Viktor & Rolf…allusione di particolare effetto data la location milanese. Gli espedienti espressivi che danno vita a questo capovolgimento della realtà sono archi, colonne e mobili di ispirazione neoclassica.

SZI Design

Tussen de Bogen 40
1013JB Amsterdam
The Netherlands
www.szidesign.com

Photos by Andrea Martiradonna

Viktor & Rolf Boutique

Via Sant Andrea 14
20121 Milan
Italy
www.viktor-rolf.com

126 | Viktor & Rolf Boutique

Viktor & Rolf Boutique | 127

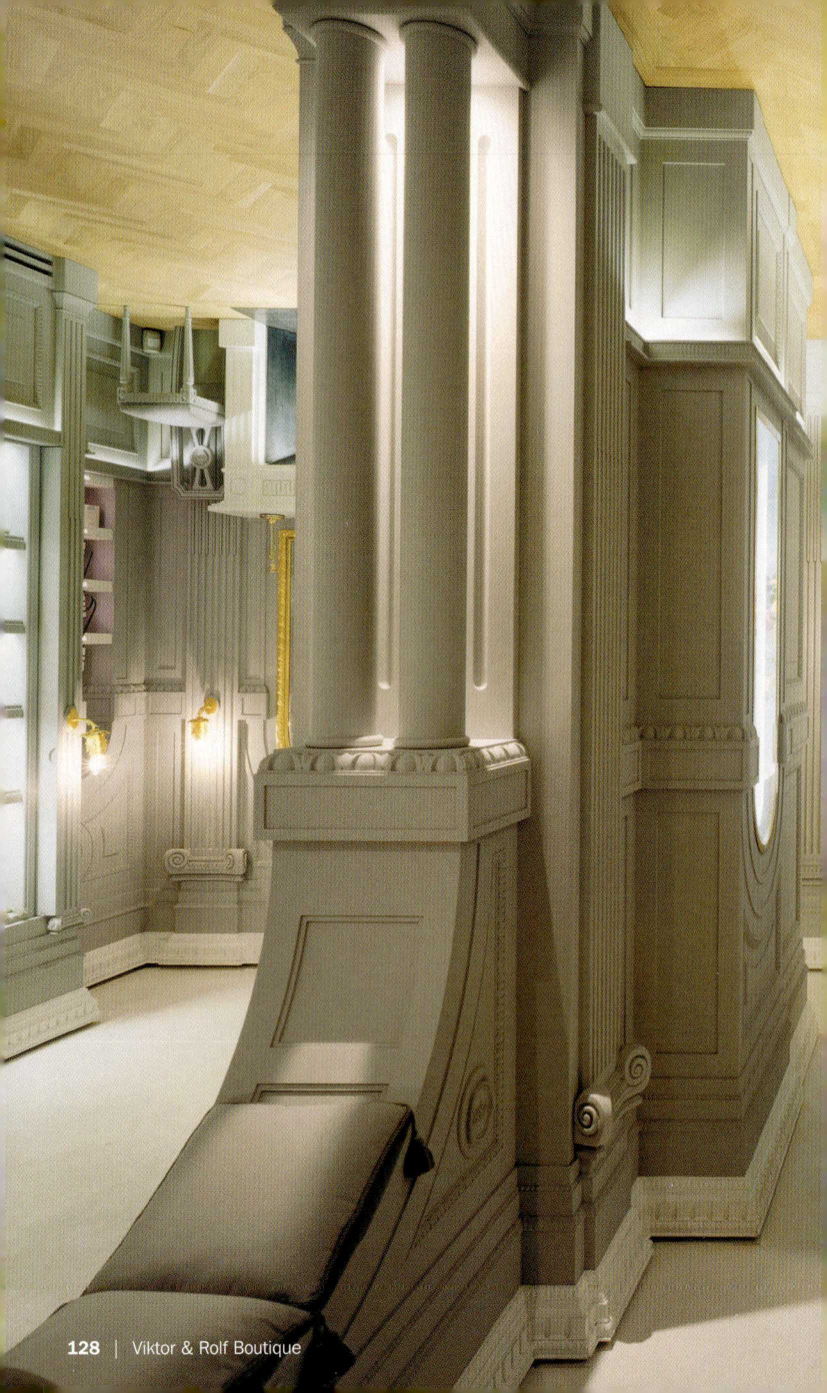

Viktor & Rolf Boutique | **129**

130 | Viktor & Rolf Boutique

Viktor & Rolf Boutique | 131

The name of the boutique for books and accessories defines the design theme: vases and hand-tied floral sprays set the scene for a suggestive ambience, which is close to nature. The architect, Vincent Van Duysen, also keeps the basic harmony of the colors in the soft tones of tea and roses.

Der Name der Boutique für Bücher und Accessoires gibt das gestalterische Thema vor: Vasen und Blumengebinde inszenieren ein naturnahes, anmutiges Ambiente. Auch beim Grundakkord der Farben hält sich der Architekt Vincent Van Duysen an die sanften Töne von Tee und Rosen.

Le nom de ce magasin de livres et d'accessoires définit le thème du design : des vases et des compositions florales créent une atmosphère agréable, proche de la nature. Dans son choix des couleurs de base l'architecte Vincent Van Duysen conserve les tons délicats du thé et de la rose.

El nombre de esta *boutique* de libros y accesorios determina el diseño del interior: las vasijas y las composiciones florales son los elementos decorativos de un agradable ambiente cercano a la naturaleza. En la composición cromática el arquitecto Vincent Van Duysen emplea los tonos suaves del té y de las rosas.

È il nome stesso della boutique di libri ed accessori a dettare la filosofia di fondo dello shop design: vasi e composizioni floreali contribuiscono a creare una leggiadra atmosfera ispirata alla natura. Anche per gli accostamenti cromatici l'architetto Vincent Van Duysen si attiene alle tonalità delicate del tè e delle rose.

Vincent Van Duysen Architects

Lombardenvest 34
2000 Antwerp
Belgium
www.vincentvanduysen.com

Photos courtesy tearose

tearose

Via Italia 5
20052 Monza
Italy
www.tearose.it

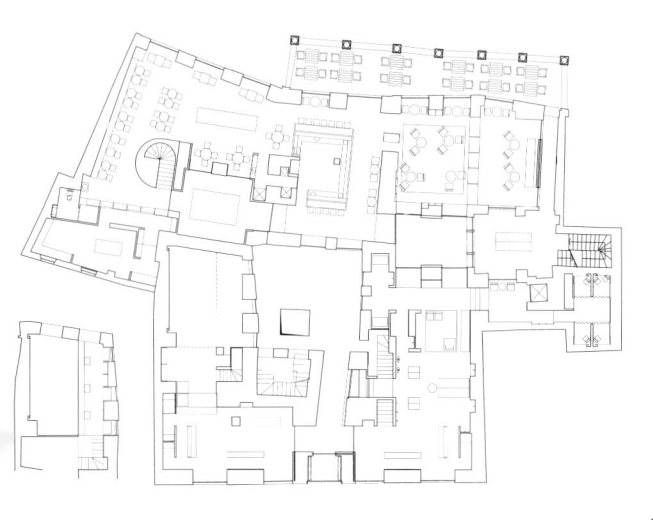

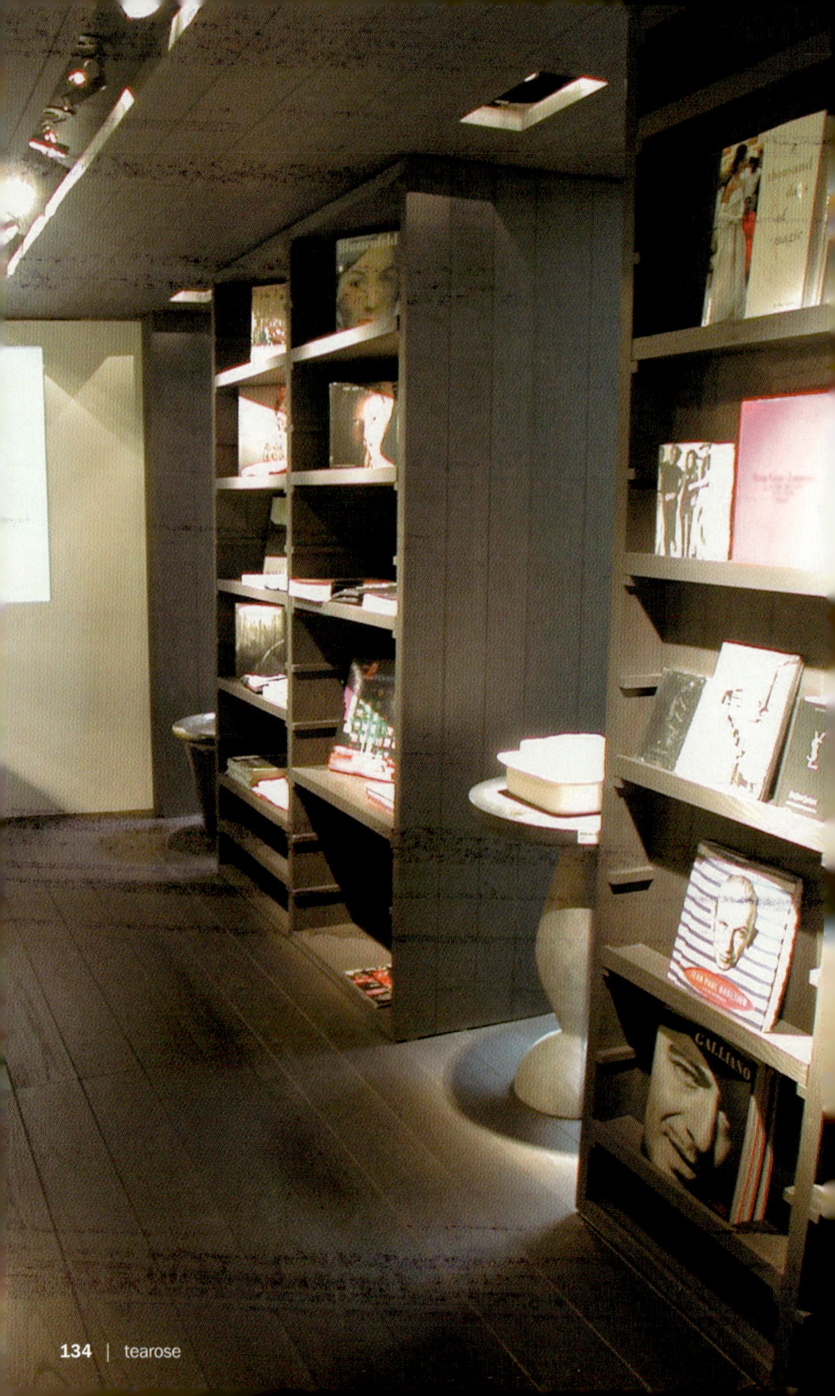
GALLIANO

tearose | 135

The interplay of strong colors with the cool white of the marble defines the sophisticated ambience of the boutique at La Perla in Rome. The rather narrow room is structured with clarity and in cubist style. Niches are created, where the individual outfits are displayed to optimal effect.

Das Zusammenspiel kräftiger Farben mit dem kühlen Weiß von Marmor bestimmt das mondäne Ambiente der Boutique von La Perla in Rom. Der eher schmale Raum ist klar und kubistisch gegliedert. Es entstehen Nischen, in denen die einzelnen Outfits optimal in Szene gesetzt werden.

L'interaction de couleurs vives avec la froideur du marbre blanc caractérise l'atmosphère sophistiquée du magasin La Perla à Rome. L'espace plutôt étroit bénéficie d'une articulation claire et cubiste. Des niches se créent, dans lesquelles les toilettes sont individuellement et idéalement mises en scène.

El juego entre los colores fuertes y el frío blanco del mármol determina el mundano ambiente de la *boutique* de La Perla en Roma. La superficie más bien reducida se caracteriza por las líneas claras y su distribución cubista, que crea pequeños espacios donde se presentan de forma óptima las prendas.

Il contrasto cromatico fra le tonalità decise ed il freddo bianco del marmo è l'elemento predominante dell'atmosfera mondana della boutique La Perla a Roma. All'ambiente stretto e lungo è stata conferita una struttura geometrica ben definita. Nelle nicchie così ricavate singole creazioni trovano la giusta valorizzazione.

Buratti + Battiston Architects

Via Cellini 5
20020 Busto Garolfo – Milan
Italy
www.burattibattiston.it

Photos by Matteo Piazza

La Perla

Via Condotti 79
00187 Rome
Italy
www.laperla.com

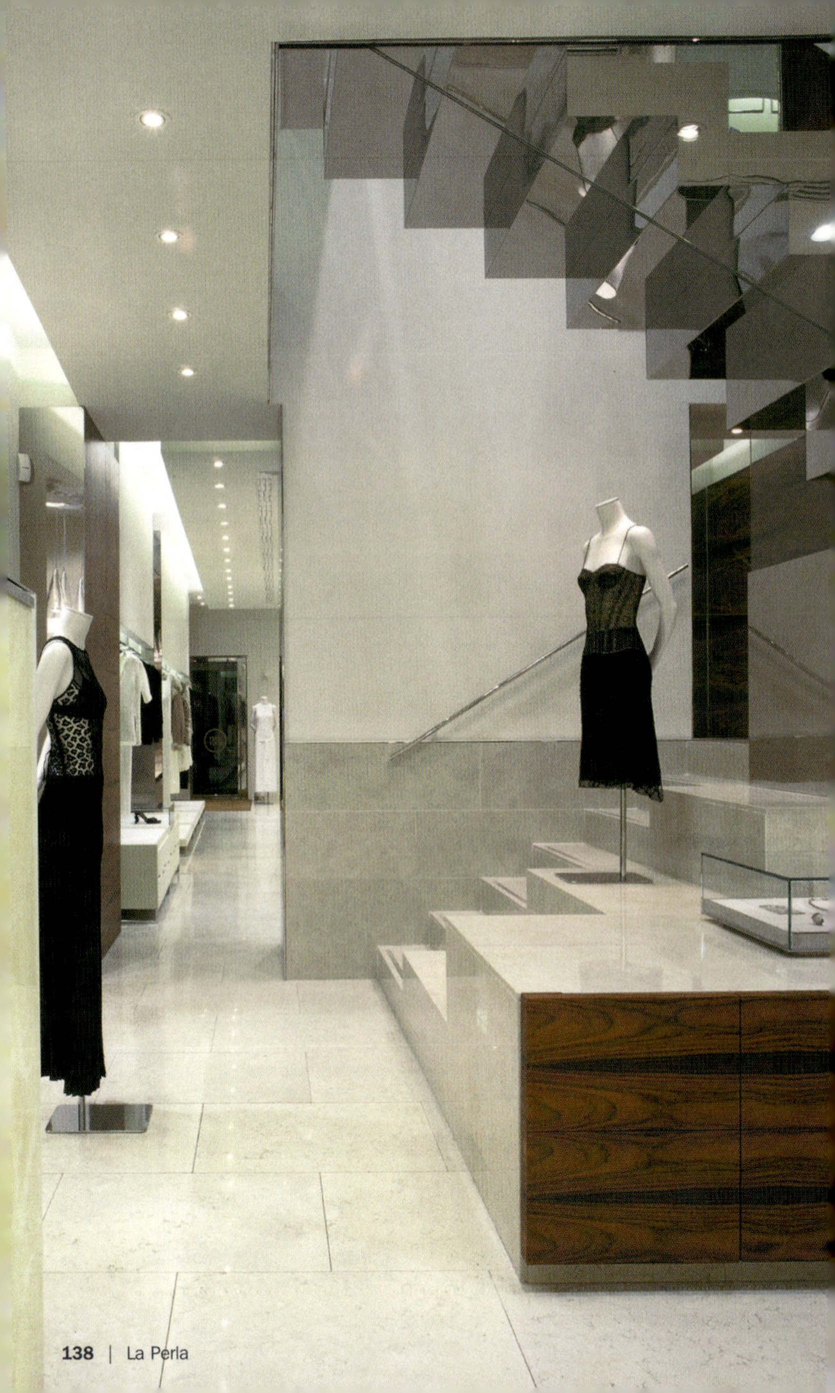

La Perla | 139

140 | La Perla

La Perla | 141

The logo and design of this store speak the same style language. The label's signature therefore defines the boutique's design criteria. On the one hand, this means clarity, which is achieved by light, well-illuminated spaces. On the other hand, long, extending arches and sharp edges characterize the interior.

Logo und Design dieses Stores sprechen die gleiche Stilsprache. So gibt der Schriftzug des Labels die gestalterischen Maßstäbe für die Boutique vor. Das bedeutet einerseits Klarheit – realisiert durch helle, gut ausgeleuchtete Räume. Auf der anderen Seite prägen die lang gezogenen Bögen und scharfen Kanten das Interieur.

Le logo et le design de ce magasin parlent le même langage stylistique. L'écriture du nom de la marque fournit les repères pour la conception du magasin. D'une part, la clarté, concrétisée par des pièces lumineuses et bien éclairées. D'autre part, les arches étirées et les arêtes prononcées caractérisant l'intérieur.

El lenguaje del estilo del logotipo coincide con el del diseño de esta tienda. El tipo de letra de la marca determina la pauta en la decoración interior de la *boutique*. Esto supone, por un lado, claridad, que se consigue con unos espacios bien iluminados. Y por otro, los largos arcos y los afilados bordes caracterizan el interior.

Logo e design di questo store parlano lo stesso linguaggio espressivo. I caratteri del marchio suggeriscono i parametri referenziali dello shop design. Questo si traduce da una parte in uno stile ben definito che trova realizzazione negli ambienti luminosi e illuminati a giorno. Dall'altra in arcate oblunghe e linee spigolose che conferiscono loro carattere.

Sean Dix

Alzaia Naviglio Grande 14
20144 Milan
Italy
www.seandix.com

Photos by Ramak Fazel

Byblos

Krasnogrsk 4
143400 Moscow
Russia
www.byblos.it

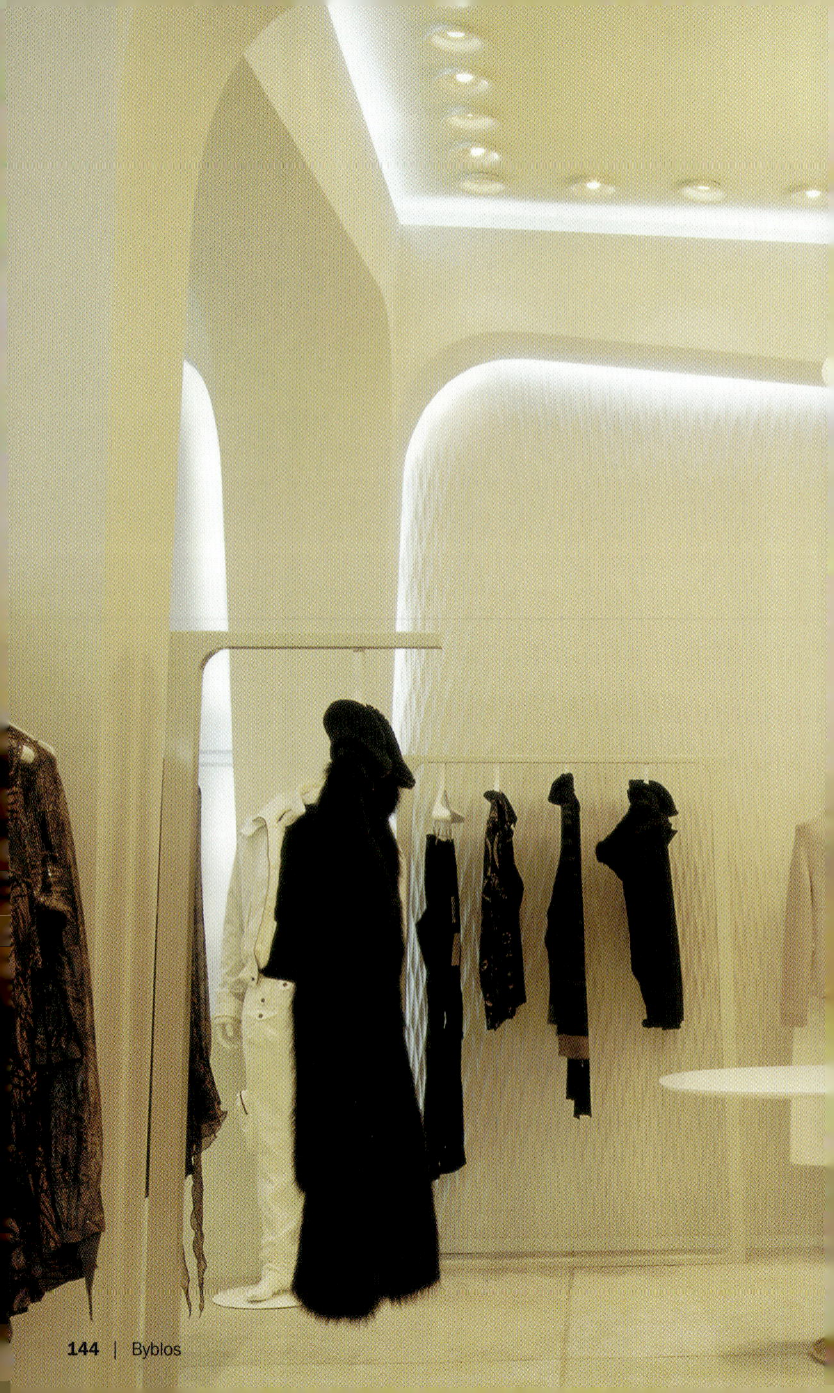

Byblos | 145

Moschino's entrance as a store is distinctive for the monumental mix of old and new, a coincidence of Baroque and modern styling elements, and the use of fabrics in architecture. This principle is on show at the Gum-store with large, red fabric spirals serving as fitting rooms.

Markant für den Store-Auftritt von Moschino ist der monumentale Mix aus Altem und Neuem, der Zusammenfluss von barocken und modernen Stilelementen sowie die Verwendung von Stoffen in der Architektur. Ein Prinzip, das sich im Gum-Store an den großen roten Stoffspiralen verdeutlicht, die als Umkleidekabinen dienen.

L'entrée en scène de Moschino avec un magasin frappe par le mélange monumental d'ancien et de nouveau, la rencontre d'éléments baroques et modernes ainsi que l'emploi d'étoffes dans l'architecture. Un principe réalisé dans le magasin du Gum avec les grandes spirales d'étoffe rouges qui servent de cabines d'essayage.

Lo llamativo del diseño de la tienda de Moschino es la impresionante mezcla entre lo antiguo y lo nuevo, la amalgama de los elementos de estilo barroco y moderno, y el empleo de tejidos en la arquitectura. Un principio que encuentra su expresión en las rojas espirales de tela de la tienda Gum que actúan como probadores.

L'elemento di maggior impatto del Moschino store è la mescolanza monumentale di vecchio e nuovo, la fusione di elementi espressivi barocchi e moderni nonché l'utilizzo delle stoffe come elemento architettonico. Un principio che nello store situato all'interno dei magazzini Gum si concretizza in cabine di prova costituite da enormi spirali rosse in stoffa.

Sean Dix

Alzaia Naviglio Grande 14
20144 Milan
Italy
www.seandix.com

Photos by Sergei Artemiev

Moschino Gum

3, Red Square
Moscow
Russia
www.bosco.ru

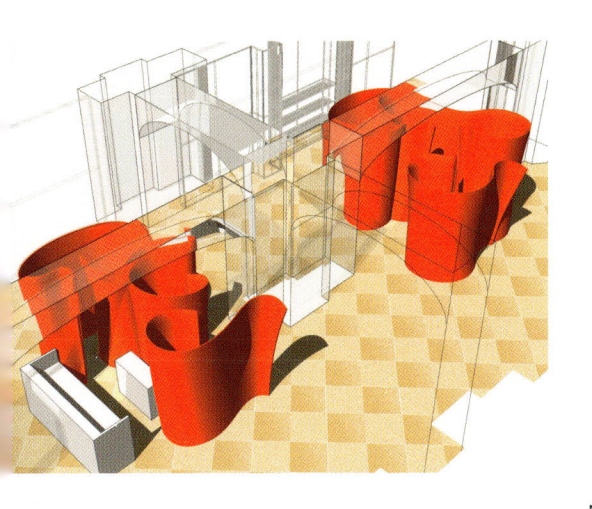

148 | Moschino Gum

Moschino Gum | 149

In the London Porsche Design store, black, titanium and dark brown ensure a timelessly elegant design experience. At the same time, this distinctive tonality underlines Porsche's high-end technology standard. Plasma screens epitomize this and project multi-perspective, visual images of all products.

Im Londoner Porsche Design Store sorgen Schwarz, Titan und Dunkelbraun für ein zeitlos-edles Design-Erlebnis. Zugleich unterstreicht diese markante Tonalität den Anspruch von Porsche auf High-End-Technologie. Paradigmatisch stehen dafür die Plasma-Monitore, die perspektivenreich alle Produkte visualisieren.

Dans le magasin londonien Porsche Design, noir, titane et marron foncé nous donnent à voir un design élégant et intemporel. Cette tonalité prononcée souligne l'exigence de Porsche en terme de technologie haut de gamme. Les écrans plasma qui permettent de visualiser tous les produits en perspective en témoignent.

En la tienda londinense de Porsche Design, el negro, el titanio y el marrón oscuro crean un elegante diseño intemporal. Al mismo tiempo, esta acentuada tonalidad subraya la pretensión de Porsche de ofrecer tecnología punta, por eso se emplean pantallas de plasma donde se visualizan todos los productos desde diversas perspectivas.

Nel Porsche Design Store di Londra lo shop design è tutto giocato sui colori nero, titanio e marrone scuro. L'accostamento cromatico conferisce all'ambiente un'atmosfera di eterna eleganza, non mancando di sottolineare il rimando alla tecnologia high-end cui si ispira il marchio. Paradigmatici pertanto i monitor al plasma sui quali sono visualizzati tutti i prodotti da svariate prospettive.

Matteo Thun

Via Appiani 9
20121 Milan
Italy
www.matteothun.com

Photos courtesy Porsche Design

Porsche Design Store London

New Bond Street 119
London W1S 1EP
United Kingdom
www.porsche-design.com

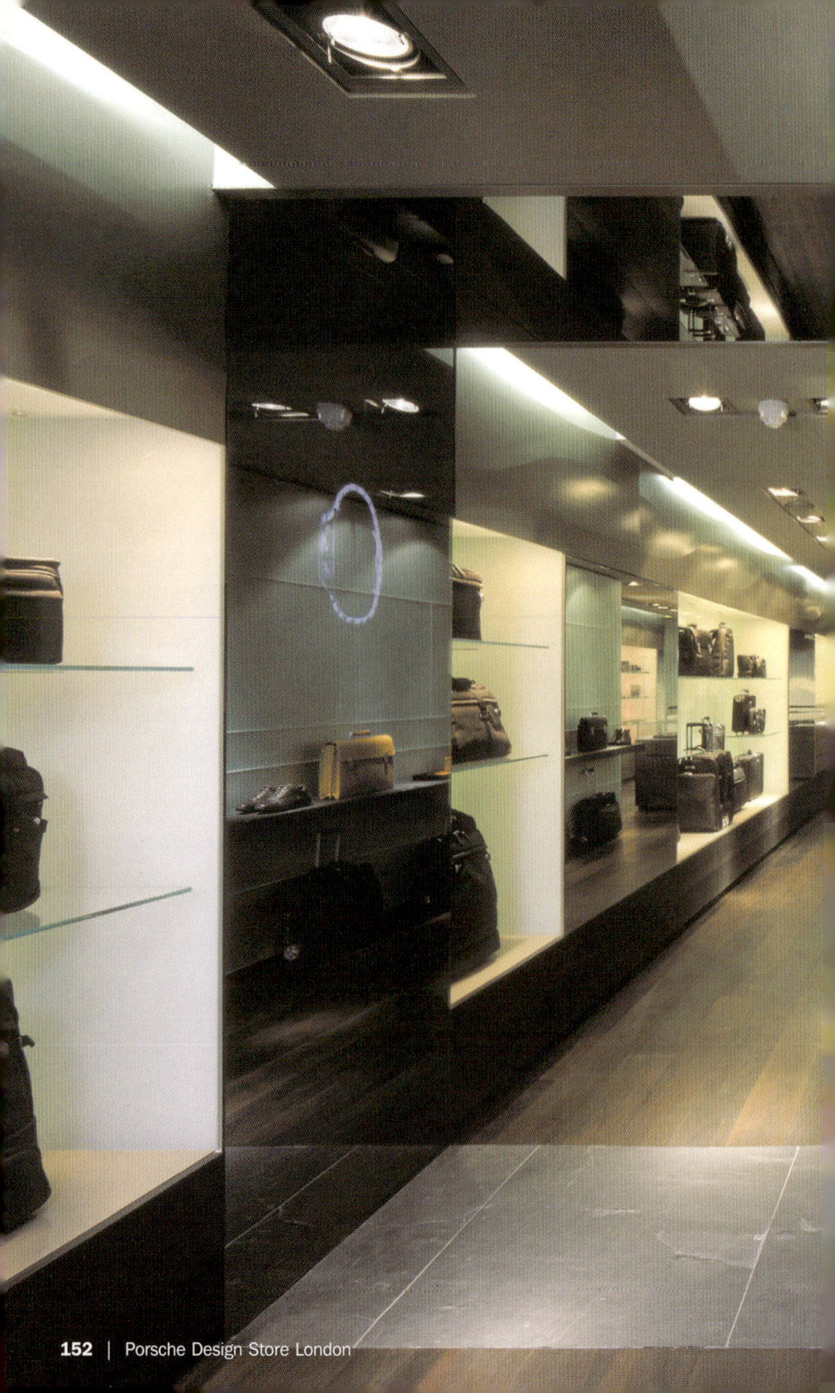

Porsche Design Store London | 153

Hardly any other designer label presents such multi-faceted store design as Stella McCartney. But certain elements are constantly repeated: an emphatically feminine design, as well as expansive spatial organization with the impact of landscaping. In the London store, foliage patterns cover the walls and virtually take root right down to the floor.

Kaum ein Label zeigt sich so vielfältig im Store-Design wie Stella McCartney. Dennoch gibt es Elemente, die immer wieder auftauchen: eine betont feminine Gestaltung sowie eine weite Raumordnung, die landschaftlich wirkt. Im Londoner Store überziehen Strauch-Motive die Wände, die sich regelrecht bis in den Boden hinein fortpflanzen.

Presque aucune autre marque n'affiche une telle diversité dans le design de ses magasins que Stella McCartney. Cependant, certains éléments se répètent : une décoration résolument féminine ainsi qu'une organisation généreuse de l'espace donnant une impression de paysage. Dans le magasin londrais, des motifs d'arbustes couvrent les murs allant jusqu'à prendre racine dans le sol.

Pocas marcas poseen un diseño tan polifacético en sus tiendas como Stella McCartney. Y aun así hay elementos que siempre se repiten: una marcada presentación femenina y una amplia distribución del espacio con la que se consigue un efecto paisajístico. En la tienda de Londres formas arborescentes recorren las paredes, que parecen introducirse en el suelo.

Come nessun'altra griffe Stella McCartney sa presentarsi in veste sempre nuova. Lo shop design è contraddistinto tuttavia da elementi ricorrenti, come la spiccata femminilità degli interni e l'ampia spazialità. Nello Stella McCartney Store di Londra motivi di ispirazione vegetale si avviluppano sulle pareti, in un intreccio che sembra spuntare dal pavimento.

Universal Design Studio Ltd.

Ground Floor
35 Charlotte Road
London E2CA 3PG
United Kingdom
www.universaldesignstudio.com

Photos by Richard Davies / Universal Design Studio

Stella McCartney

30 Bruton Street
London W1J 6QR
United Kingdom
www.stellamccartney.com

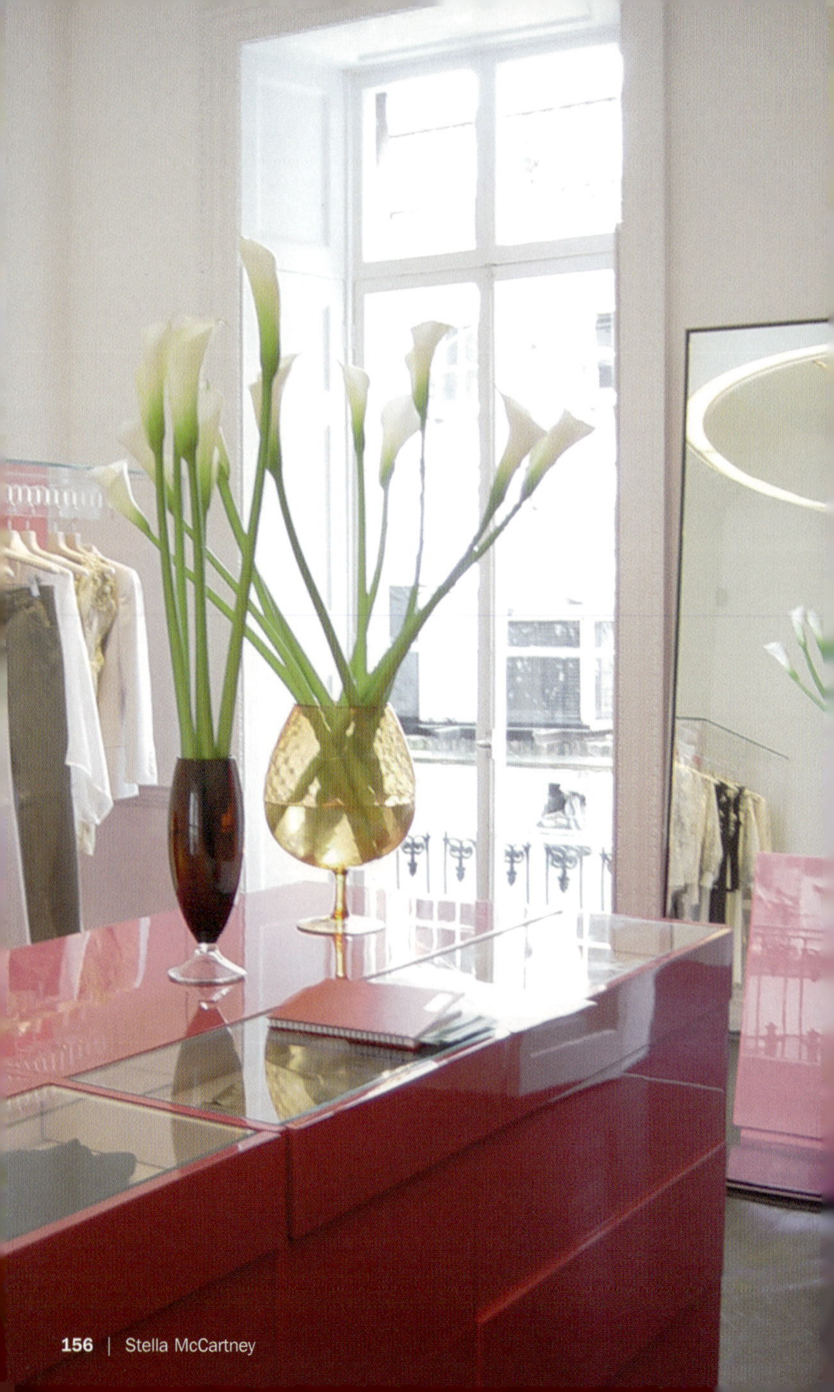

Stella McCartney | **157**

Tranquility in motion prevails in Isay Weinfeld's design. The walkways lead clearly through the boutique—you stroll past rows of outfits like on the catwalk. The walled shelves are ordered at the sides in a fine, repetitive rhythmic flow. In-between, traditional furnishing sets tranquil notes.

In Isay Weinfelds Design herrscht Ruhe in der Bewegung. Klar führen die Wege durch die Boutique – wie bei einem Defilee schlendert man an aufgereihten Outfits entlang. In feiner, wiederkehrender Rhythmik gliedern sich seitlich die Regalwände. Dazwischen setzen traditionelle Möbel Ruhepunkte.

Le design d'Isay Weinfeld, c'est la tranquillité dans le mouvement. Le magasin est parcouru d'allées claires – comme dans un défilé on déambule devant les toilettes alignées. De part et d'autre, les étagères murales rythment l'agencement du magasin. Des meubles traditionnels offrent des îlots de calme.

En el diseño de Isay Weinfeld domina la tranquilidad en el movimiento. Los caminos conducen de forma clara a lo largo de la tienda mientras que, como si de un desfile se tratara, los clientes van pasando lentamente al lado de las prendas expuestas en fila. Las paredes con las estanterías están dispuestas siguiendo un delicado y repetitivo ritmo. En medio, los muebles antiguos actúan como zonas de descanso.

Nello shop design firmato Isay Weinfeld prevale l'idea di quiete nel movimento. Percorsi ben definiti guidano attraverso la boutique, come in un défilé ci sfilano accanto creazioni moda ben allineate. Lateralmente le scaffalature scandiscono un ritmo sottile e ricorrente, interrotto quà e là da elementi d'arredo tradizionali che sembrano come fissare il movimento.

Isay Weinfeld

Rua Andre Fernandes, 175
04536-020
São Paulo / SP
Brazil
www.isayweinfeld.com

Photos by Álvaro Povoa

Forum Rio

Rua Barão da Torre, 422
22441-000
Rio de Janeiro / RJ
Brazil
www.forum.com.br

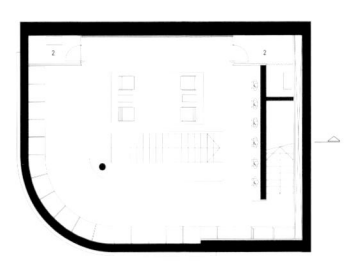

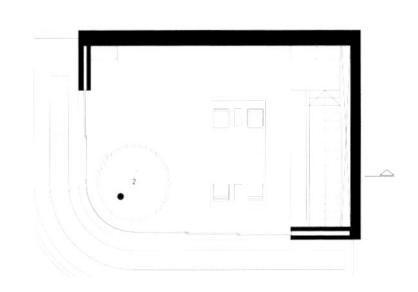

Forum Rio

Forum Rio | **161**

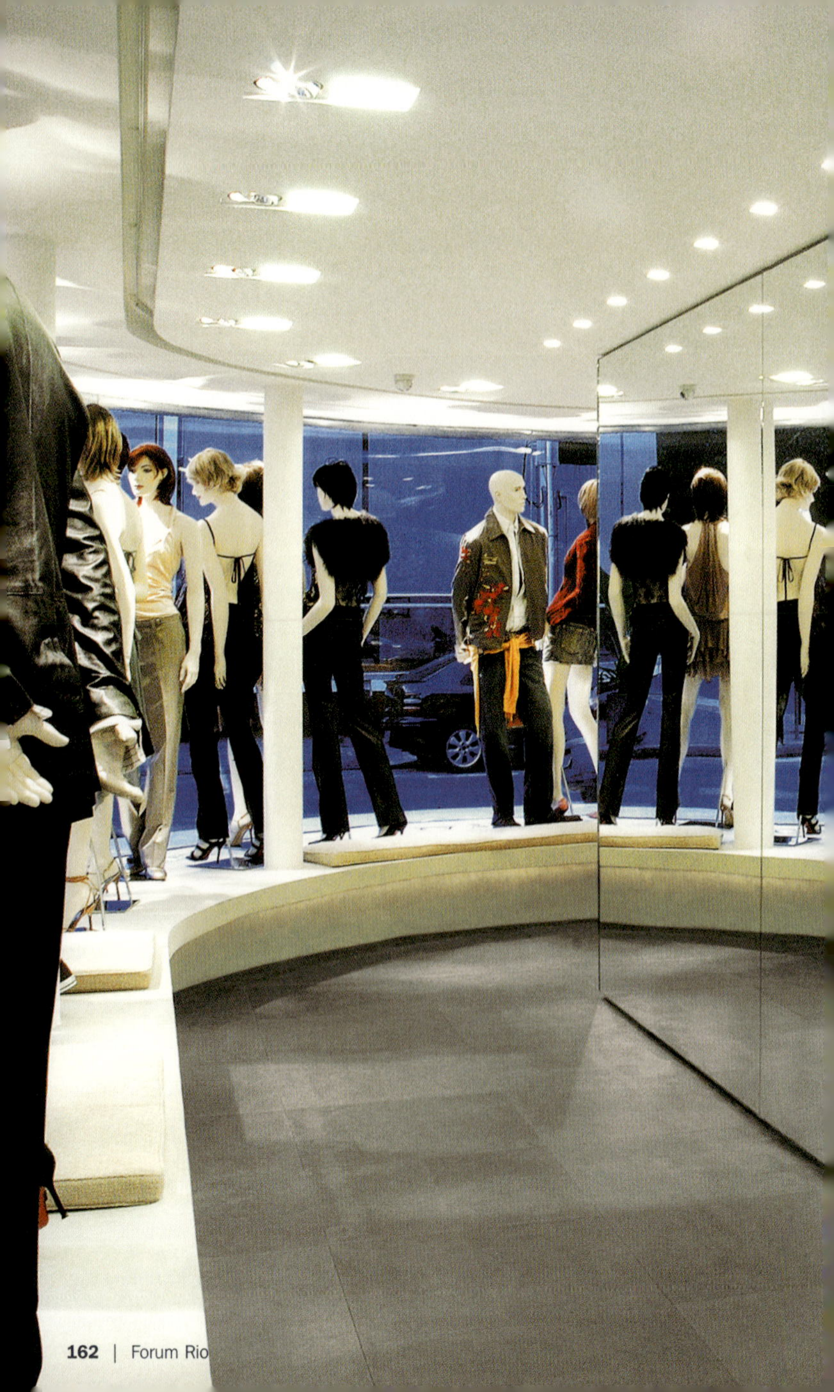

Forum Rio | 163

164 | Forum Rio

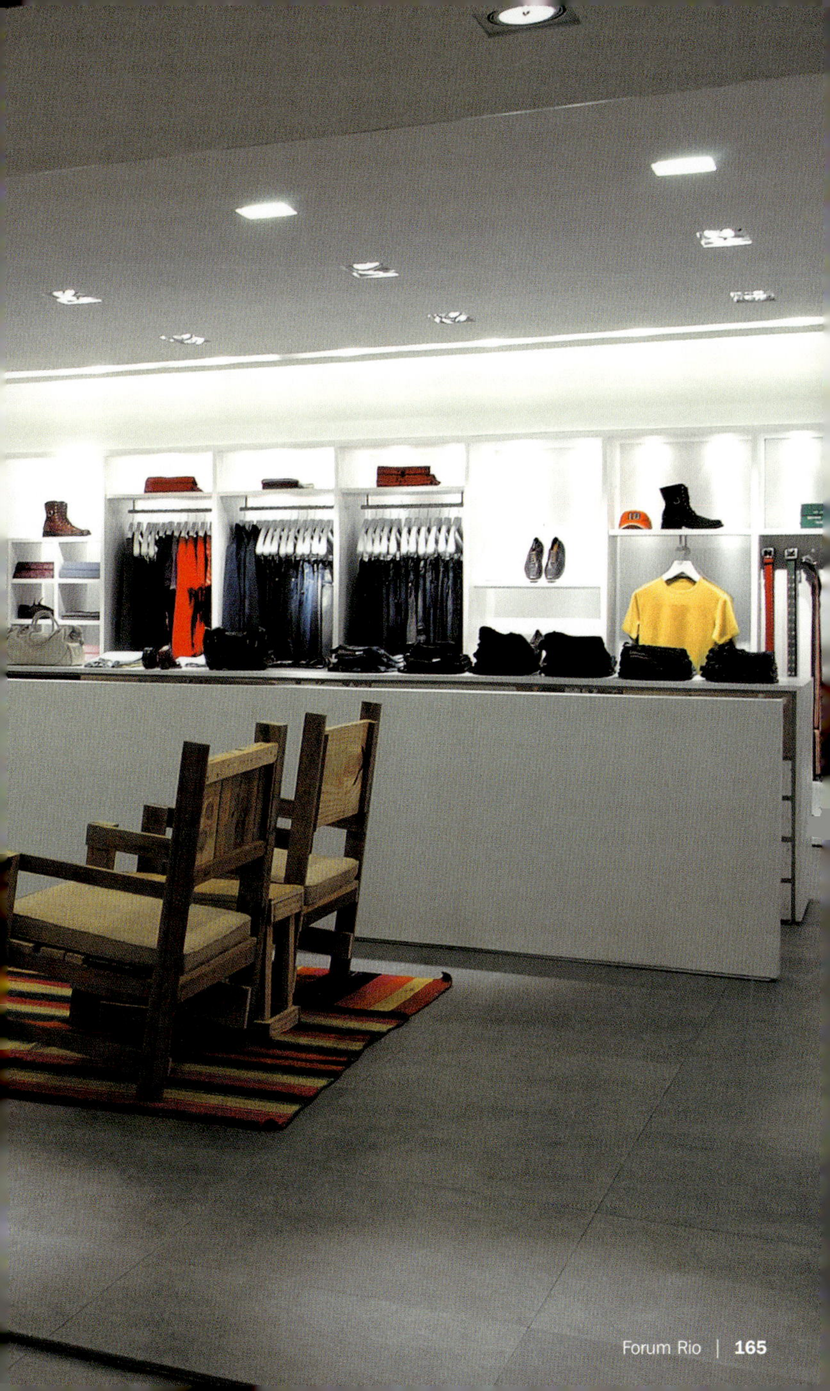

Clube Chocolate represents conceptual design: wooden-slatted frontage and disciplined rhythm influence the ambience. Elements such as white mosaic stones, or the repetitive palm decoration create an outdoor atmosphere. The slender, reflecting spiral staircase is the most striking design feature.

Der Clube Chocolate steht für Konzeptdesign: Stabholzfronten und strenge Rhythmik prägen das Ambiente. Eine Atmosphäre wie im Freien erzeugen Elemente wie Mosaike aus weißen Steinen oder die wiederkehrende Palmendekoration. Auffälligstes Objekt des Designs ist die schlanke, spiegelnde Wendeltreppe.

Le Clube Chocolate incarne le design conceptuel: un habillage de bois et un rythme strict caractérisent l'atmosphère. Des éléments tels que des mosaïques de pierres blanches ou l'emploi répété de palmiers pour la décoration créent une impression de plein air. L'objet le plus frappant du design est l'escalier miroitant en colimaçon.

El Clube Chocolate es sinónimo de diseño conceptual: Los frentes de listones de madera y la severidad del ritmo caracterizan el ambiente. Elementos como los mosaicos de piedras blancas y una repetitiva decoración de palmeras recrean una atmósfera que evoca un espacio abierto. El objeto más llamativo del diseño de este interior es la esbelta escalera de caracol reflectante.

Il Clube Chocolate è sinonimo di concept design: superfici in legno a listarelle e ritmo rigoroso definiscono lo stile. I mosaici di tasselli bianchi e la presenza ricorrente di palme decorative ricreano l'atmosfera di uno spazio all'aperto. L'emento di maggior rilievo nel design è costituito dalla sottile scala a chiocciola con parete riflettente.

Isay Weinfeld

Rua Andre Fernandes, 175
04536-020
São Paulo / SP
Brazil
www.isayweinfeld.com

Photos by Tuca Reinés, Álvaro Povoa

Clube Chocolate

Rua Oscar Freire, 913
01426-001
São Paulo / SP
Brazil
www.clubechocolate.com

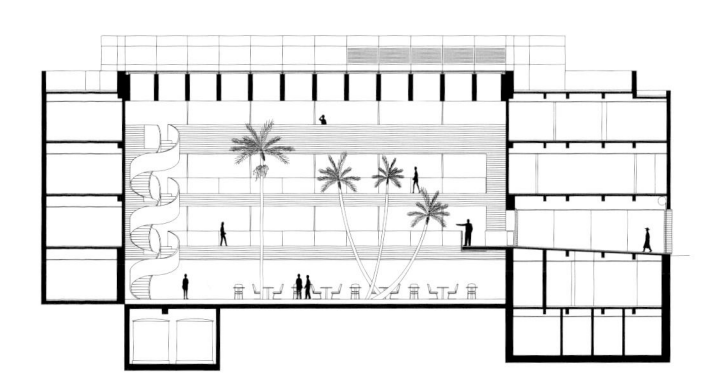

CLUBE CHOCOLATE

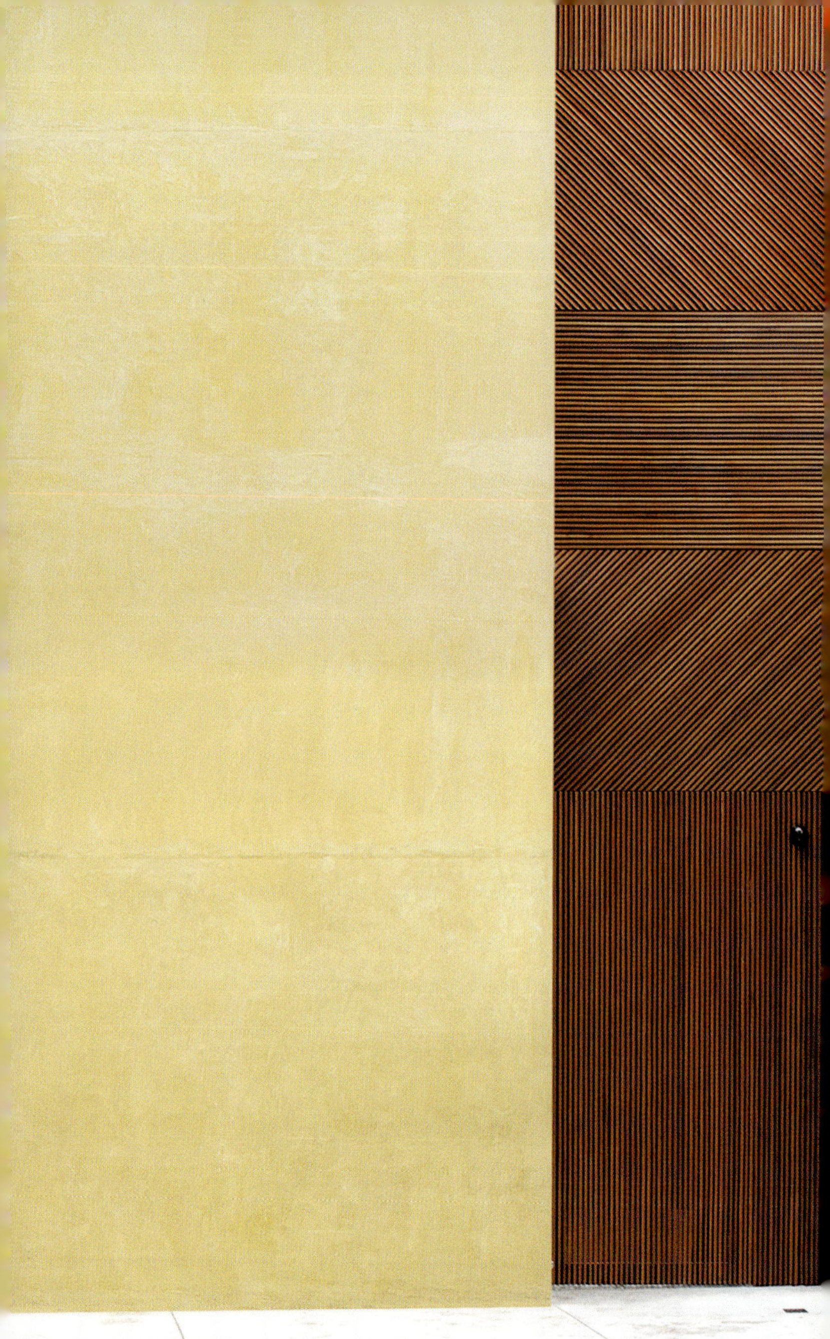

170 | Clube Chocolate

Clube Chocolate | 171

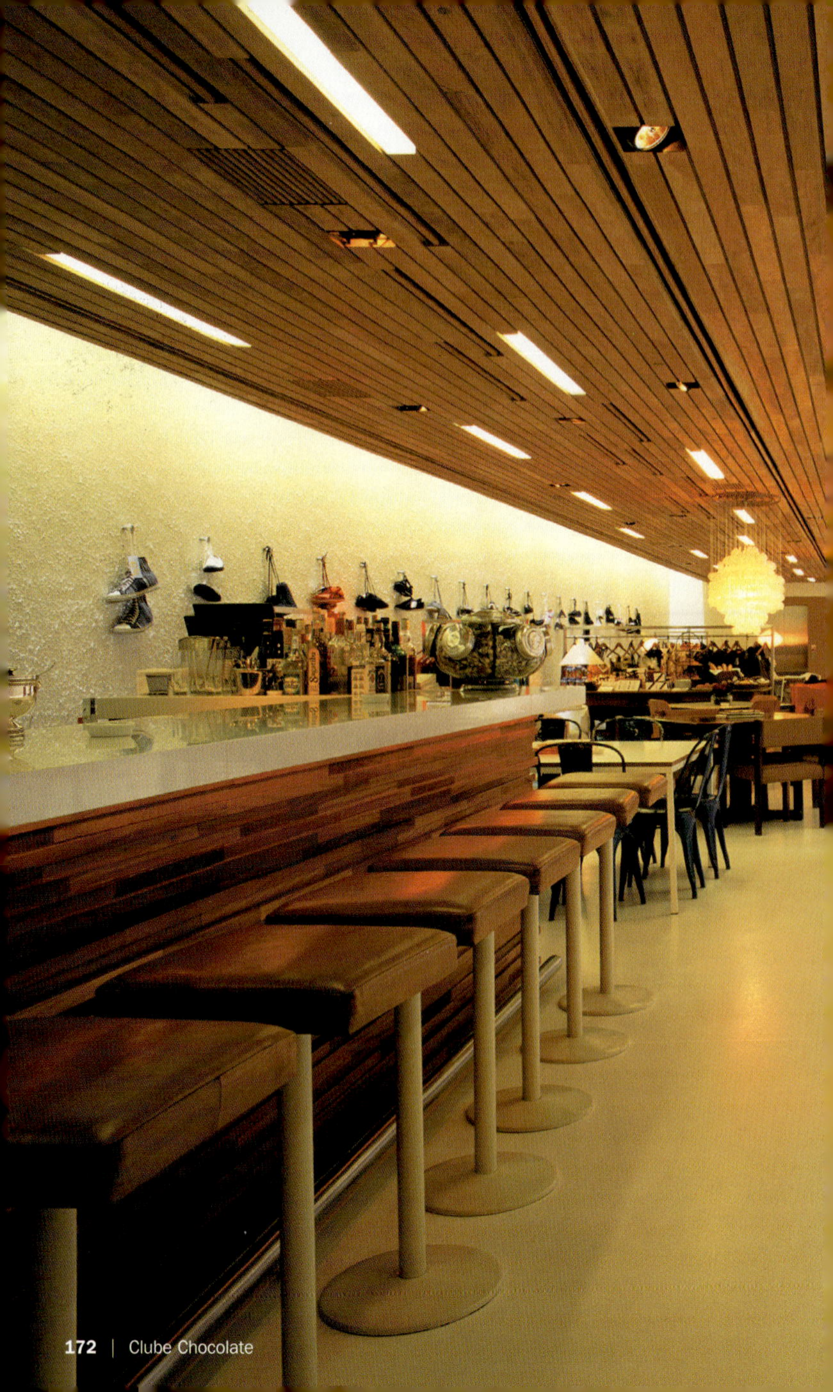

Clube Chocolate

In Weinfeld's architectural design, what dominates is the spatial expanse for the Forum SP: long, extending cuboids and hallways and an external staircase fitted with red glass mosaic tiles. In the open scenery, Weinfeld's taste for discreet and equally distinctive fittings is shown.

Die Weite des Raums dominiert in Weinfelds architektonischem Entwurf für das Forum SP: Lang gestreckte Quader und Flure und eine mit rotem Glasmosaik ausgelegte Freitreppe. In der offenen Inszenierung zeigt sich Weinfelds Sinn für eine dezente und gleichzeitig prägnante Ausstattung.

Dans le dessin architectural de Weinfeld pour le Forum SP, le plus frappant est l'étendue de l'espace : des parallélépipèdes rectangles et des couloirs étirés et un perron carrelé de mosaïque en verre rouge. Cette mise en scène ouverte témoigne du goût de Weinfeld pour une décoration discrète et cependant originale.

La amplitud del espacio es el elemento dominante de la proyección arquitectónica de Weinfeld para el Forum SP: sillares y pasillos alargados y una escalera exenta cubierta con mosaicos de vidrio rojos. En la escenificación abierta se muestra el sentido de Weinfeld para el equipamiento discreto a la vez que preciso.

L'ampiezza è l'elemento predominante nella concezione architettonica realizzata per il Forum SP: parallelepipedi e corridoi oblunghi ed una scalinata esterna ricoperta di mosaici di vetro rosso. La scenografia aperta mostra al meglio la tendenza spiccata di Weinfeld di firmare i suoi interni con pochi ma significativi dettagli.

Isay Weinfeld

Rua Andre Fernandes, 175
04536-020
São Paulo / SP
Brazil
www.isayweinfeld.com

Photos by Tuca Reinés

Forum SP

Rua Oscar Freire, 916
01426-000
São Paulo / SP
Brazil
www.forum.com.br

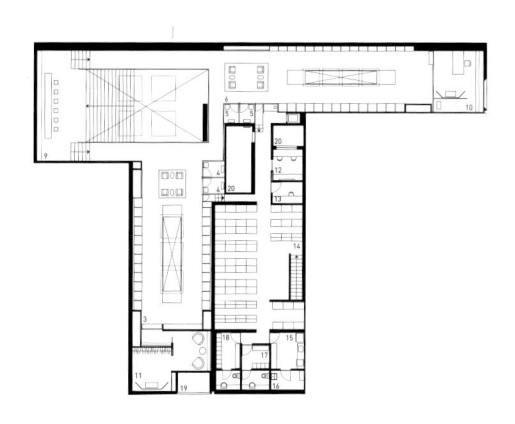

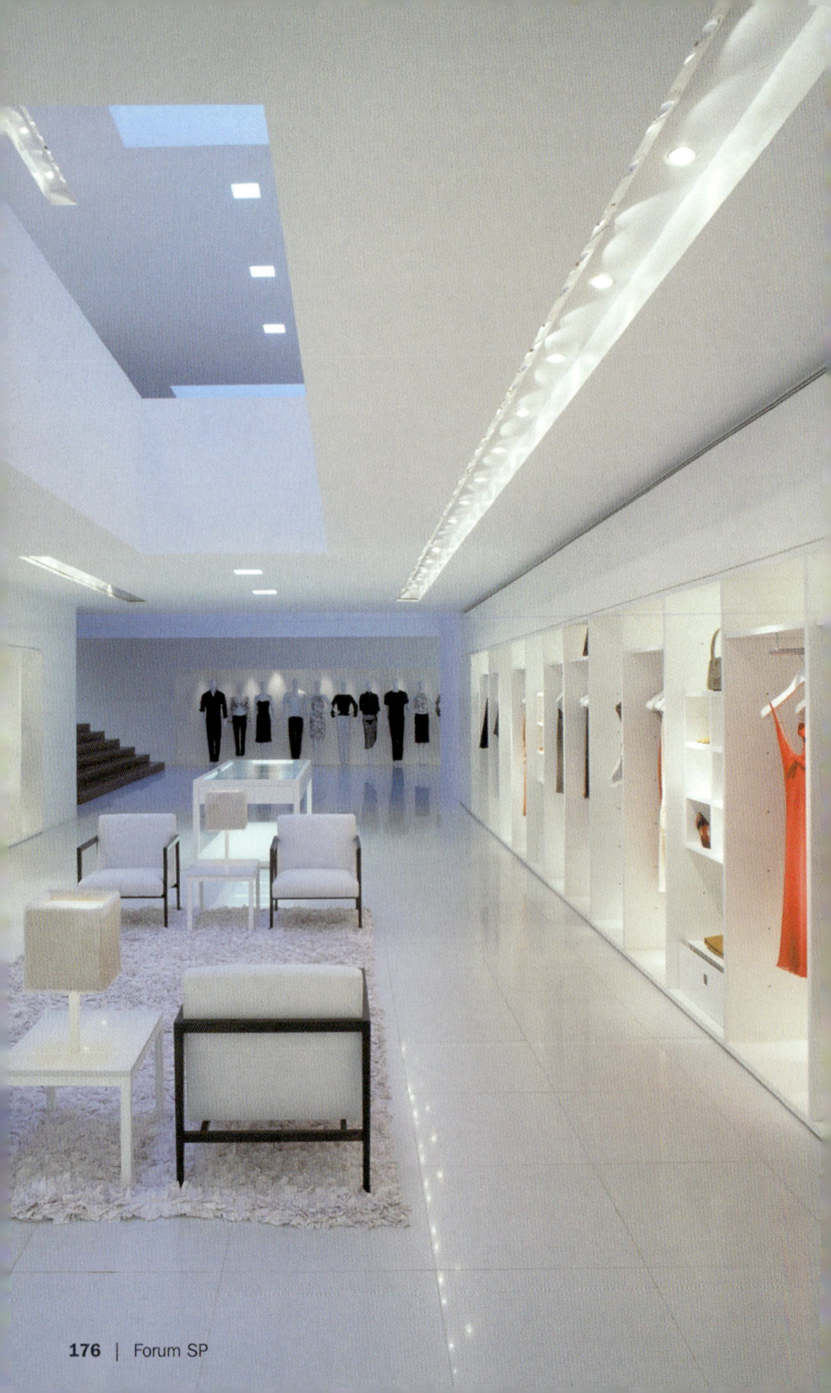

Forum SP | **177**

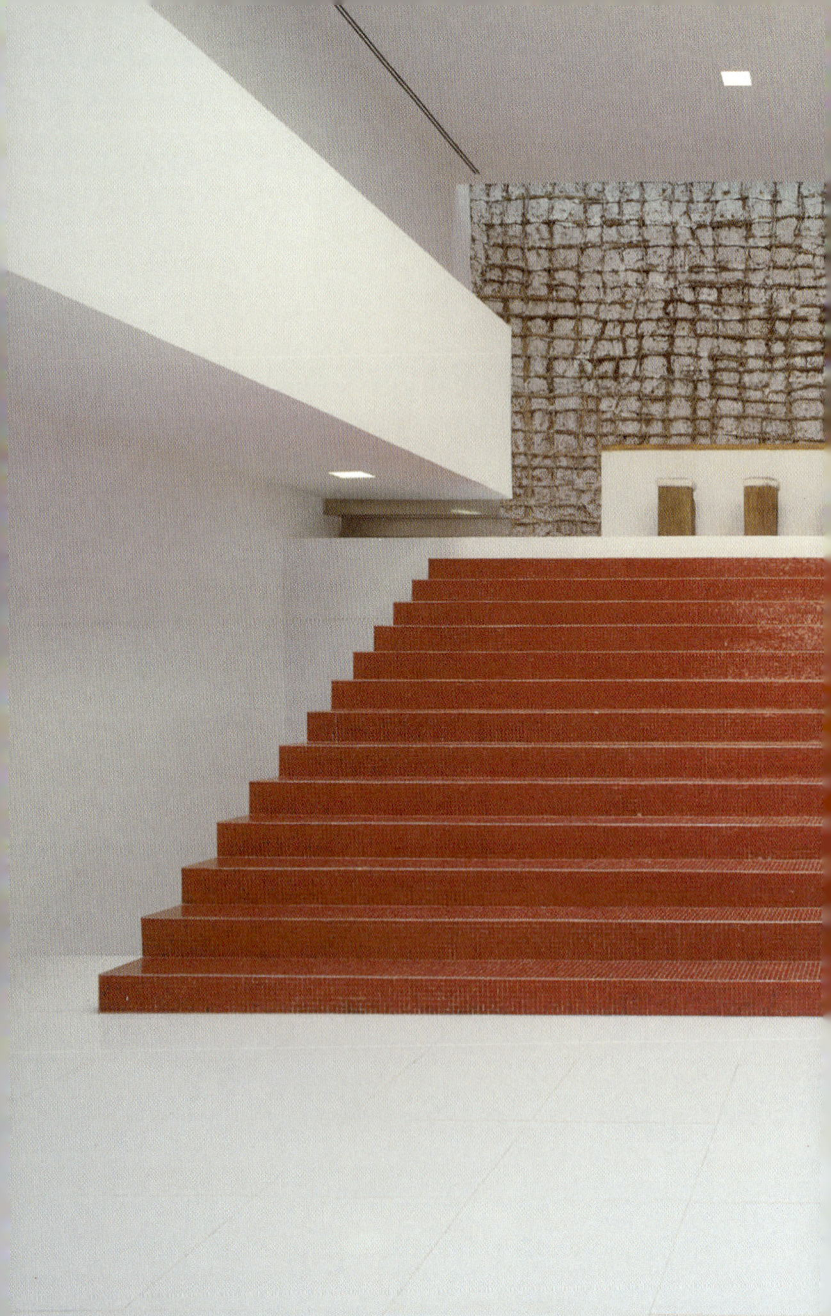

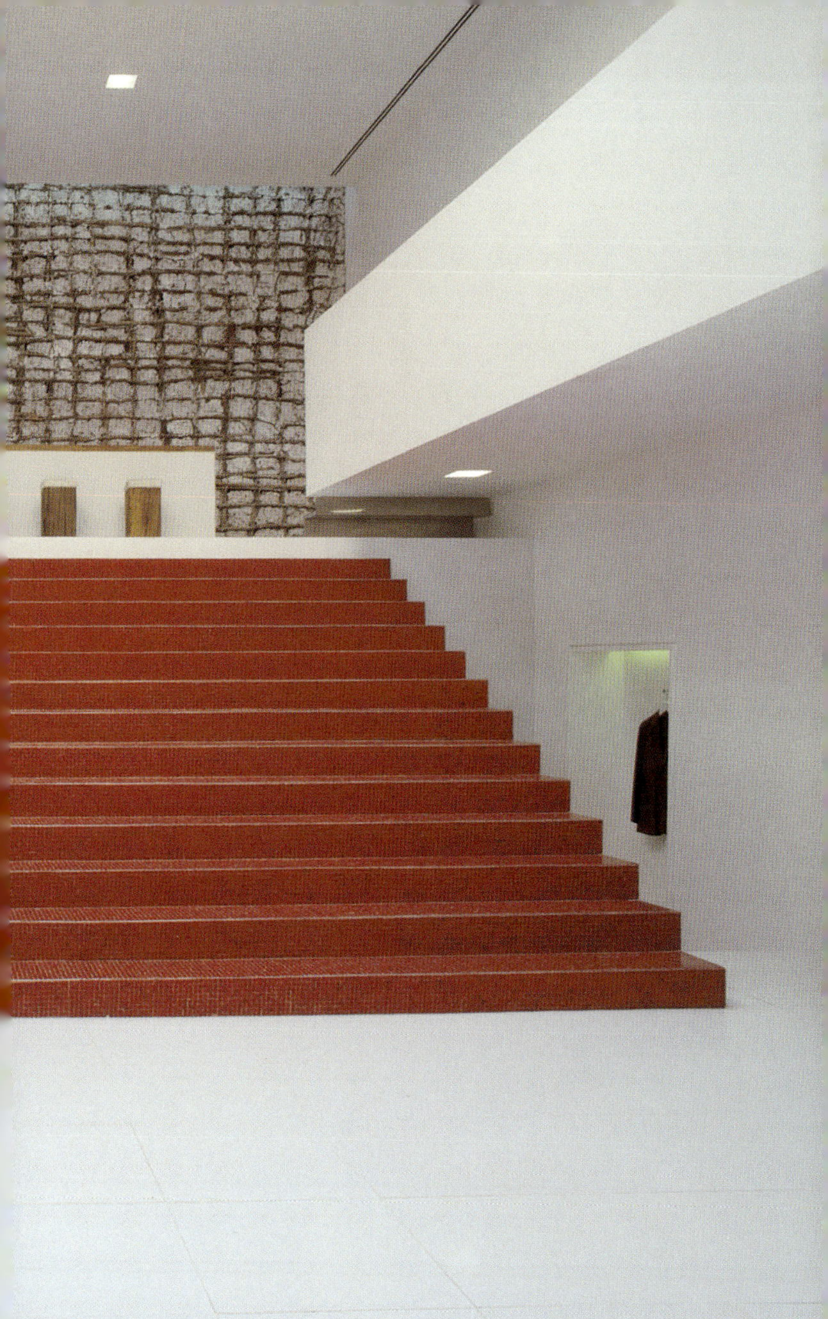

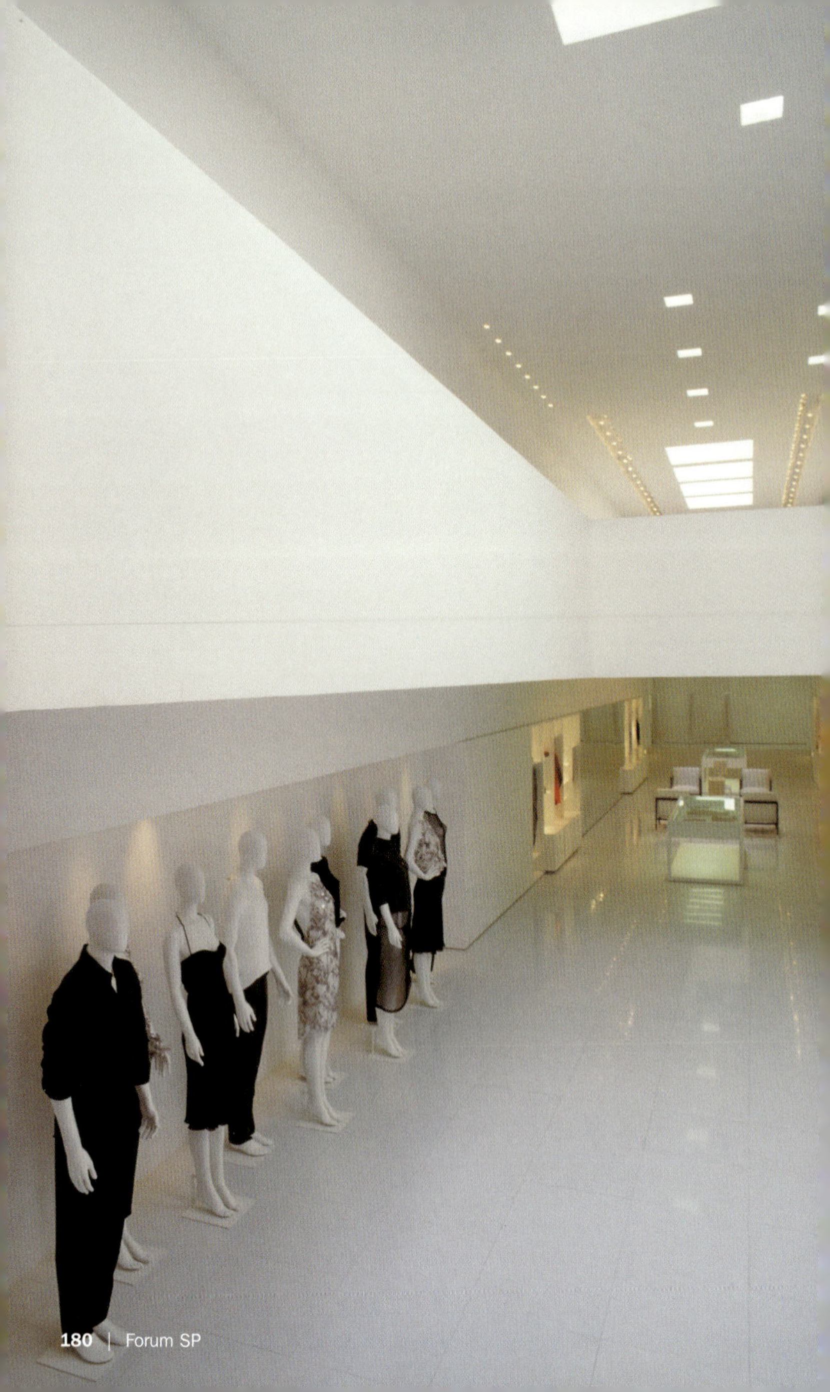

Forum SP

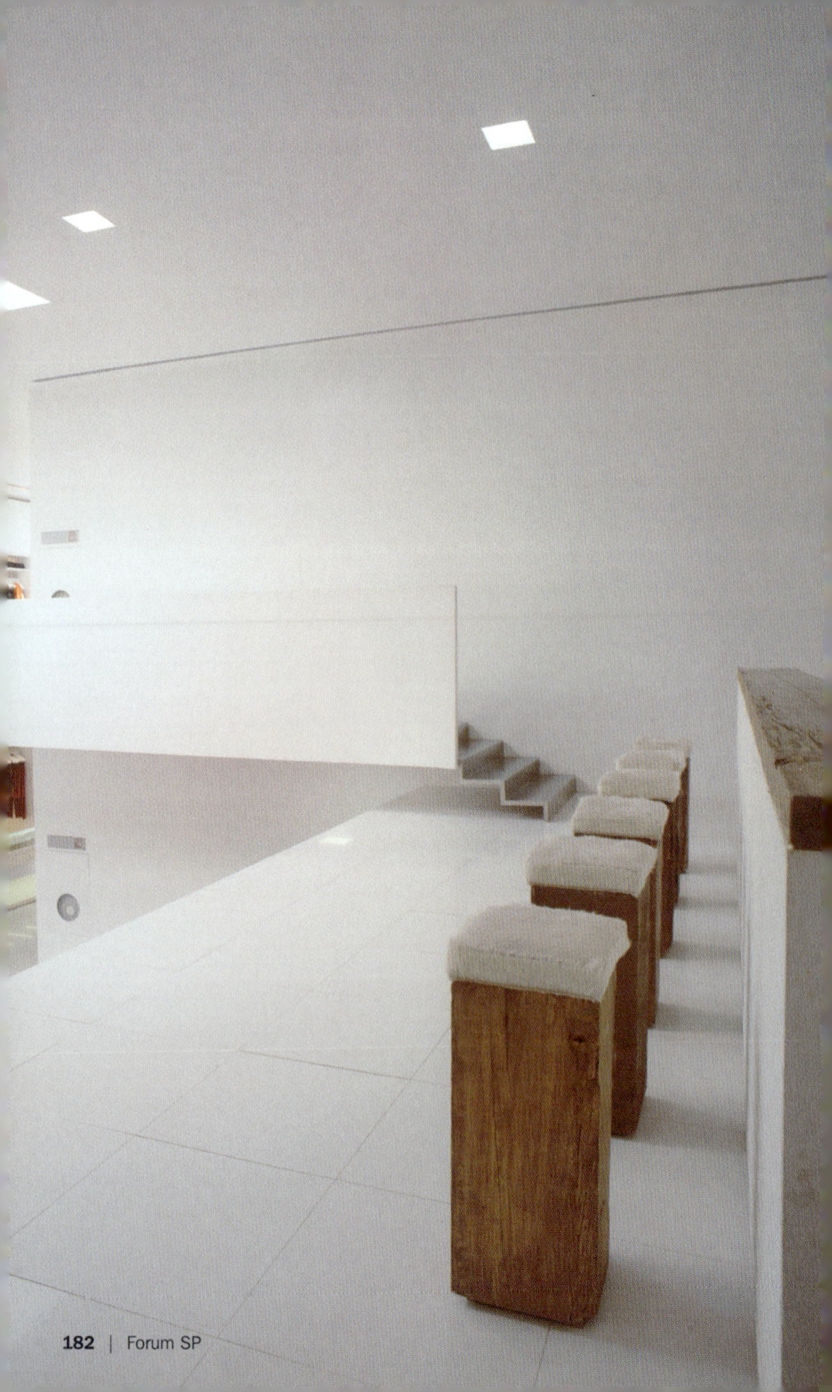

Forum SP | **183**

Sheer luxury needs to be achieved appropriately. For this floor of the shop, the designers adopt historic references, such as the boudoir. But all retrospectives enjoy contemporary interpretations. A room-dividing partition wall made of mirrors unfolds like a concertina and is full of symbolic power.

Höchster Luxus will angemessen in Szene gesetzt sein. Im Falle dieser Shop-Etage greifen die Designer historische Bezüge auf – etwa die des Boudoirs. Doch alle Rückgriffe erfahren zeitgemäße Interpretationen. Voller Symbolkraft entfaltet sich eine Raum teilende Spiegelwand wie eine Ziehharmonika.

Le luxe pur se doit d'être convenablement mis en scène. Pour cet étage du magasin les designers adoptent des références historiques, comme le boudoir. Mais ces reprises font l'objet d'interprétations contemporaines. Pleine de force symbolique, une cloison constituée de miroirs séparant l'espace s'étire comme un accordéon.

El lujo superlativo requiere una presentación adecuada. En el caso de esta planta de la tienda, los diseñadores se sirven de las referencias históricas como las del *boudoir*. Sin embargo, todas las alusiones se someten a la interpretación de la época actual. Como un acordeón se despliega un tabique de espejos dividiendo el espacio con la fuerza del simbolismo.

Il lusso all'ennesima potenza necessita di un contesto in grande stile. Nel caso dell'Holt Renfrew Montréal i designer si sono serviti di dettagli storici, come per esempio i boudoir, rivisitandoli in chiave contemporanea. Di grande forza simbolica la parete a specchio che, aprendosi come una fisarmonica, delimita gli spazi.

burdifilek

183 Bathurst St. Suite 300
M5t 2R7 Toronto
Canada

Photos by Ben Rahn – A Frame

Holt Renfrew Montréal – Women's Couture Room

1300 Sherbrooke Street West
H3G 1H9 Montréal
Canada
www.holtrenfrew.com

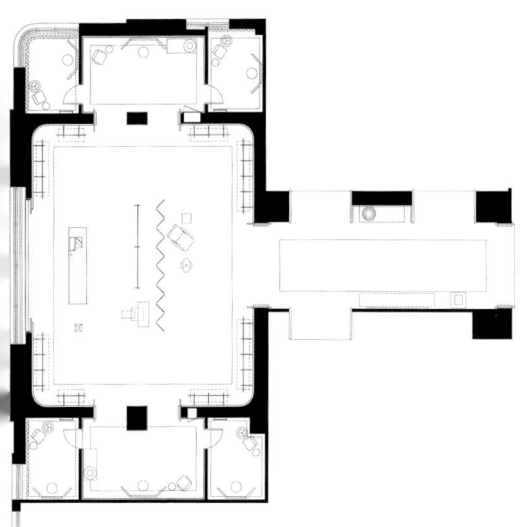

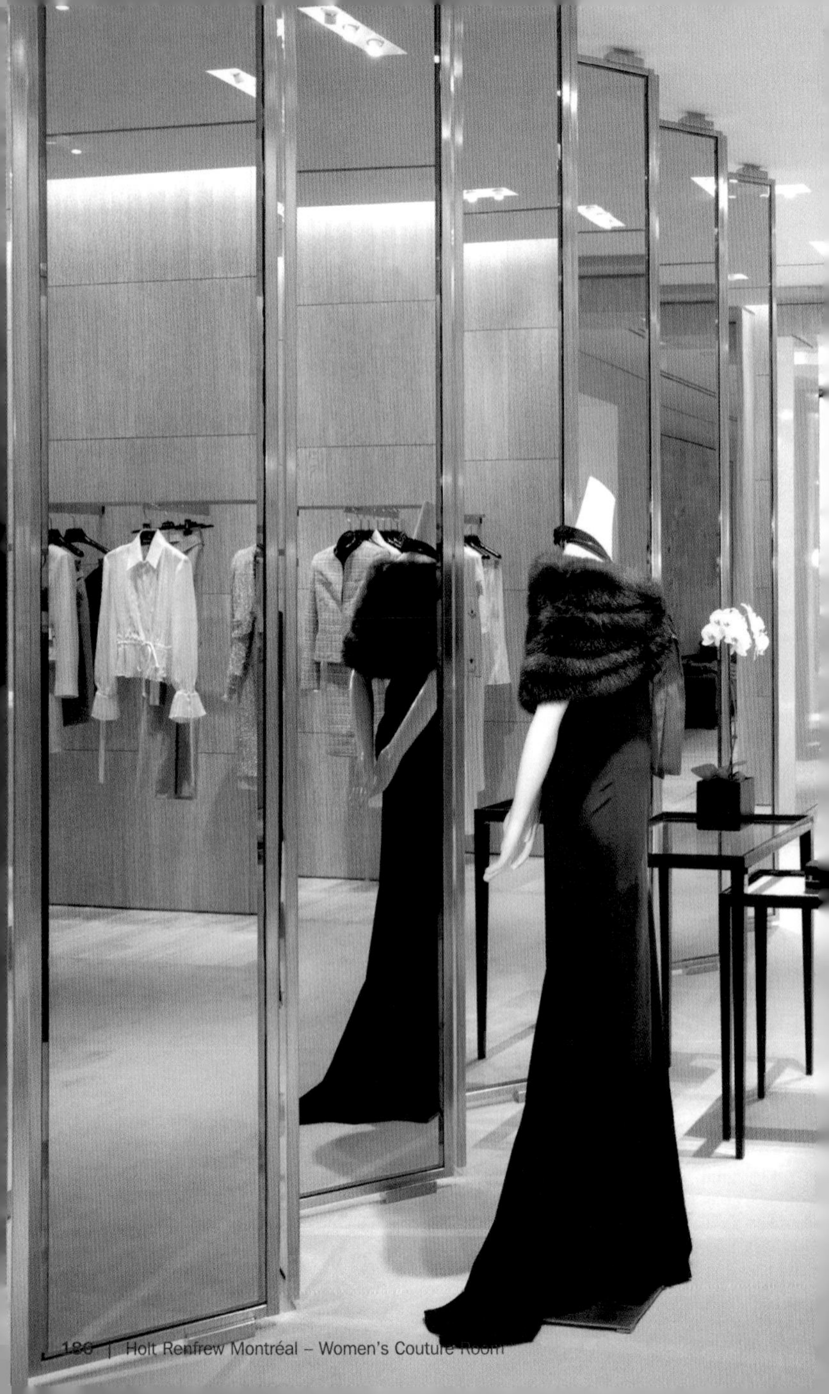

Holt Renfrew Montréal – Women's Couture Room | **187**

188 | Holt Renfrew Montréal – Women's Couture Room

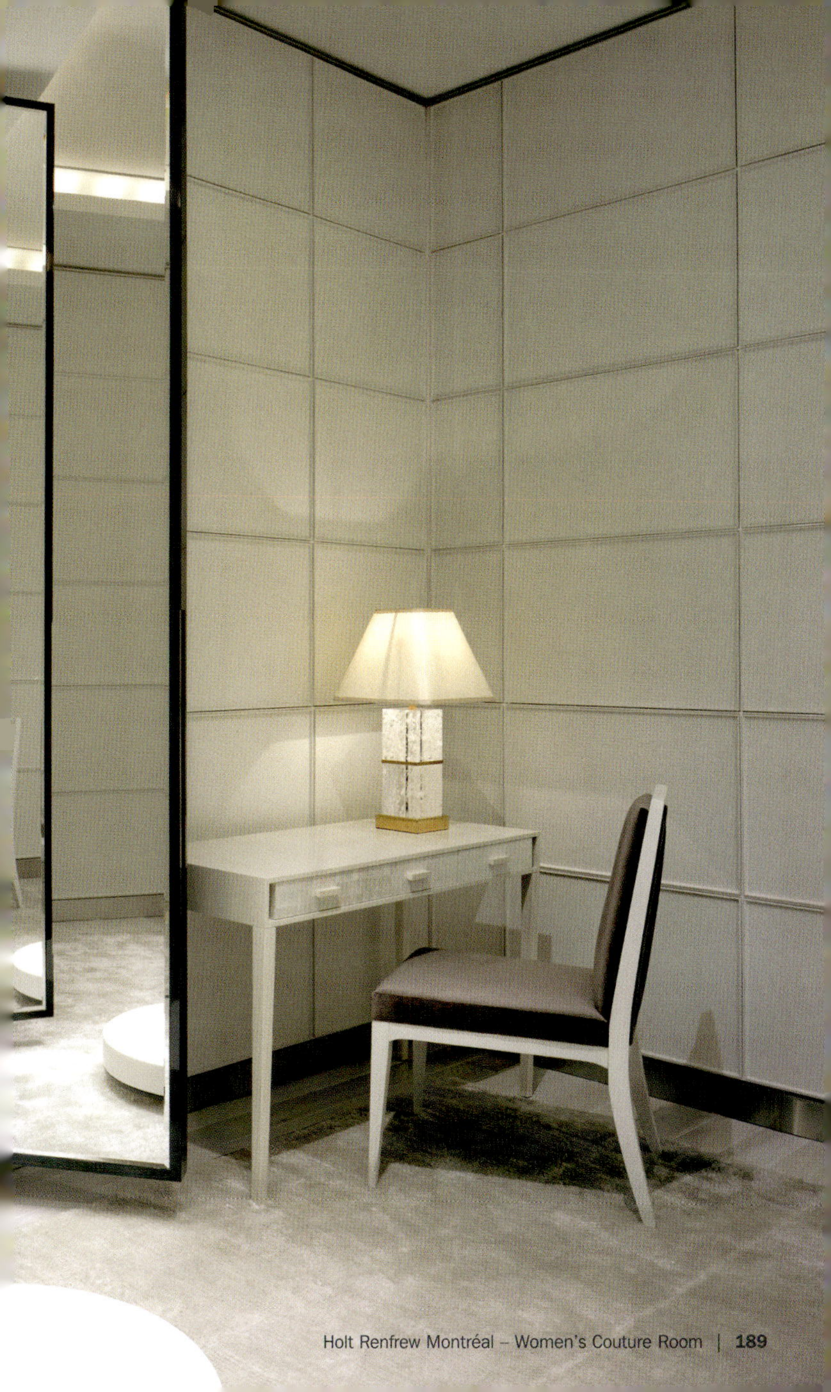

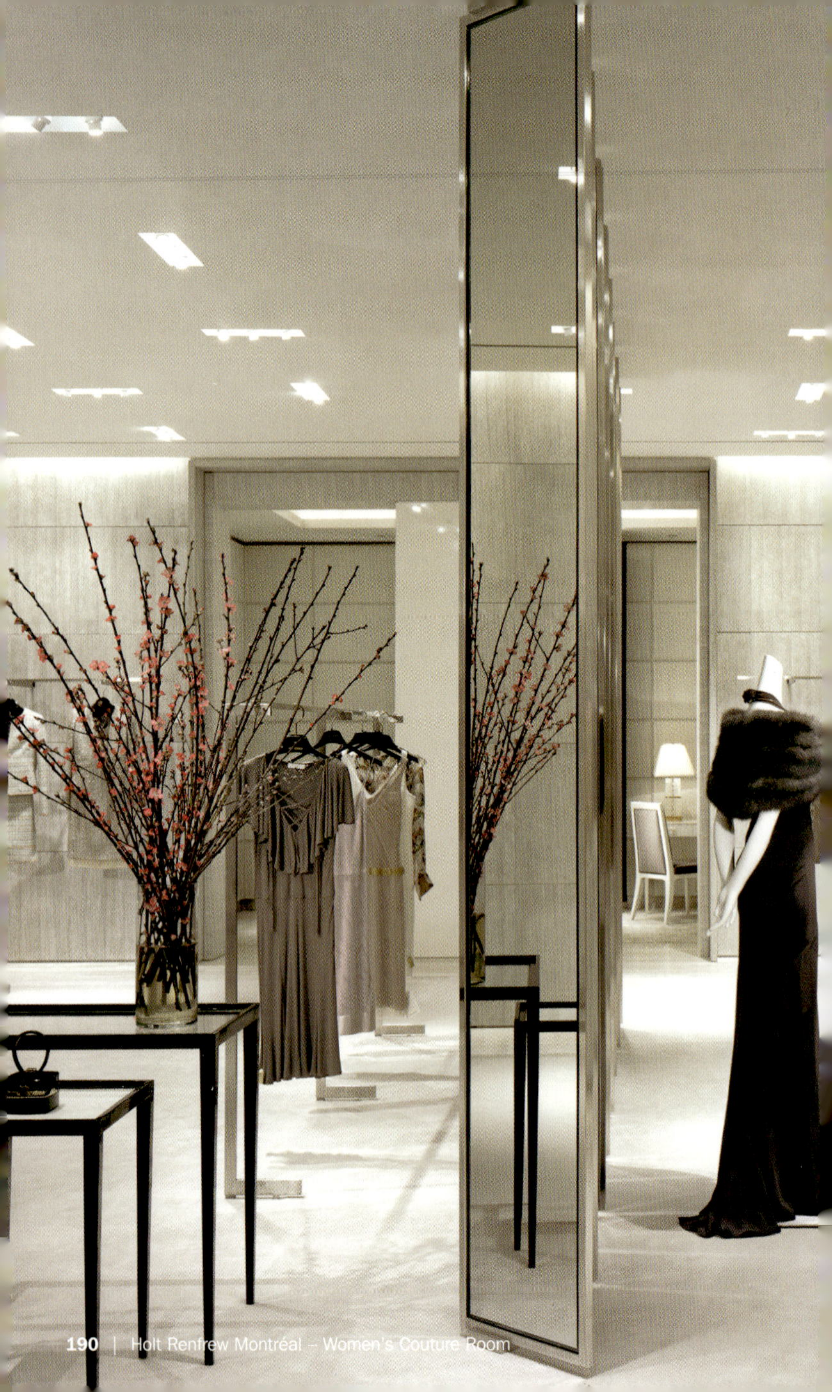

Holt Renfrew Montréal – Women's Couture Room | **191**

The burdifilek studio views the store design as reminiscent of the luxurious portfolio of the Holt Renfrew brand. An exclusive landscape therefore unravels in front of gray shimmering walls with modern artworks: refined-looking show cabinets and displays of exotic woods. At the center: a tranquility zone, designed like a room at the club.

Das Büro burdifilek versteht das Design des Stores als eine Reminiszenz an das luxuriöse Portfolio des Hauses Holt Renfrew. So öffnet sich vor grau schimmernden Wänden mit modernen Kunstwerken eine exklusive Landschaft: edel wirkende Vitrinen und Auslagen aus exotischen Hölzern. Mittendrin: eine Ruhezone, gestaltet wie ein Clubzimmer.

Le bureau burdifilek envisage le design du magasin comme une réminiscence du luxueux portfolio de la maison Holt Renfrew. Devant des murs gris scintillants avec des œuvres d'art moderne s'ouvre ainsi un paysage exclusif : des vitrines raffinées et des produits en bois exotiques. Au milieu : un espace de tranquillité aménagé comme le salon d'un club.

El despacho de arquitectos burdifilek entiende el diseño de esta tienda como una reminiscencia de la lujosa cartera de valores de la casa Holt Renfrew. Así, ante unas paredes de brillante color gris decoradas con obras de arte se abre un exclusivo paisaje de vitrinas y escaparates de maderas exóticas. En medio: un espacio para la tranquilidad concebido como una habitación cúbica.

Lo studio burdifilek interpreta lo shop design di questo store come una reminiscenza della gamma prestigiosa del marchio Holt Renfrew. Così, sullo sfondo di lucide pareti grigie impreziosite da moderne opere d'arte, si apre una scenografia all'insegna dell'esclusività. Eleganti elementi espositivi e complementi in legni esotici esaltano l'effetto d'insieme. Al centro: un'area relax dalle sembianze di una sala club.

burdifilek

183 Bathurst St. Suite 300
M5t 2R7 Toronto
Canada

Photos by Ben Rahn – A Frame

Holt Renfrew Toronto – Ground Floor

50 Bloor Street West
ON M4W 1A1 Toronto
Canada
www.holtrenfrew.com

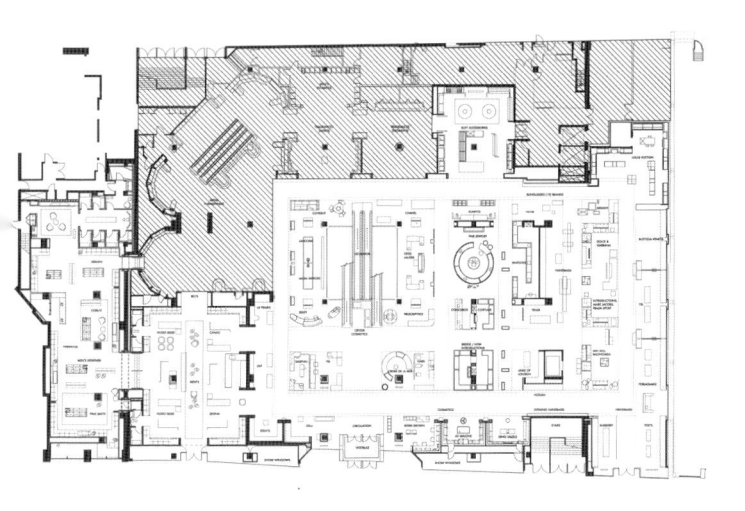

194 | Holt Renfrew Toronto – Ground Floor

Holt Renfrew Toronto – Ground Floor | **195**

196 | Holt Renfrew Toronto – Ground Floor

Holt Renfrew Toronto – Ground Floor | 197

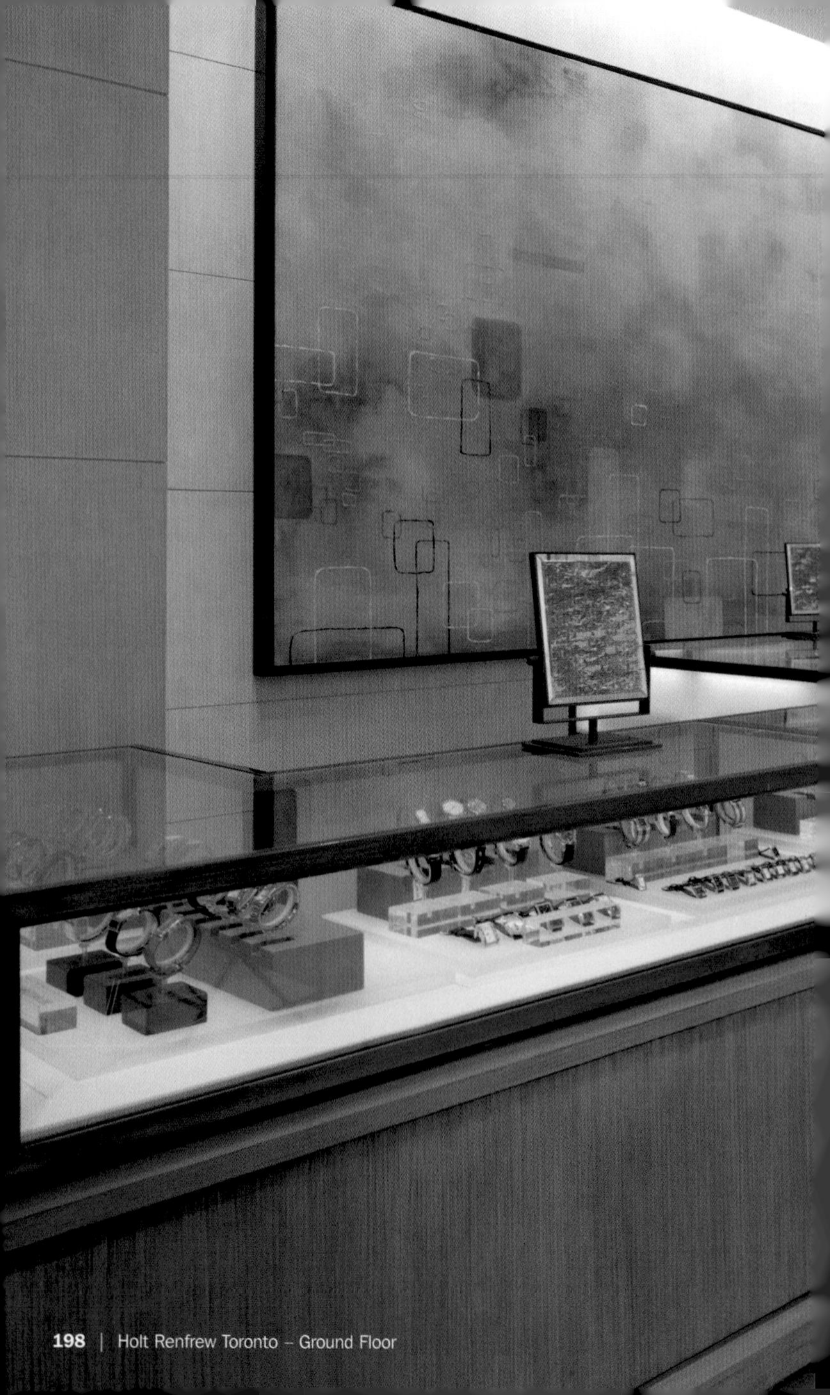

Holt Renfrew Toronto – Ground Floor | **199**

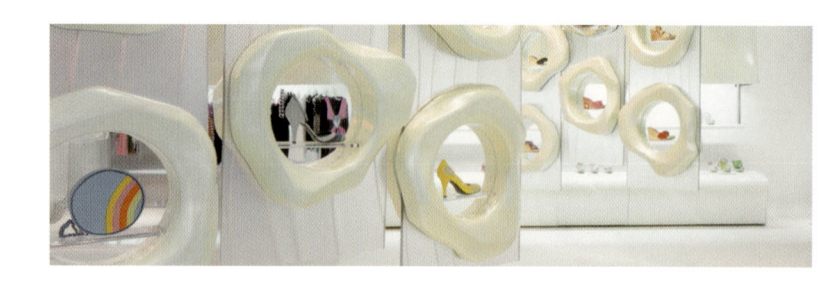

The design of this shop is meant to feast the eyes and other senses on, and to attract attention to itself. Architect Giorgio Borruso relies on organic forms, which he jazzes up for the launch: tentacle-shaped lighting elements, as well as displays that are reminiscent of eyes and eyelids.

Ein Erlebnis für Augen und sonstige Sinne will die Gestaltung dieses Shops bieten und damit die Aufmerksamkeit auf sich ziehen. Dafür greift der Architekt Giorgio Borruso auf organische Formen zurück, die er poppig in Szene setzt: tentakelartige Strahlerobjekte sowie Displays, die an Augen und Lider erinnern.

Une fête pour les yeux et les sens, tel est l'aménagement de ce magasin qui focalise ainsi l'attention sur lui. L'architecte Giorgio Borruso a recours à des formes organiques qu'il met en scène de façon voyante : des spots lumineux tentaculaires ou des présentoirs rappelant yeux et paupières.

Una experiencia para la vista y demás sentidos es lo que ofrece el diseño de esta tienda para atraer la atención sobre sí mismo. Para ello, el arquitecto Giorgio Borruso emplea formas orgánicas que presenta con una ambientación pop: objetos iluminados con forma de tentáculos y vitrinas semejantes a ojos y párpados.

Un'esperienza di grande impatto non solo visivo ma a tutto tondo, ecco l'effetto polarizzante a cui punta lo shop design di questo store firmato Giorgio Borruso. Il architetto ricorre a forme organiche che propone in chiave pop: proiettori luce tentacolari ed elementi espositivi che evocano le forme di occhi e palpebre.

Giorgio Borruso Design

333 Washington Blvd #352
Marina Del Rey, CA 90292
USA
www.borrusodesign.com

Photos by Benny Chan

Fornarina

Mandalay Place
3930 Las Vegas Blvd So.
Las Vegas, NV 89119
USA
www.fornarina.com

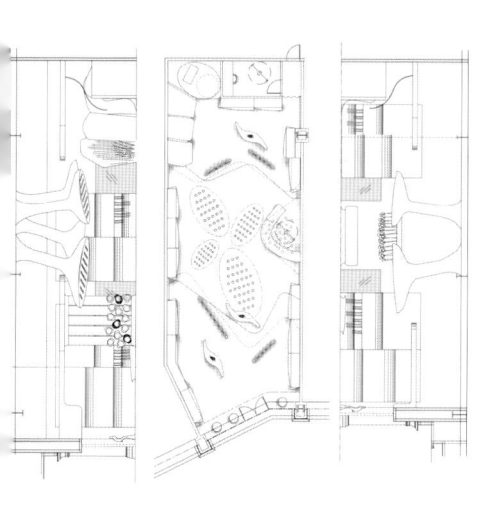

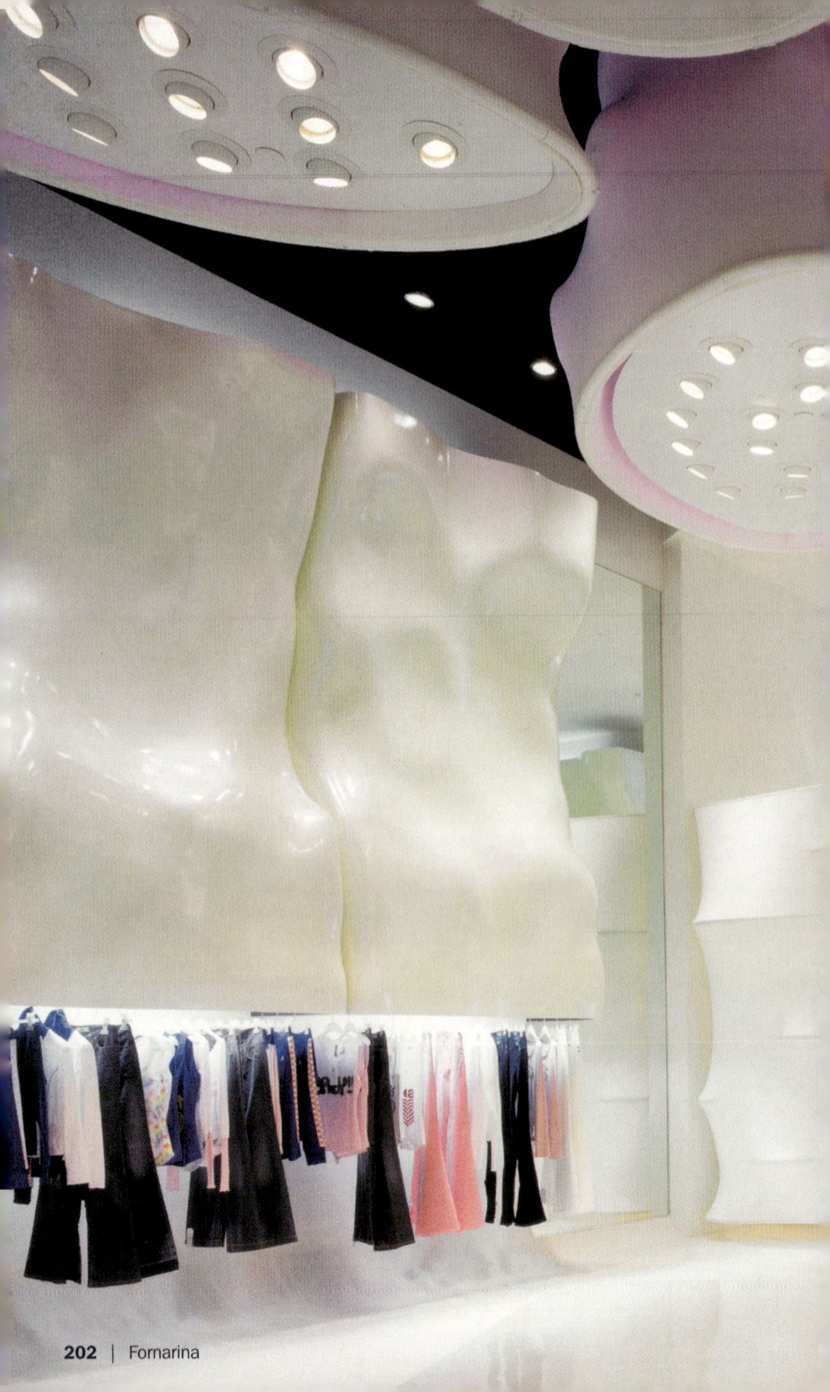

Fornarina | **203**

Fornarina

Fornarina | 205

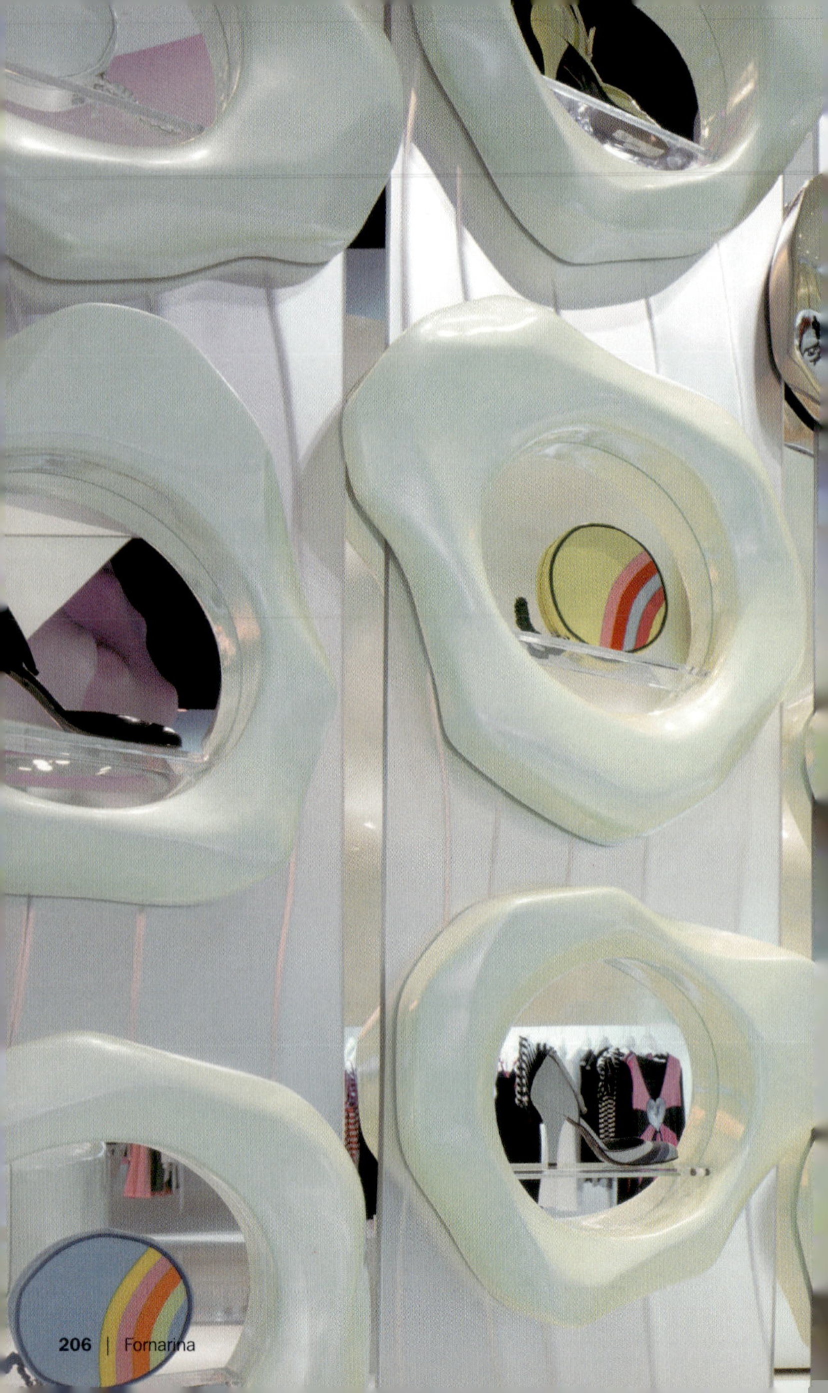

Fornarina

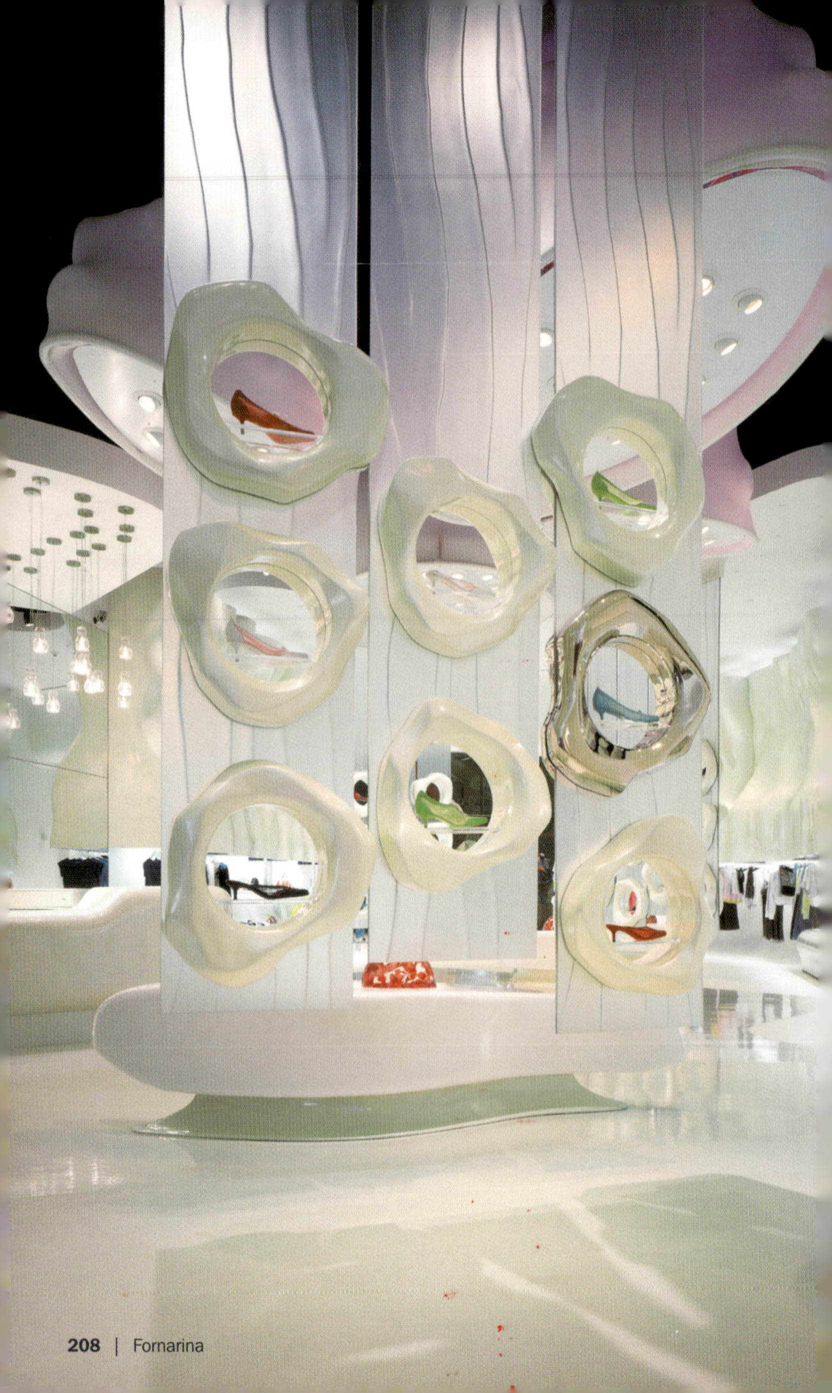

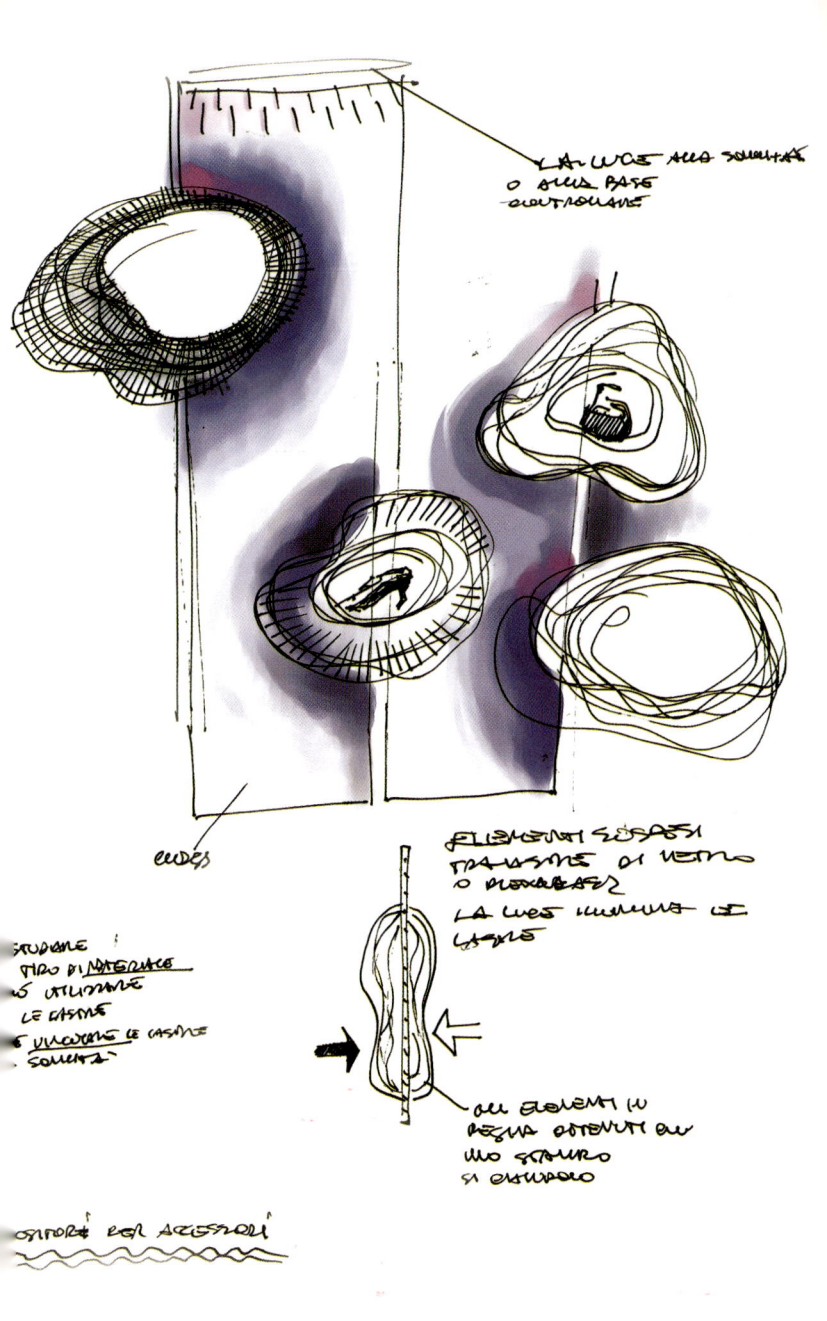

Fornarina | 209

The purpose of the ceiling construction at Snaidero's showroom is to highlight the integrative feature of multiplicity. The spiral element in Snaidero's label's colors define room perception and structures its division. In their diverse style, the kitchens also find their singular focus.

Das Verbindende in der Vielfalt aufzuzeigen ist die Aufgabe der Deckenkonstruktion in Snaideros Showroom. Das Spiralengebilde in den Farben der Marke Snaidero bestimmt die Wahrnehmung des Raumes und strukturiert die Aufteilung. Die Küchen in ihrer unterschiedlichen Stil finden so ihren singulären Fokus.

La construction du plafond dans le showroom de Snaidero fait fonction d'élément intégrant de la diversité. La spirale aux couleurs de la marque Snaidero détermine la perception de l'espace et en structure la séparation. Dans leurs différents styles, les cuisines trouvent ainsi leur propre expression.

La función de la construcción del techo es mostrar el nexo de unión en la diversidad en el showroom de Snaidero. La figura con forma de espiral en los colores de la marca Snaidero determina la percepción del espacio y estructura la división. Así, las cocinas en sus diferentes estilos, disponen de su foco particular.

La funzione della superficie strutturata del soffitto dello showroom Snaidero è di esaltare l'elemento comune nella diversità. La costruzione a spirale nei colori del marchio Snaidero predomina nella percezione dell'ambiente cui conferisce una struttura spaziale valorizzando al meglio le svariate cucine, ognuna nel suo stile differente.

Giorgio Borruso Design

333 Washington Boulevard #352
Marina Del Rey, Ca 90292
USA
www.borrusodesign.com

Photos by Benny Chan

Snaidero Showroom

370 N Robertson Boulevard
Los Angeles, CA 90048
USA
www.snaidero-usa.com

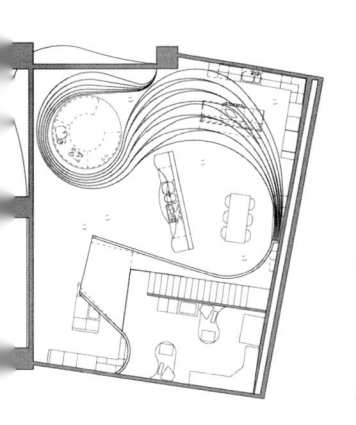

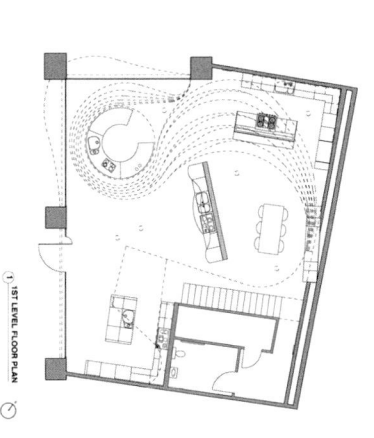

1 1ST LEVEL FLOOR PLAN

212 | Snaidero Showroom

Snaidero Showroom | 213

214 | Snaidero Showroom

Snaidero Showroom | **215**

216 | Snaidero Showroom

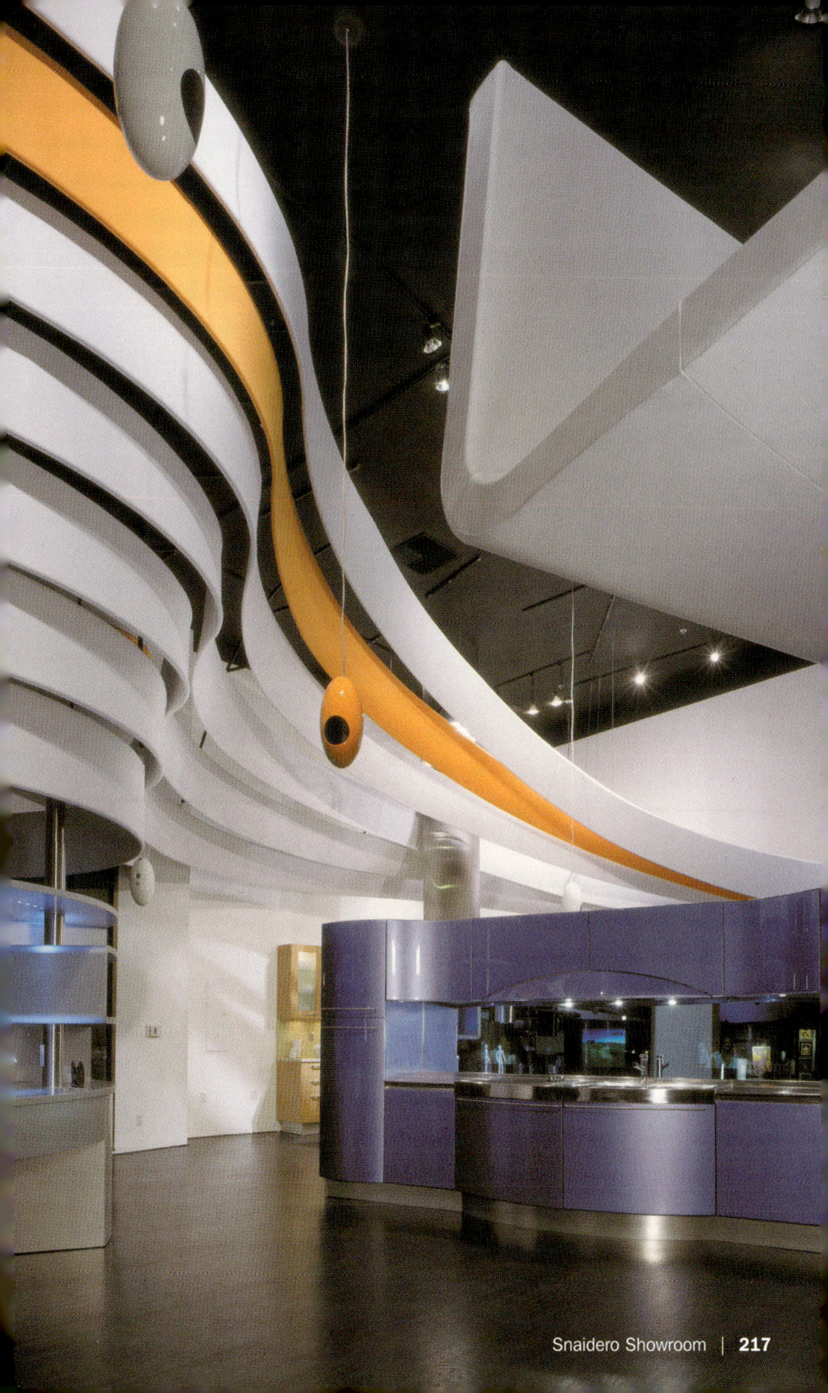

Even eyeglasses are subject to fashion trends. The architects therefore placed even more emphasis on spatial constants, which can withstand changing fashions, and yet at the same time set an individual aesthetic note. This is achieved by a strict, architectural style, both in the spatial organization and interior.

Auch Brillen sind Mode-Strömungen unterworfen. Umso mehr legten die Architekten Wert auf eine räumliche Konstante, die den modischen Schwankungen Stand zu halten weiß, zugleich aber einen eigenen ästhetischen Akzent setzt. Dies gelingt mit einem strengen architektonischen Stil, sowohl bei der Raumordnung als auch beim Interieur.

Même les lunettes sont soumises aux tendances de la mode. Les architectes ont donc davantage souligné la stabilité de l'espace qui résiste aux fluctuations de la mode mais pose aussi un accent esthétique individuel. Ceci s'illustre par un style architectural strict, tant dans l'organisation de l'espace que dans l'aménagement intérieur.

Las gafas también están sometidas a las tendencias de la moda. Por eso los arquitectos apuestan por una constante espacial que sepa estar a la altura de los cambios, al mismo tiempo que establece su propio acento estético. Esto lo consiguen con un sobrio estilo arquitectónico que se refleja tanto en la disposición del espacio como en el diseño del interior.

Anche gli occhiali non possono sottrarsi alle tendenze della moda. Per sottolineare questo aspetto gli architetti hanno voluto esaltare una costante spaziale capace di tener testa alla fugacità delle mode e nel contempo di imporsi esteticamente. Una concezione che si traduce in uno stile architettonico rigoroso tanto nella suddivisione spaziale quanto nell'arredamento.

NMDA, Inc.
Neil M. Denari Architects

12615 Washington Boulevard
Los Angeles, CA 90066
USA
www.nmda-inc.com

Photos by Benny Chan_Fotoworks

l.a. Eyeworks

7386 Beverly Boulevard
Los Angeles, CA 90036
USA
www.laeyeworks.com

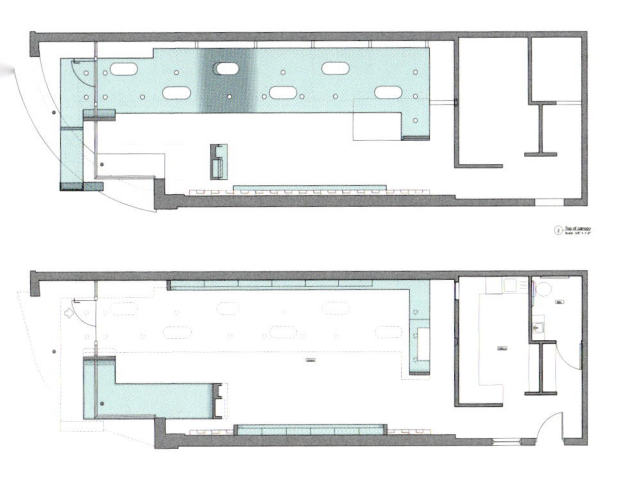

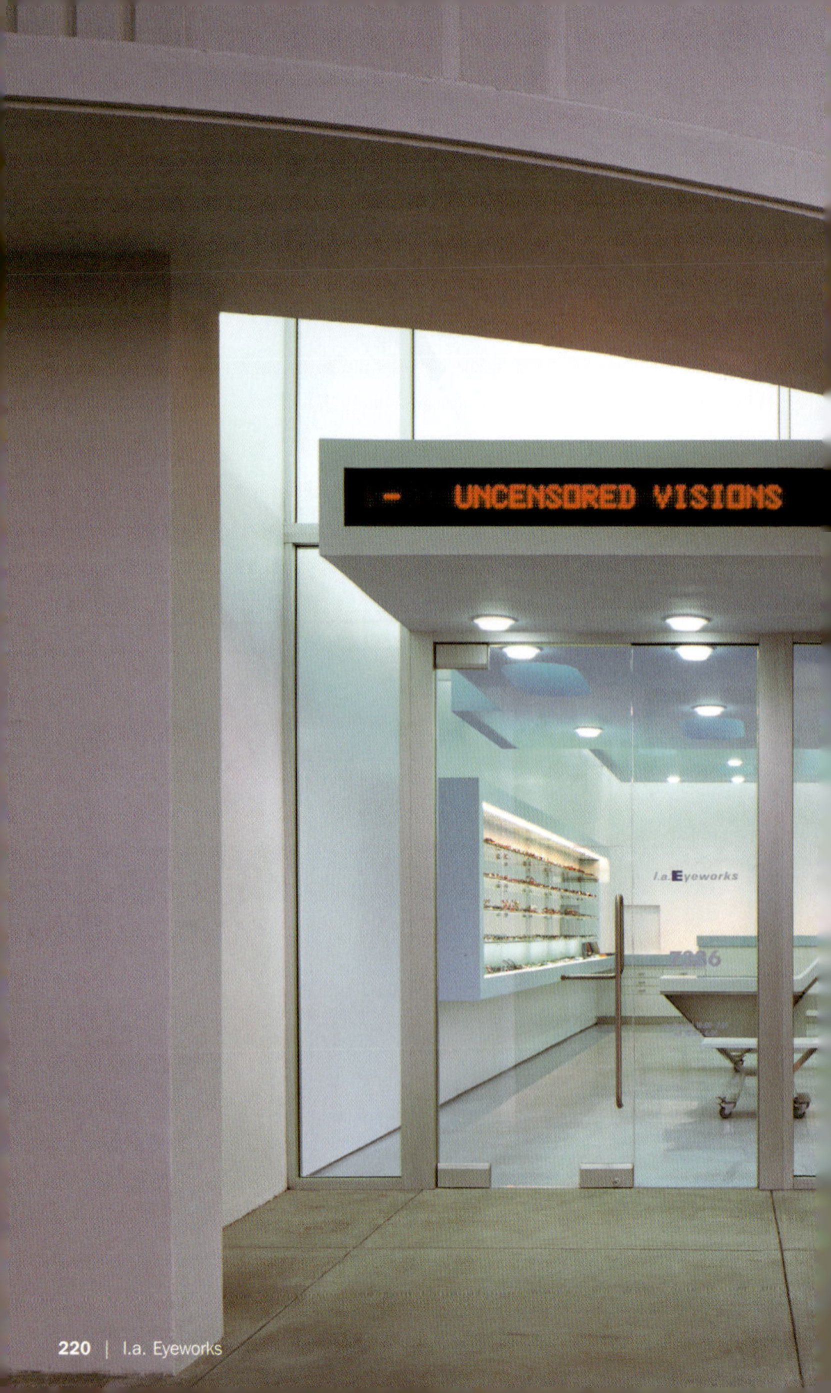
- UNCENSORED VISIONS
l.a.Eyeworks

l.a. Eyeworks

I.a. Eyeworks

l.a. Eyeworks

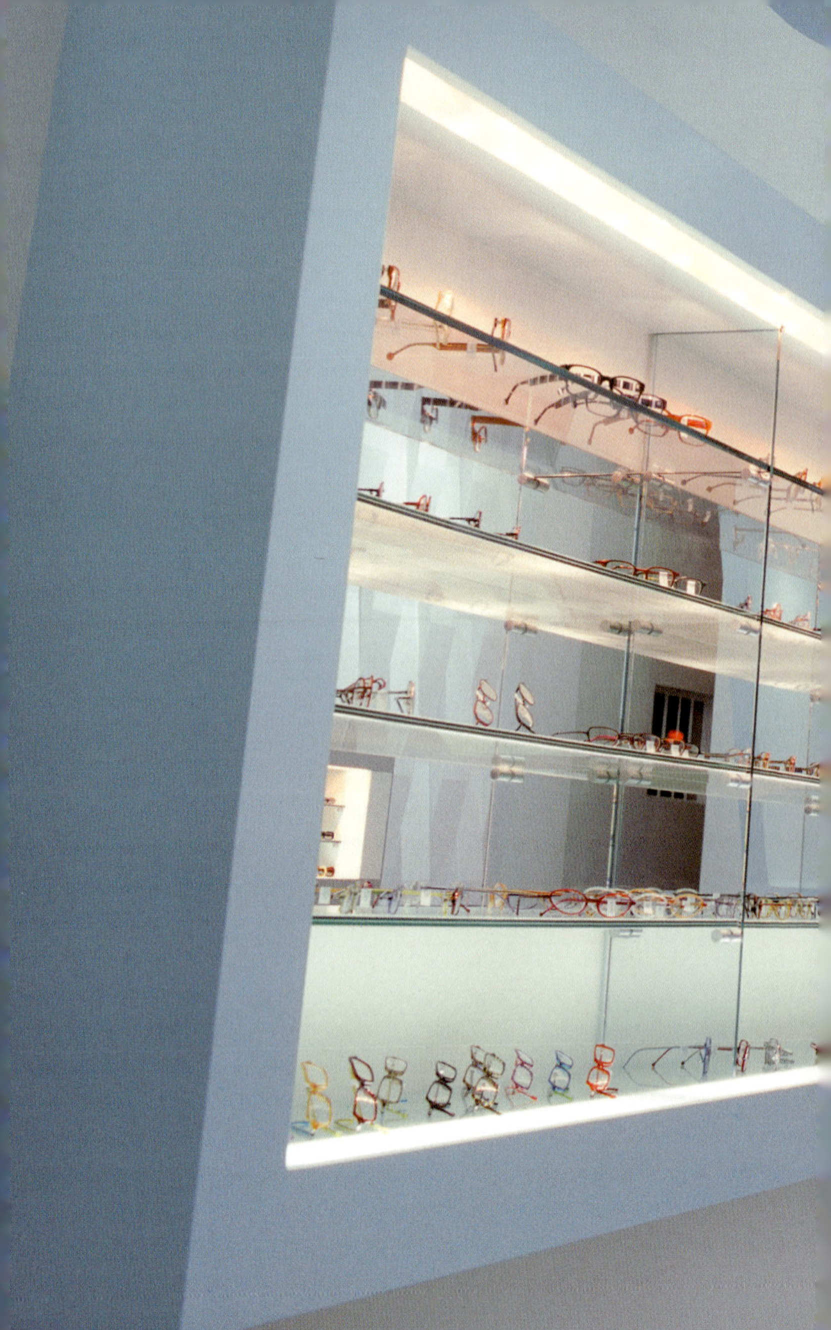

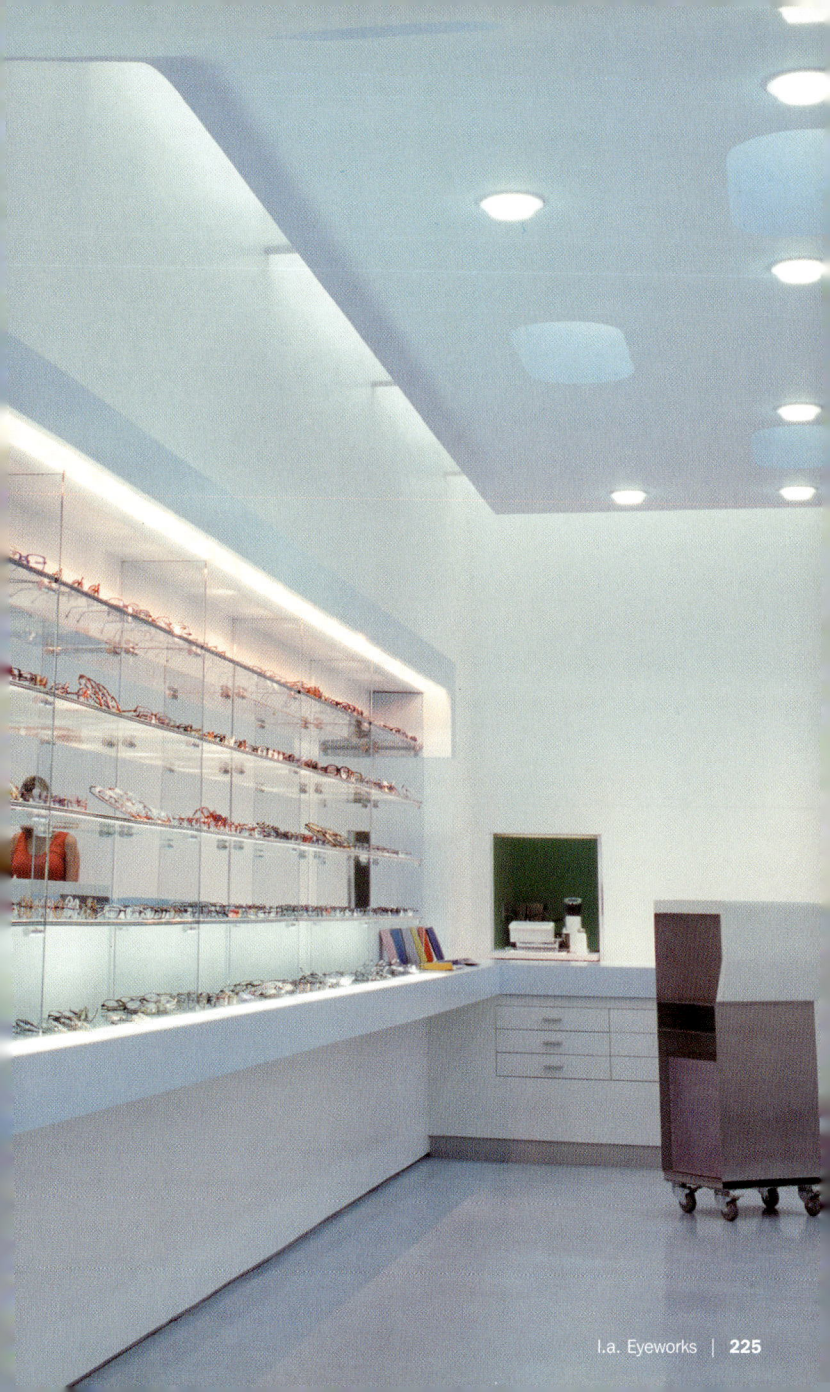

l.a. Eyeworks | 225

We might also be dealing with a spacious loft. This could be suggested by the natural light from large, framed windows, along with the parquet flooring. But the playful pipeline structures with their organic shapes serve as display elements. All of this helps to make the shop feel friendly and intimate.

Es könnte sich auch um einen geräumigen Loft handeln. Das natürliche Licht der großen gerahmten Fenster spräche dafür und auch der Parkettboden. Doch die verspielten Rohrgebilde mit ihren organischen Formen dienen als Auslage. Das alles trägt dazu bei, dass der Shop freundlich und familiär wirkt.

Il pourrait aussi bien s'agir d'un loft spacieux. La lumière naturelle pénétrant par les grandes fenêtres encadrées ainsi que le parquet pourraient le suggérer. Pourtant u assemblage espiègle de tuyaux aux formes organiques sert de portemanteaux. Cec contribue à rendre ce magasin sympathique et familier.

Igualmente podría tratarse de un amplio loft. La luz natural que pasa a través d las grandes ventanas enmarcadas y los pavimentos de parqué lo confirmarían. Si embargo, las caprichosas composiciones de los tubos de formas orgánicas hacen la veces de expositores. Todo ello dota a la tienda de un ambiente agradable y familiar

Potrebbe sembrare semplicemente un loft spazioso. Lo proverebbero la luce natural delle grandi finestre incorniciate ed il pavimento parquet. Ma come spiegare allor l'effetto contrastante con gli elementi espositivi ricavati da strutture in tubatura e form organiche? È l'efetto d'insieme a conferire al Marni store un'atmosfera accogliente familiare.

Sybarite

322 Fulham Road
London SW10 9UG
United Kingdom
www.sybarite-uk.com

Photos by Katharina Feuer

Marni

8460 Melrose Place
Los Angeles, CA 90069
USA
www.marni.com

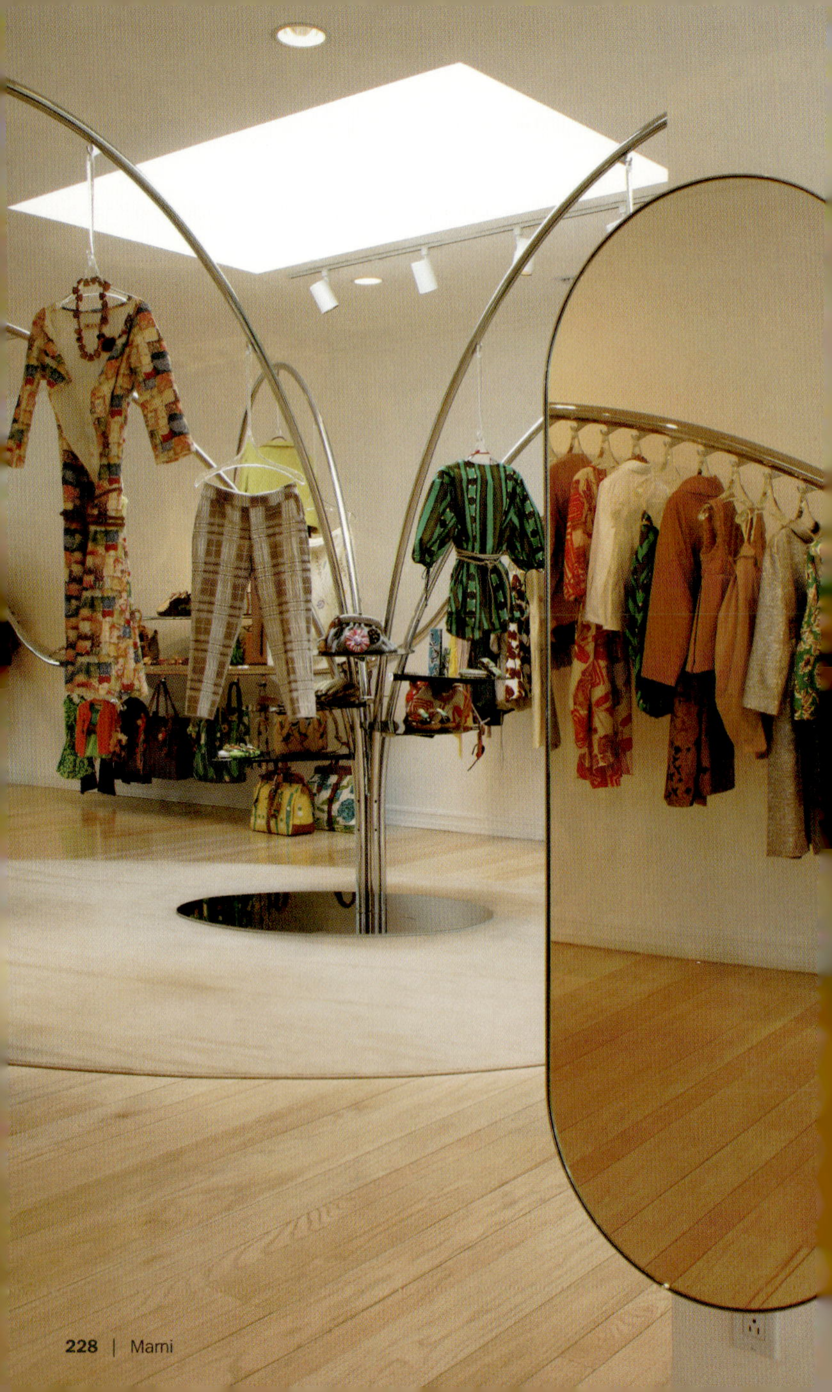

Marni | **229**

Marni

Marni | 231

"Being in a glass of pink champagne"—a summary of the brief for the shop design at Trina Turk. Alongside partially youthful and brash motifs, an elegant air defines the ambience. What takes care of this are refined materials such as marble and exclusive furnishings. Sparkling: the lamps, which hang from the ceiling like air bubbles.

„Being in a glass of pink champagne" – dies beschreibt die Vorgabe für die Shop-Gestaltung von Trina Turk. Neben teils jugendlich-schrillen Motiven ist das Ambiente bestimmt von einem eleganten Eindruck. Dafür sorgen edle Materialien wie Marmor und exklusives Mobiliar. Prickelnd: Die Lampen, die wie Luftblasen von der Decke hängen.

« Being in a glass of pink champagne – Comme dans un verre de champagne rosé » - tel est le propos affiché de l'aménagement du magasin de Trina Turk. A côté de motifs parfois juvéniles et mutins, l'atmosphère est empreinte d'une élégance que traduisent des matériaux nobles comme le marbre ainsi qu'un mobilier exclusif. Pétillant : les lampes suspendues au plafond comme des bulles d'air.

"Being in a glass of pink champagne" –como estar en una copa de champán rosado- esta es la frase que describe la pretensión para el diseño de la tienda de Trina Turk. El ambiente está determinado por motivos extravagantes y juveniles además de por una sensación de elegancia conseguida con el empleo de materiales nobles, como el mármol y un exclusivo mobiliario. Espumeante: las lámparas cuelgan del techo como burbujas de aire.

"Being in a glass of pink champagne": ecco la chiave di lettura dello shop design firmato Trina Turk. Accanto a motivi giovanili talvolta stridenti l'effetto d'insieme è quello dell'eleganza esaltata dai materiali preziosi come il marmo e dal mobilio esclusivo. Dettaglio frizzante: i lampadari che scendono dal soffitto come tante bolle d'aria.

Kelly Wearstler

317 North Kings Road
Los Angeles, CA 90048
USA
www.kwid.com

Photos by Martin Nicolas Kunz, courtesy Trina Turk LA

Trina Turk LA

8008 West Third Street
Los Angeles, CA 90048
USA
www.trinaturk.com

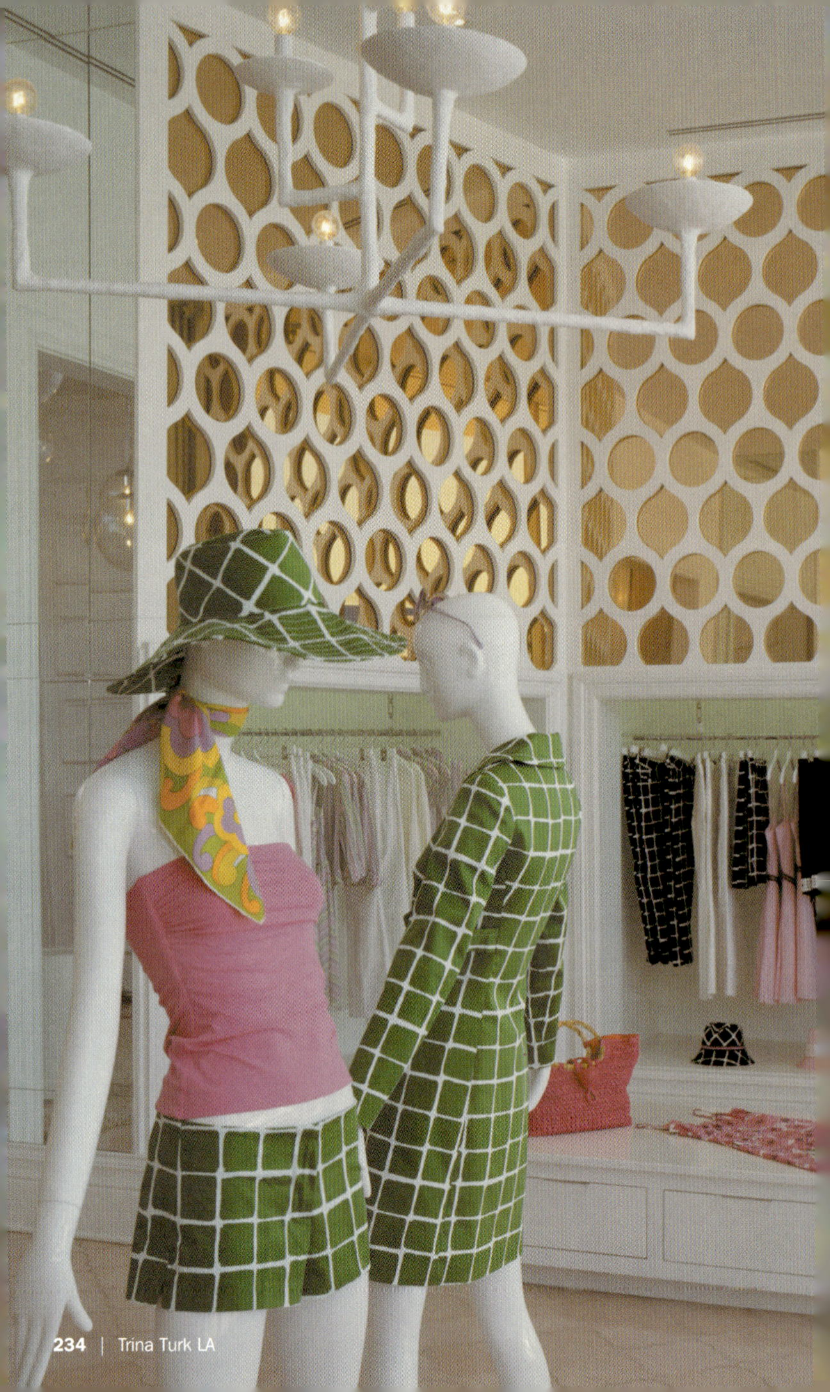

Trina Turk LA | **235**

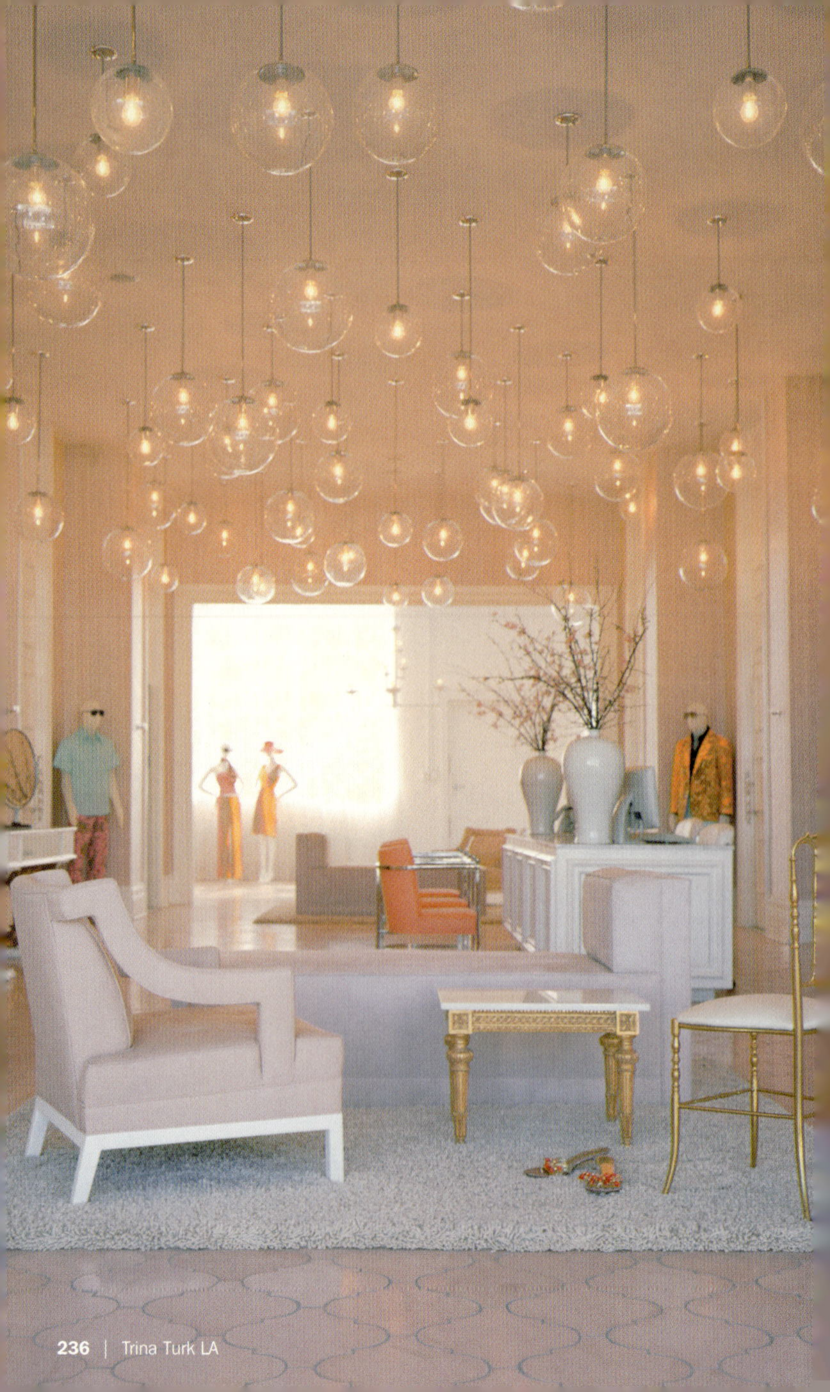

Trina Turk LA | 237

The designers at Asymptote compose a landscape shell of pure white by using corian a synthetic material. The shell is reminiscent of an igloo shape and at the same time appears modern and urban. So, the right context is created for the Brazilian's fashion which combines the most up-to-date materials with traditional forms.

Mit Corian, einem synthetischen Material, komponieren die Designer von Asymptote eine landschaftliche Hülle aus purem Weiß, die an die Formen eines Iglus erinnert und zugleich modern und urban wirkt. So entsteht der passende Rahmen für die Mode des Brasilianers, die modernste Materialien mit traditionellen Formen vereint.

Les designers d'Asymptote composent avec le Corian, matériau synthétique, un écrin paysager d'un blanc pur en forme d'igloo mais paraissant à la fois moderne et urbain. Ainsi se crée le cadre parfait pour la mode du Brésilien qui associe les matériaux les plus modernes avec les formes traditionnelles.

Empleando el corian, un material sintético, los diseñadores de Asymptote componen una envoltura de color blanco que recuerda a las formas de un iglú al tiempo que produce un efecto moderno y urbano. Así surge el marco indicado para la moda de este diseñador brasileño que une los materiales más modernos con las formas tradicionales.

Un rivestimento del materiale sintetico Corian in bianco puro dalle sembianze di un igloo moderno rivisitato in chiave urbana: ecco la cornice realizzata dai designer di Asymptote per contestualizzare le creazioni di moda dello stilista brasiliano Carlos Miele alla ricerca della sintesi perfetta fra materiali all'avanguardia e forme tradizionali.

Asymptote Architecture

160 Varick Street, 10th floor
New York, NY 10013
USA
www.asymptote.net

Photos by Paul Warchol

Carlos Miele

408 West 14th Street
New York, NY 10014
USA
www.carlosmiele.com.br

240 | Carlos Miele

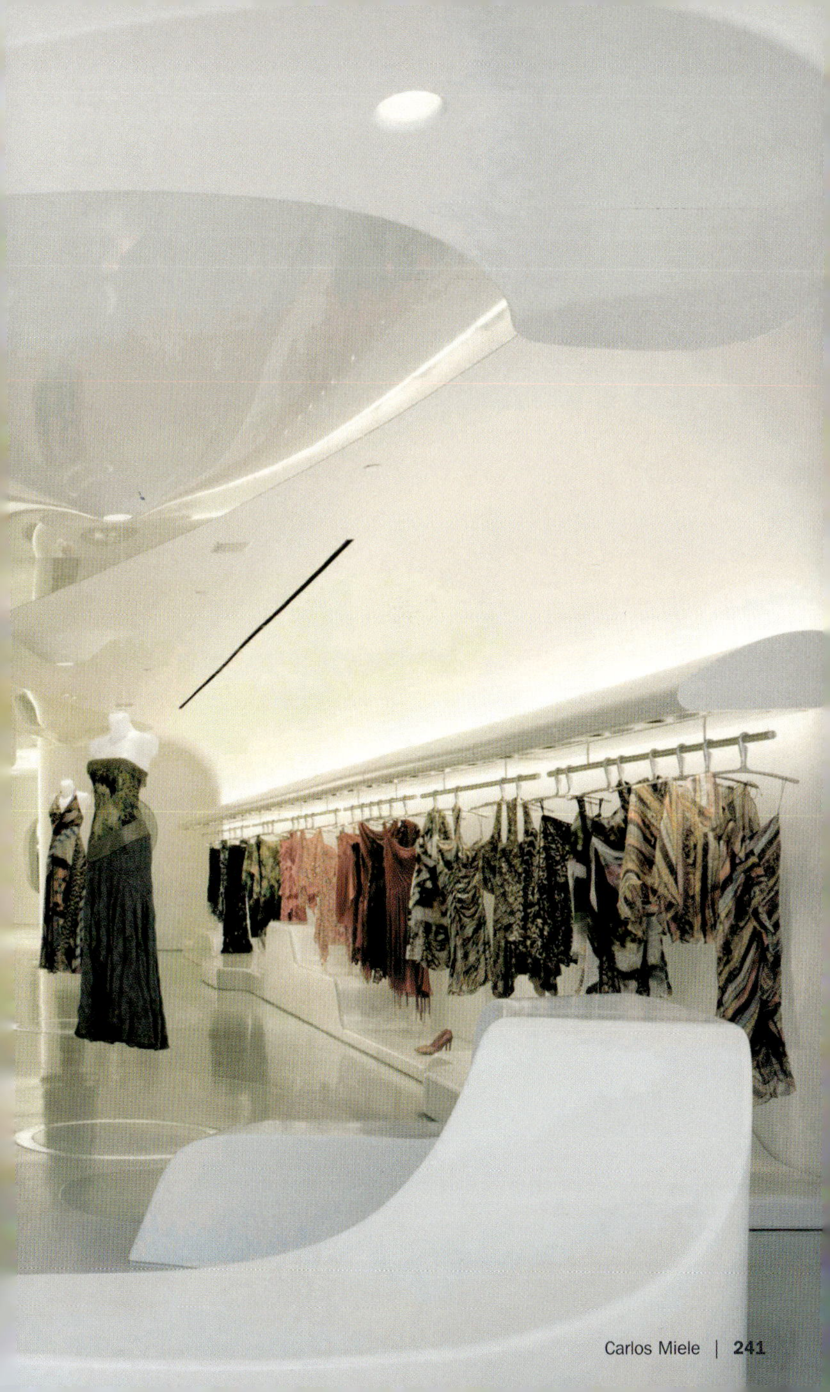

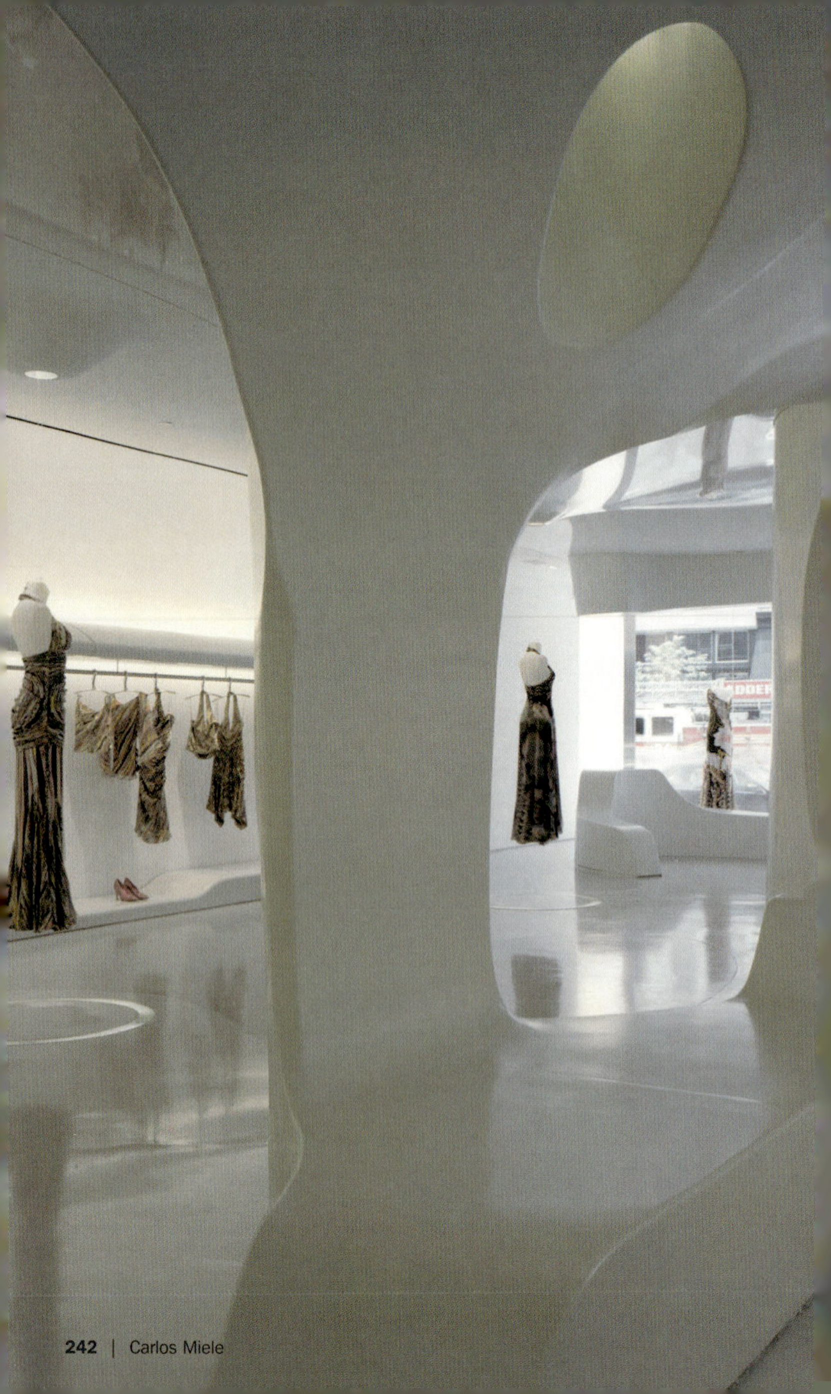

Carlos Miele | 243

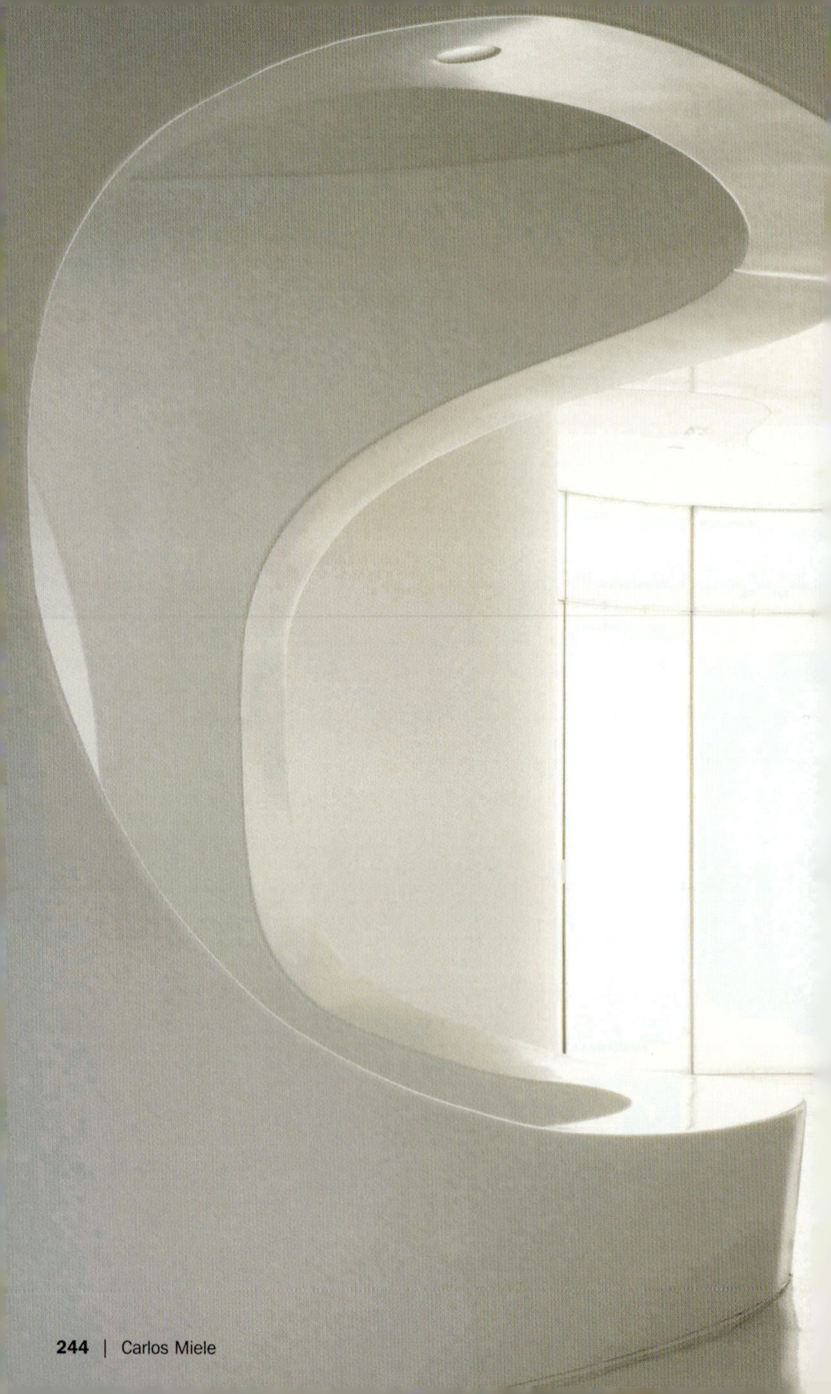

Carlos Miele | 245

Flowing or jerky forms dominate the interior at the flagship store of the Fila sportswear brand; and they symbolize movement. Many furnishing items resemble flexed muscles. The ceiling pattern even strains to reach the center of the room and shifts the sales counter towards the middle.

Fließende oder sprunghafte Formen dominieren das Interieur des Flagship-Stores der Sportmarke Fila und symbolisieren so Bewegung. Manche Möbelstücke gleichen angespannten Muskeln. Das Deckenmuster selbst strebt zum Zentrum des Raumes hin und rückt den Verkaufstresen in den Mittelpunkt.

Des formes fluides ou saccadées caractérisent l'intérieur du magasin étendard de la marque sportive Fila, symbolisant le mouvement. Certains meubles font penser à des muscles bandés. Le dessin du plafond même tend vers le centre de la pièce et déplace le comptoir au milieu.

Las formas fluidas o discontinuas dominan el interior de la tienda insignia de la marca deportiva Fila y simbolizan el movimiento. Algunos elementos del mobiliario parecer músculos en tensión. El dibujo del techo parece dirigirse hacia el centro del espacio convirtiendo los mostradores en el centro de atención.

Linee fluide e spezzate, come a simboleggiare il movimento, sono l'elemento predominante dello shop design del flagship store della griffe sportiva Fila. Alcuni elementi d'arredo somigliano a muscoli tesi nello sforzo sportivo. Il motivo decorativo sul soffitto polarizza gli sguardi verso il centro mettendo in risalto per riflesso i banconi di vendita sottostanti.

Giorgio Borruso Design

333 Washington Boulevard #352
Marina Del Rey, Ca 90292
USA
www.borrusodesign.com

Photos by Benny Chan

Fila

340 Madison Avenue
New York, NY 10017
USA
www.fila.com

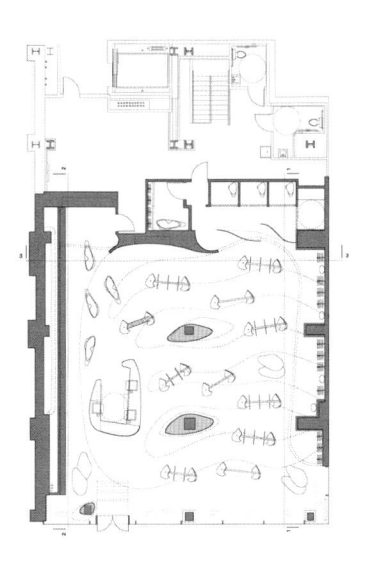

248 | Fila

Fila | 249

250 | Fila

Fila | 251

Luxury. Comfort. Quality. Craftsmanship. Art.

Fila | 253

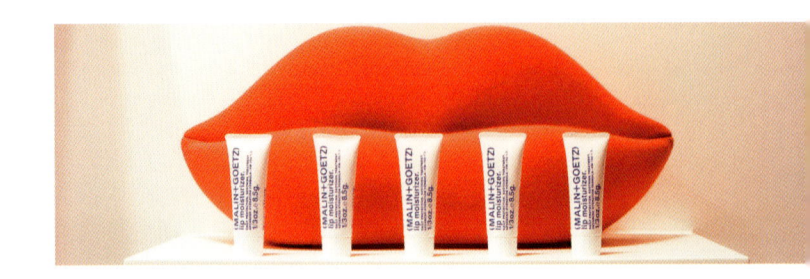

A shop design that is distinguished by its clarity, which it uses to express the high standard, required of its skin and hair products. The konyk studio used a synthetic material known as corian, in order to achieve the purest white. The exposed walls are in contrast to this and embody a natural feel.

Ein Shop-Design, das sich durch seine Klarheit auszeichnet und so den Anspruch an die Produkte für Haut und Haar zum Ausdruck bringt. Das Büro konyk setzte ein synthetisches Material namens Corian ein, um das reinste Weiß zu realisieren. Die freigelegten Wände stehen im Kontrast dazu und verkörpern Natürlichkeit.

Un design de magasin caractérisé par sa clarté, exprimant parfaitement l'exigence de qualité des produits pour la peau et les cheveux. Le bureau konyk a mis en œuvre le Corian, matériau synthétique, pour obtenir le blanc le plus pur. Le contraste créé par les murs à nu donne une impression de naturel.

Un diseño que destaca por su claridad y que transmite así la pretensión de sus productos para la piel y el cabello. El estudio konyk empleó el material sintético corian para obtener el blanco más puro. Las paredes, sin revoque, establecen el contraste representan la naturalidad.

Uno shop design in cui l'elemento marcato della purezza delle linee sottolinea un'analogia espressiva di fondo con i prodotti per la cura della pelle e dei capelli che trovano la giusta collocazione. Per la realizzazione del bianco più puro lo studio konyk ha utilizzato un materiale sintetico chiamato Corian. La sua purezza artificiosa crea un effetto di contrasto con la naturalezza ispirata dalle pareti con muro a vista.

konyk

61 Pearl Street #509 (Dumbo)
New York, NY 11201-8339
USA
www.konyk.net

Photos by Roland Bauer, courtesy Malin + Goetz

Malin + Goetz

177 7th Avenue
New York, NY 10011
USA
www.malinandgoetz.com

Malin + Goetz

(MALIN+GOETZ)

advanced skin and hair care.
HYDRATION SCIENCE. ABSORPTION SCIENCE.
PAIRED PERFORMANCE SYSTEMS.

new york.

258 | Malin + Goetz

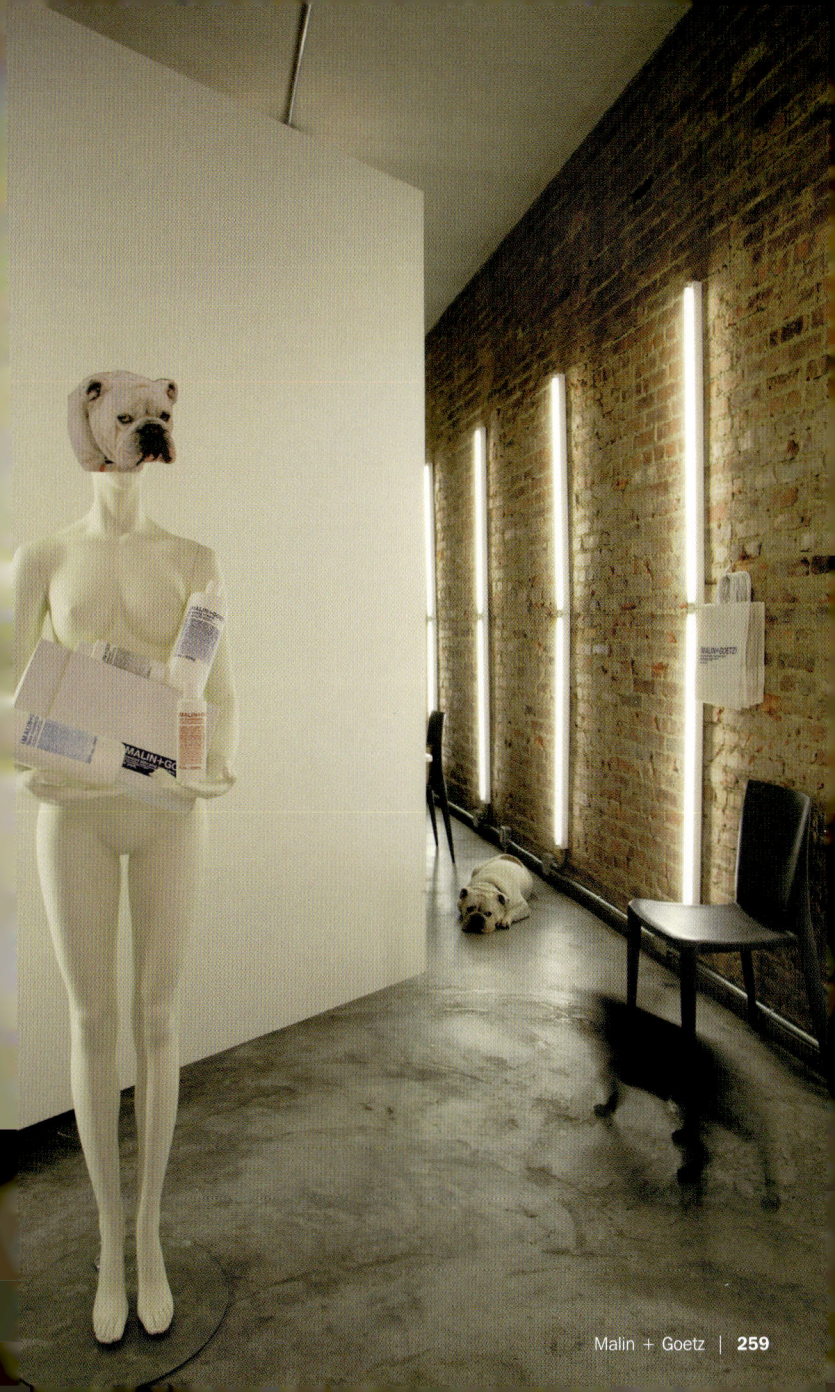

Malin + Goetz | 259

Not only sports' footwear is sold in this studio, but customers can even create their own sports' shoes. The shop is more reminiscent of a lounge with its designer furniture and printed wallpapers. The dark wood gives the rooms depth.

In diesem Studio werden nicht nur Sportschuhe verkauft, hier können die Kunden ihre sportive Fußbekleidung sogar selbst kreieren. Der Shop erinnert mit seinen Designmöbeln und bedruckten Tapeten eher an eine Lounge. Das dunkle Holz gibt den Räumen Tiefe.

Ce studio ne vend pas seulement des chaussures de sport: ici, les clients peuvent eux-mêmes créer leurs souliers de sport. Avec ses meubles design et ses tapisseries imprimées le magasin fait plutôt penser à un salon. Le bois sombre donne de la profondeur aux pièces.

En este estudio además de venderse zapatos deportivos los clientes pueden diseñar su propio calzado. La tienda, con sus muebles de diseño y el empapelado de sus paredes recuerda más a un *lounge*. La madera oscura dota a los espacios de profundidad.

In questo atelier non si vendono solamente calzature sportive ma si interagisce con il cliente nell'intento di sperimentare una nuova formula di vendita personalizzata che coinvolge attivamente il fruitore. I mobili design e la tappezzeria conferiscono all'ambiente l'aspetto di una lounge. Il legno scuro trasmette profondità prospettica.

Lynch / Eisinger / Design

224 Centre Street, 4th Floor
New York, NY 10013
USA
www.LynchEisingerDesign.com

Photos by Paul Warchol

Nike iD Studio

255 Elizabeth Street
New York, NY 10012
USA
www.nikeid.com

262 | Nike iD Studio

Nike iD Studio | 263

264 | Nike iD Studio

Nike iD Studio | **265**

A women's lingerie store should keep out curious looks from prying eyes. The store design at Catriona MacKechnie can alternate between discretion and open display. Various different atmospheric room zones guarantee this. The structured walls are not only refined in an optical, but also in a tactile sense.

Ein Shop für Damenunterwäsche sollte allzu neugierige Blicke abhalten. Das Store-Design von Catriona MacKechnie versteht es, zwischen Diskretion und offener Darbietung zu changieren. Dafür sorgen stimmungsvoll variierte Raumzonen. Die strukturierten Wände sind nicht nur in optischer, sondern auch in taktiler Hinsicht raffiniert.

Un magasin de lingerie féminine se doit d'éloigner les regards par trop indiscrets. Le design du magasin de Catriona MacKechnie alterne parfaitement discrétion et présentation ostensible. Divers espaces d'atmosphère différente le traduisent. Les murs à structure en relief sont raffinés, tant visuellement que tactilement.

Una tienda de ropa interior femenina debería mantener las miradas curiosas alejadas. El diseño de la tienda de Catriona MacKechnie sabe mantener el equilibrio entre la discreción y la presentación abierta con unos espacios que varían llenos de expresividad. La sofisticación de los tabiques estructurados no sólo es óptica sino también táctil.

Una boutique di biancheria intima femminile dovrebbe nascondersi agli sguardi indiscreti pur sapendosi presentare con un pizzico di esibizionismo. Lo shop design della boutique Catriona MacKechnie è la sintesi sapiente fra discrezione e sfoggio, creata dall'alternarsi suggestivamente cangevole degli spazi espositivi. Le pareti strutturate presentano espedienti raffinati di grande impatto tattile oltre che visivo.

Universal Design Studio Ltd.

Ground Floor
35 Charlotte Road
London E2CA 3PG
United Kingdom
www.universaldesignstudio.com

Photos by Frank Oudeman

Catriona MacKechnie

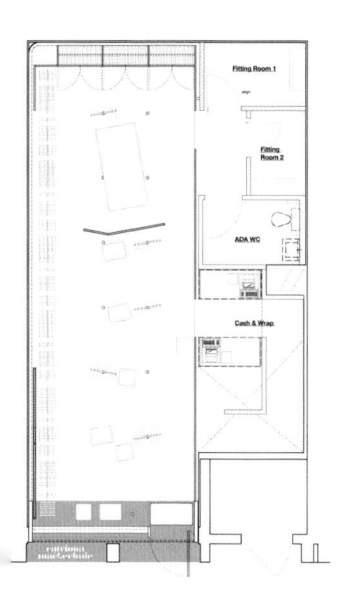

400 West 14th Street
New York, NY 10014
USA
www.catrionamackechnie.com

catriona maKechnie

268 | catriona MacKechnie

Catriona MacKechnie

270 | Catriona MacKechnie

Catriona MacKechnie | 271

At Stella McCartney's flagship New York store generosity is top of the list. A large area is devoted to displaying outfits, which are arranged in individual scenes. Hand-made curtains and wall-coverings with high-quality inlays serve as an exquisite backdrop.

Großzügigkeit steht bei Stella McCartneys Flagship-Store in New York an erster Stelle. Die Outfits sind weitläufig aufgestellt und zu einzelnen Szenen arrangiert. Als exquisiter Hintergrund dienen von Hand gefertigte Vorhänge und Wände mit wertvollen Intarsienarbeiten.

Dans le magasin étendard new-yorkais de Stella McCartney, la générosité tient la première place. Beaucoup d'espace est consacré à l'exposition des toilettes, agencées en tableaux individuels. Le décor exclusif est constitué de rideaux faits main et de murs décorés de marqueteries précieuses.

La amplitud es lo primordial en la tienda insignia de Stella McCartney en Nueva York. Las prendas se exponen muy distanciadas entre sí formando escenas individuales. Como exquisito telón de fondo se han empleado cortinas hechas a mano y paredes decoradas con valiosa taracea.

L'elemento più marcato dello Stella McCartney flagship store di New York è la spaziosità. La disposizione spaziosa consente di far risaltare le creazioni moda e di contestualizzarle con effetti scenici. Sullo sfondo raffinato tendaggi manufatti e pareti con preziosi intarsi.

Universal Design Studio Ltd.

Ground Floor
35 Charlotte Road
London E2CA 3PG
United Kingdom
www.universaldesignstudio.com

Photos by Frank Oudeman

Stella McCartney

429 West 14th Street
New York, NY 10014
USA
www.stellamccartney.com

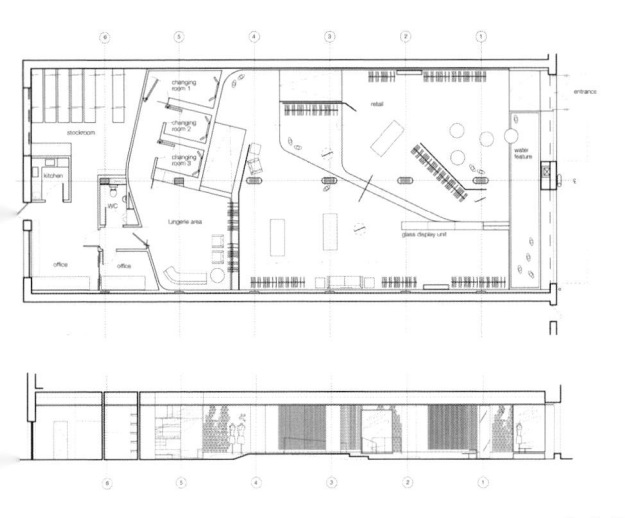

Stella McCartney

Stella McCartney | 275

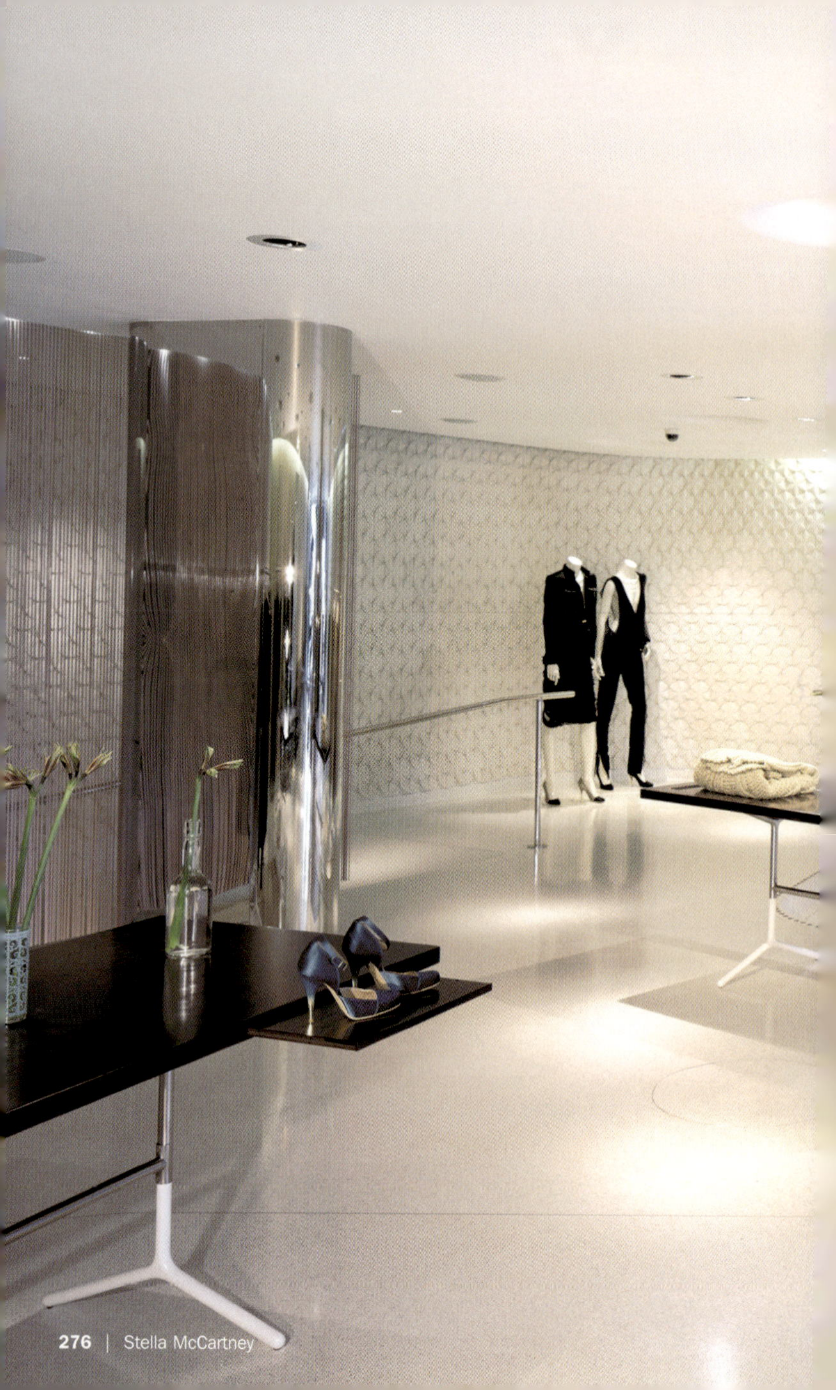

Stella McCartney

In this shop, Christian Biecher shows a uniquely successful crossover of styles: golden shelves and fittings, brash, bright patterns, then again magnificent mosaics with arabesques. Biecher's ideas form an exhilarating counterpart to Harvey Nichols' fashion.

Ein einzigartig gelungenes Stil-Crossover zeigt Christian Biecher in diesem Shop: goldene Regale und Fassungen, schrille, bunte Muster, dann wieder großartige Mosaike mit Arabesken. Zur Mode von Harvey Nichols bilden die Ideen Biechers einen beflügelnden Gegenpol.

Dans ce magasin, Christian Biecher réussit un croisement de styles unique : des étagères et des supports dorés, des motifs voyants et colorés, puis de nouveau, de magnifiques mosaïques à arabesques. Les idées de Biecher sont le contre-pied grisant de la mode de Harvey Nichols.

En esta tienda, Christian Biecher muestra una mezcla de estilos única y lograda: estanterías y marcos dorados, dibujos extravagantes y multicolores y magníficos mosaicos con arabescos. Las ideas de Biecher son el alado polo puesto de la moda de Harvey Nichols.

L'Harvey Nichols Store si presenta come un singolare crossover di stili firmato Christian Biecher: scaffalature e profili dorati, motivi audaci e policromi, ed ancora magnifici mosaici con motivi arabescati. Uno sfondo stimolante sul quale le creazioni di moda Harvey Nichols risaltano per contrasto.

Christian Biecher & Associes

14 Rue Crespin-du-Gast
75011 Paris
France
www.biecher.com

Photos by William Furniss

Harvey Nichols Store

15 Queen's Rd Central
Hong Kong
China
www.harveynichols.com

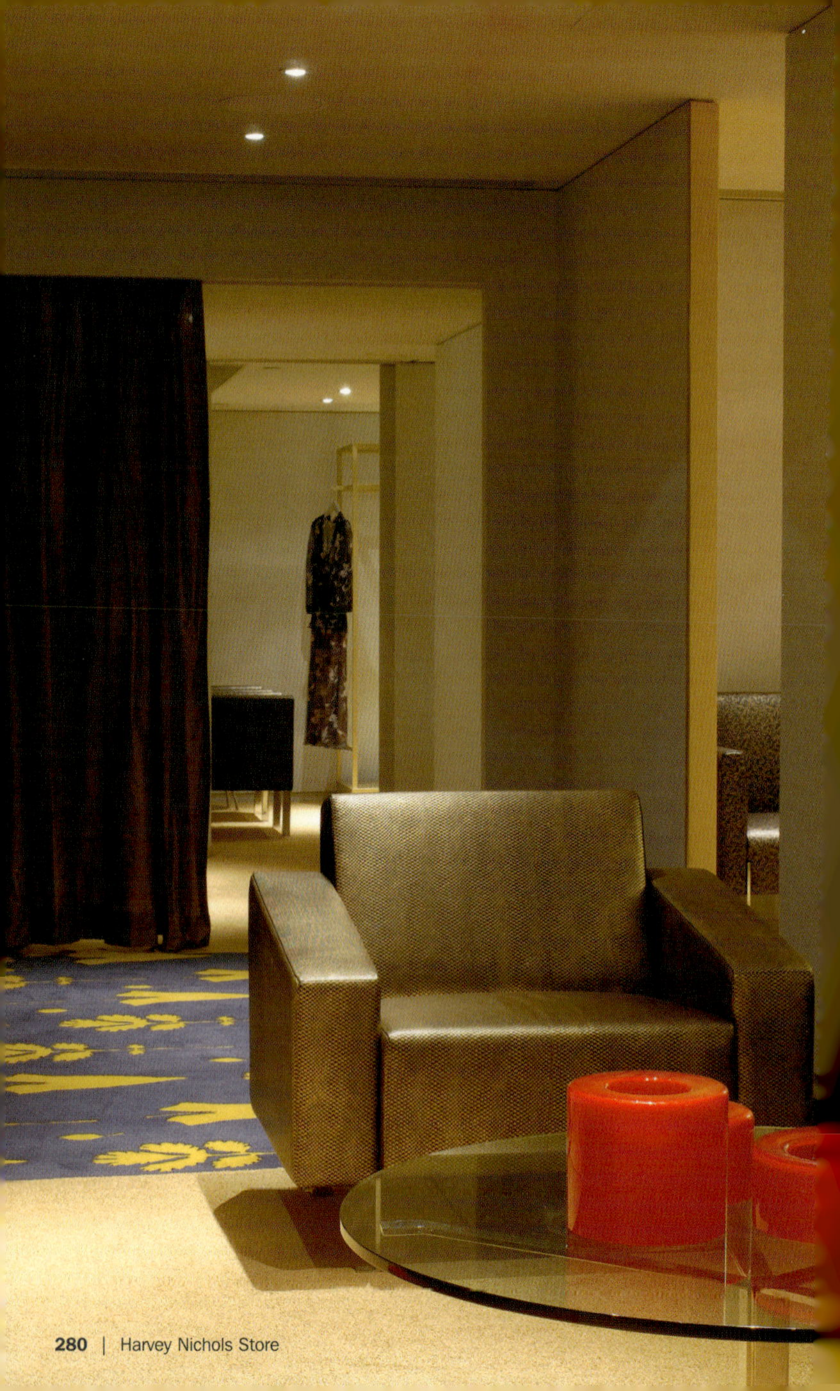

Harvey Nichols Store | 281

| Harvey Nichols Store

Harvey Nichols Store | **283**

Harvey Nichols Store

Harvey Nichols Store | **285**

Armani's mega-store in Hong Kong is a virtual stream of magic. The designers Massimiliano Fuksas and Doriana O. Mandrelli created a translucent shell made of plinths and walls. A fascinating element: the serpentine red, fiberglass ribbon that winds its way around the room and is finally used to create the bar in the restaurant.

Von geradezu fließender Magie ist Armanis Megastore in Hongkong. Die Designer Massimiliano Fuksas und Doriana O. Mandrelli gestalteten dafür eine transluzide Hülle aus Stelen und Wänden. Ein Faszinosum: das gewundene rote Fiberglas-Band, das sich durch den Raum schlängelt und aus dem schließlich die Bar im Restaurant entsteht.

Le megastore d'Armani à Hong Kong est d'une fluidité quasi magique. Les designers Massimiliano Fuksas et Doriana O. Mandrelli ont créé une gaine translucide faite de plinthes et de cloisons. Un élément fascinant : le serpentin en fibre de verre rouge qui ondule à travers la pièce pour donner finalement naissance au bar dans le restaurant.

En la megatienda de Armani en Hong Kong fluye la magia. Para conseguirlo, los diseñadores Massimiliano Fuksas y Doriana O. Mandrelli crearon un recubrimiento translúcido de columnas a media altura y paredes. Un elemento fascinante es la sinuosa banda roja de fibra de vidrio que serpentea por el espacio dando forma a la barra en la zona del restaurante.

Come pervaso da una magia quasi fluida, ecco la sensazione trasmessa dal megastore Armani di Hong Kong, opera dei designer Massimiliano Fuksas e Doriana O. Mandrelli. I rivestimento traslucido di elementi verticali e pareti ne potenzia l'effetto. Emozionante il nastro rosso realizzato in fiber glass che, con movimento sinuoso, costruisce gli spazi delimitando per esempio il bar all'interno del ristorante.

Massimiliano Fuksas, Doriana O. Mandrelli

Piazza del Monte di Pietà 30
00186 Rome
Italy
www.fuksas.it

Photos by Ramon Prat

Emporio Armani

Chater Road
Hong Kong
China
www.emporioarmani.com

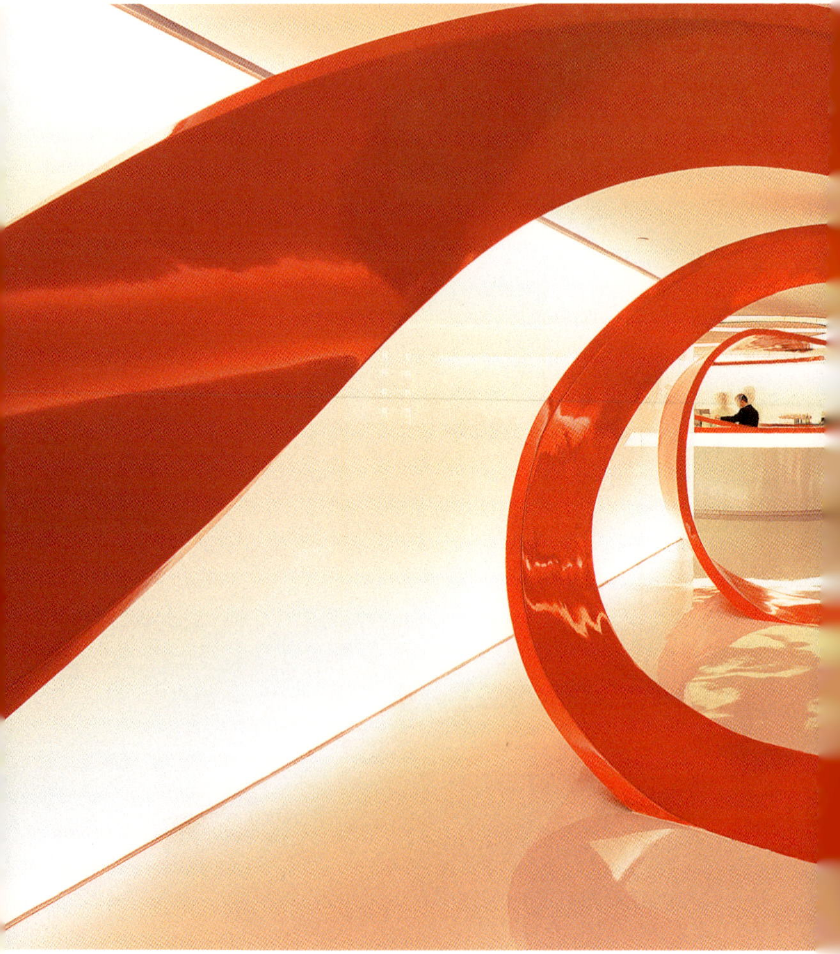

Emporio Armani

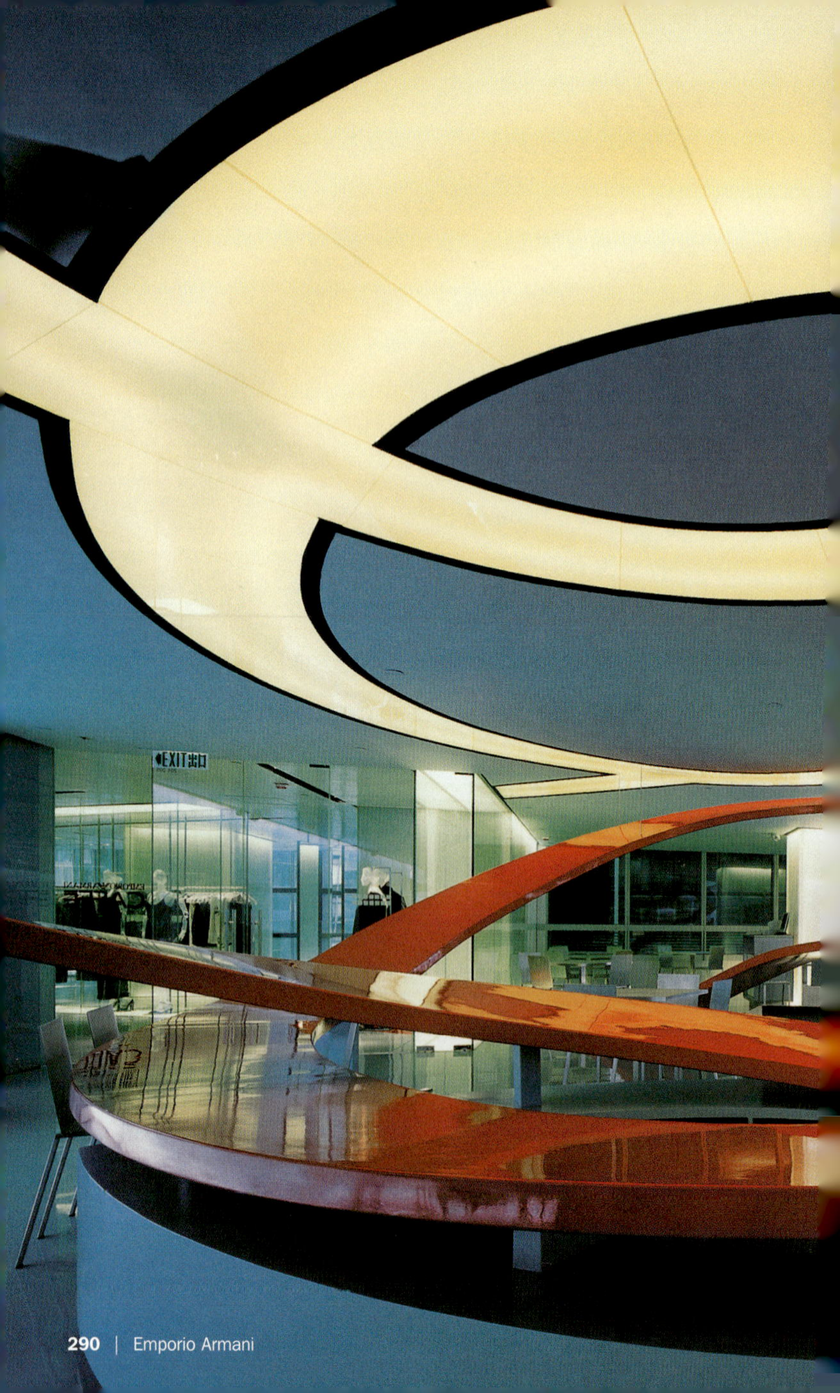
EXIT出口

Emporio Armani | 291

| Emporio Armani

Emporio Armani | 293

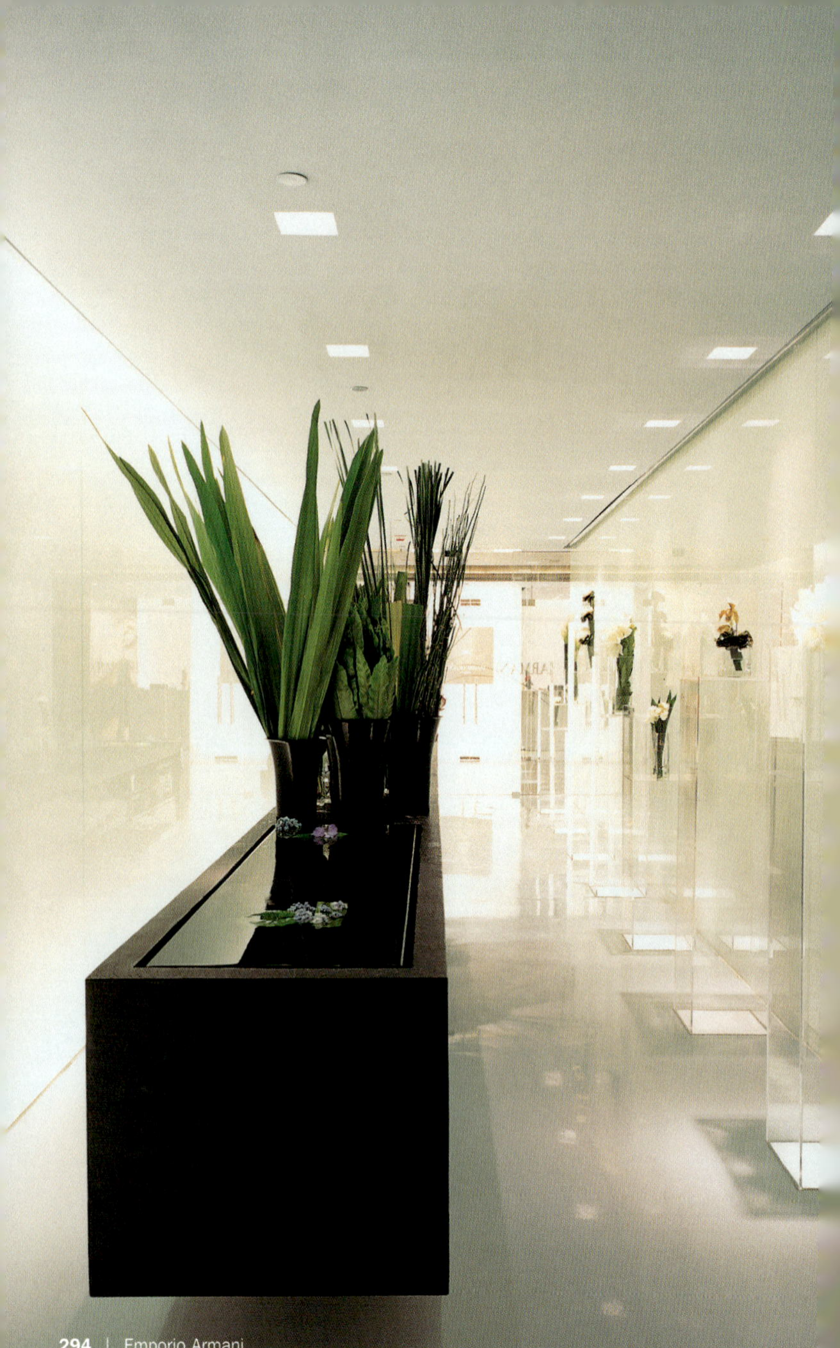

Emporio Armani | 295

Design and architecture by Yasui Hideo are defined by form-discipline and light-emphasized scene-setting in the rooms. Especially favorable to the fashion store in a rather dimly-lit mall: the thoroughly transparent materials made of artificial resin, which are arranged in concentrated fashion and radiate coolness and temptation.

Design und Architektur von Yasui Hideo sind bestimmt von Formenstrenge und licht betonter Inszenierung der Räume. Was dem Fashion-Store in der eher düsteren Mall besonders zugute kommt: durch und durch transparente Materialien aus Kunstharz, die – konzentriert angeordnet – kühl und verlockend erstrahlen.

Le design et l'architecture de Yasui Hideo sont caractérisés par l'austérité des formes et la mise en lumière accentuée des pièces. Particulièrement bénéfique à ce magasin de mode situé dans un mall plutôt sombre : des matériaux entièrement transparents en résine artificielle qui, dans leur agencement concentré, irradient froideur et tentation.

El diseño y la arquitectura de Yasui Hideo están determinados por la austeridad de las formas y la escenificación de los espacios a través de la luz. Esta tienda de moda, con una ambientación más bien sombría, saca provecho de la transparencia de la resina sintética de su mobiliario, cuyos elementos, con un brillo frío y tentador, están dispuestos de modo concentrado.

Design e progetto, firmati Yasui Hideo, sono caratterizzati dal rigore estetico e da una scenografia tutta giocata sugli effetti luce. Elementi che risaltano particolarmente nel fashion store D-Grace Hakata, ubicato in uno shopping mall un po' cupo, esaltati dall'uso coerente di materiali in resina sintetica che, disposti con ordine minimalista, rilucono di una trasparenza lunare ed invitante.

Yasui Hideo Atelier

4-3-27 Shibuya
Shibuya-ku
Tokyo 150-0002
Japan
www.yasui-atr.com

Photos by Nacása & Partners Inc.

D-Grace Hakata

Tenjin 1-11-1
Fukuoka-shi
Fukuoka-ken 810-0001
Japan

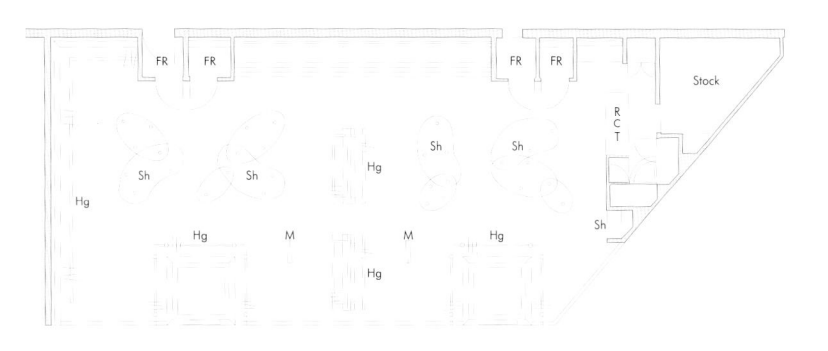

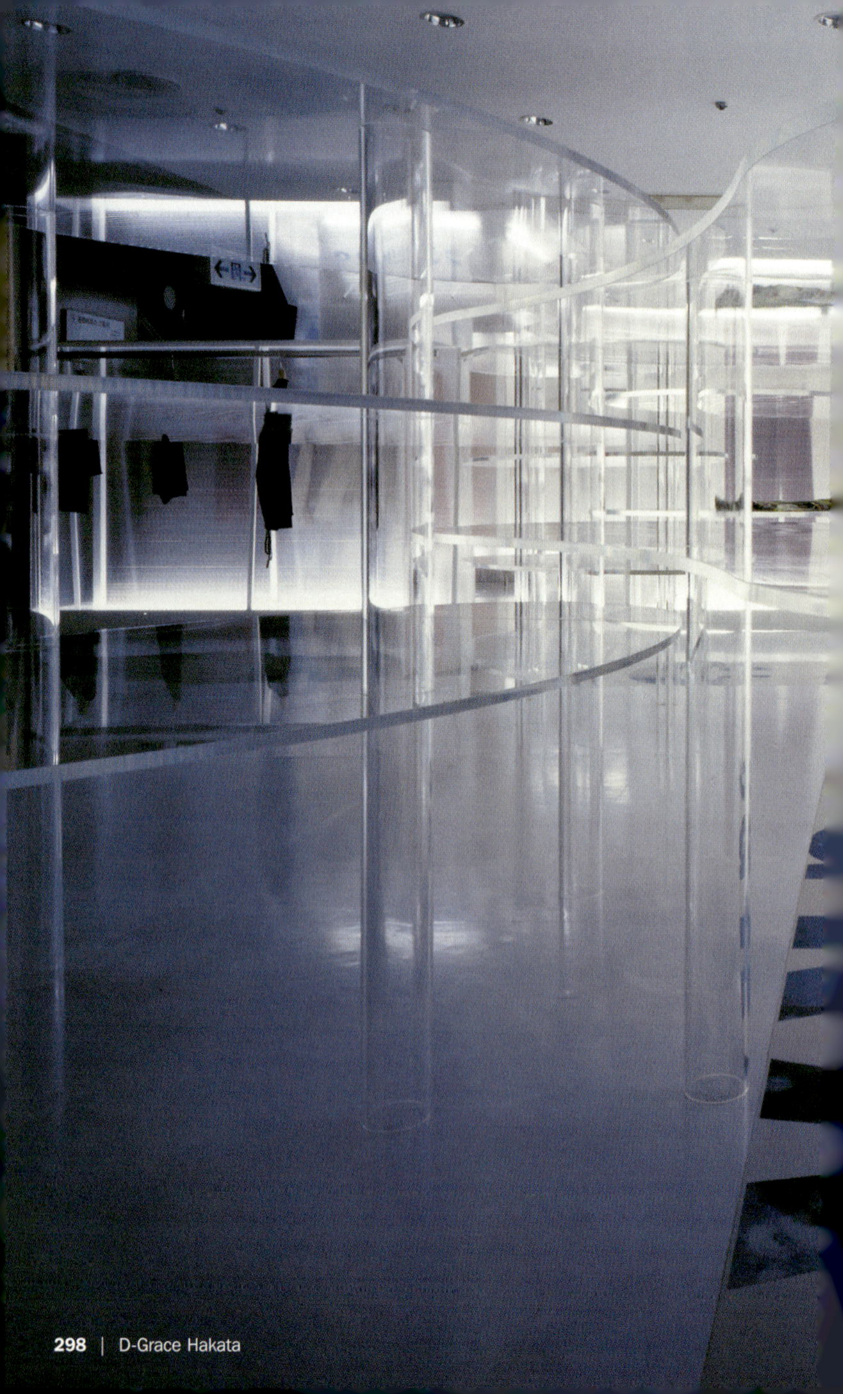

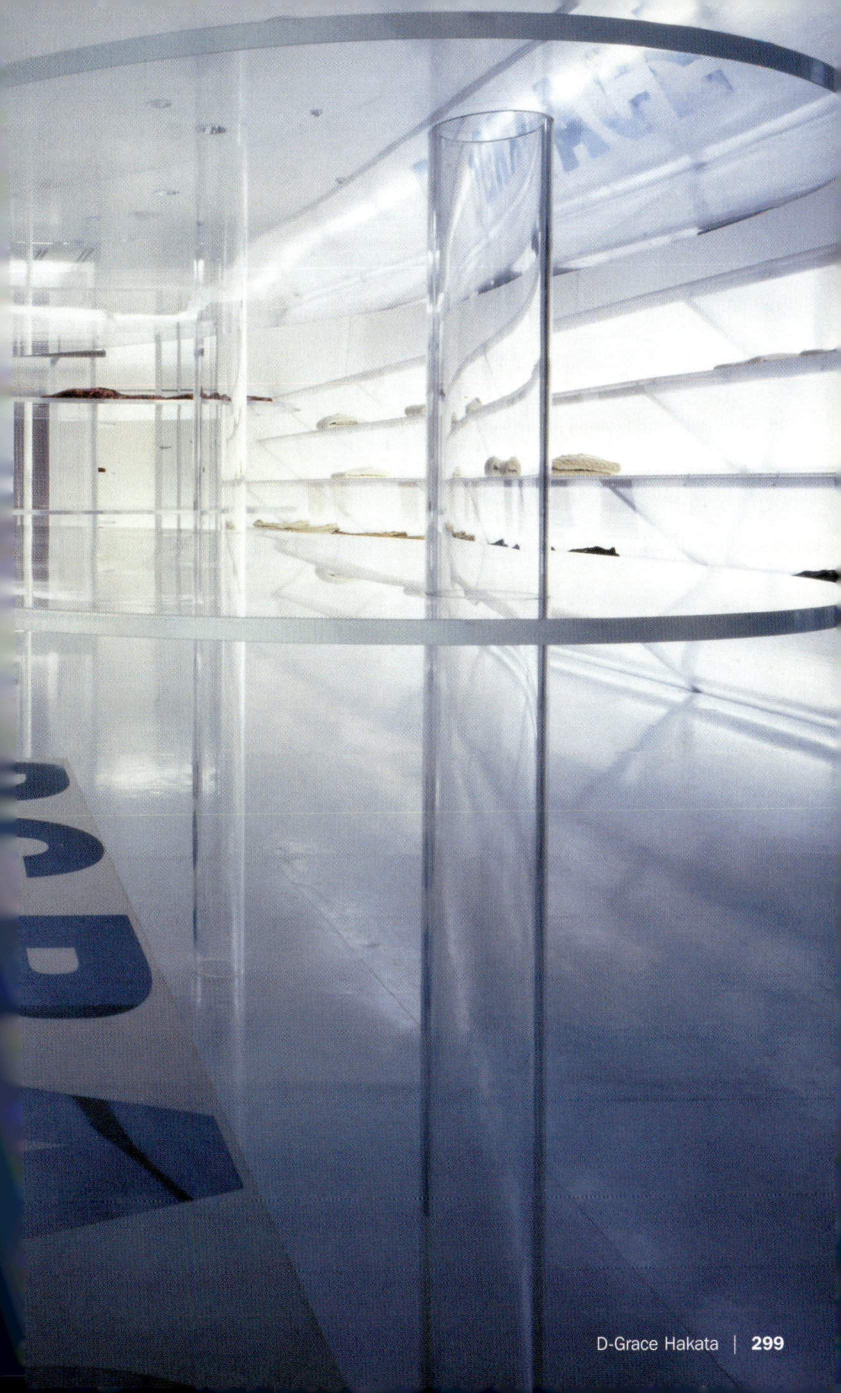

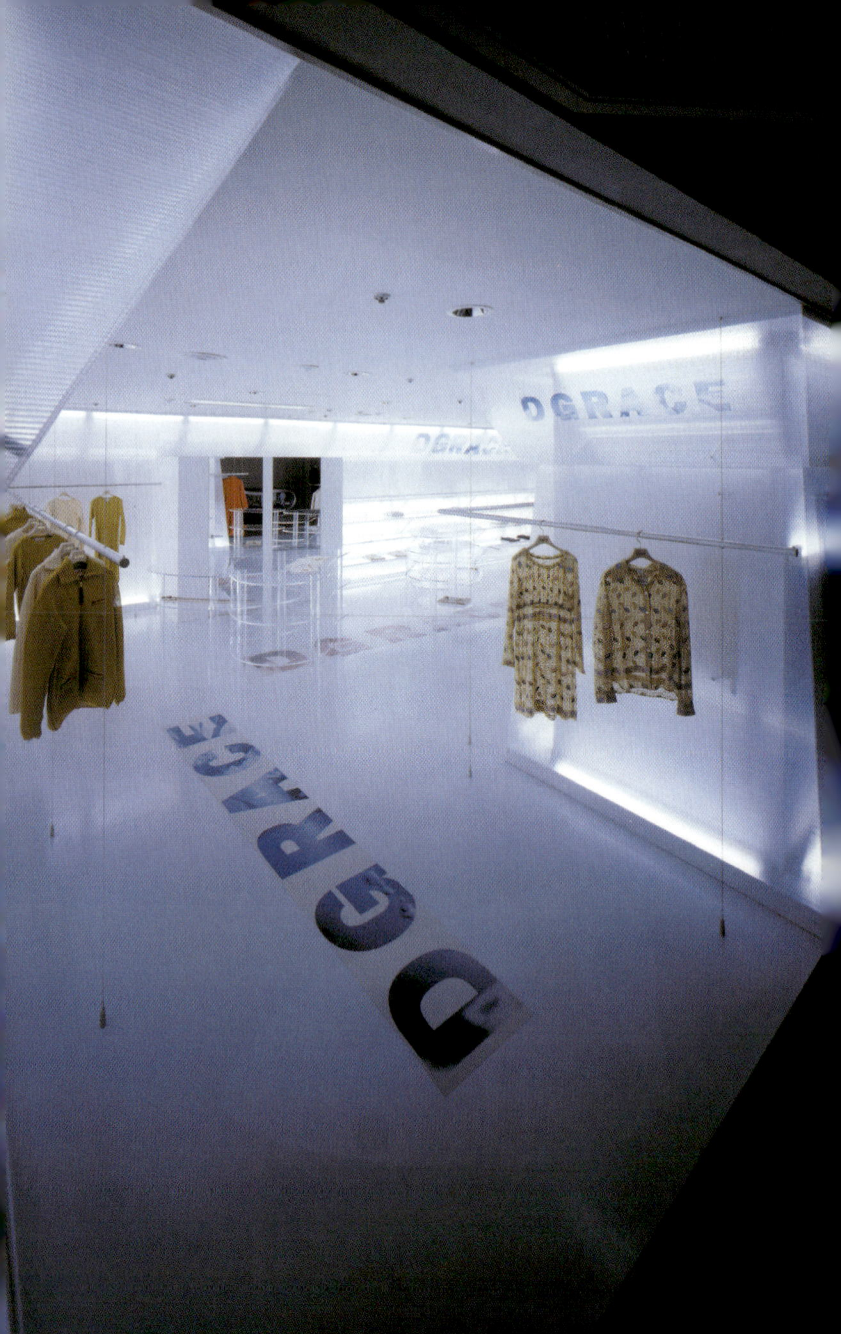
DGRACE
DGRACE
DGRACE

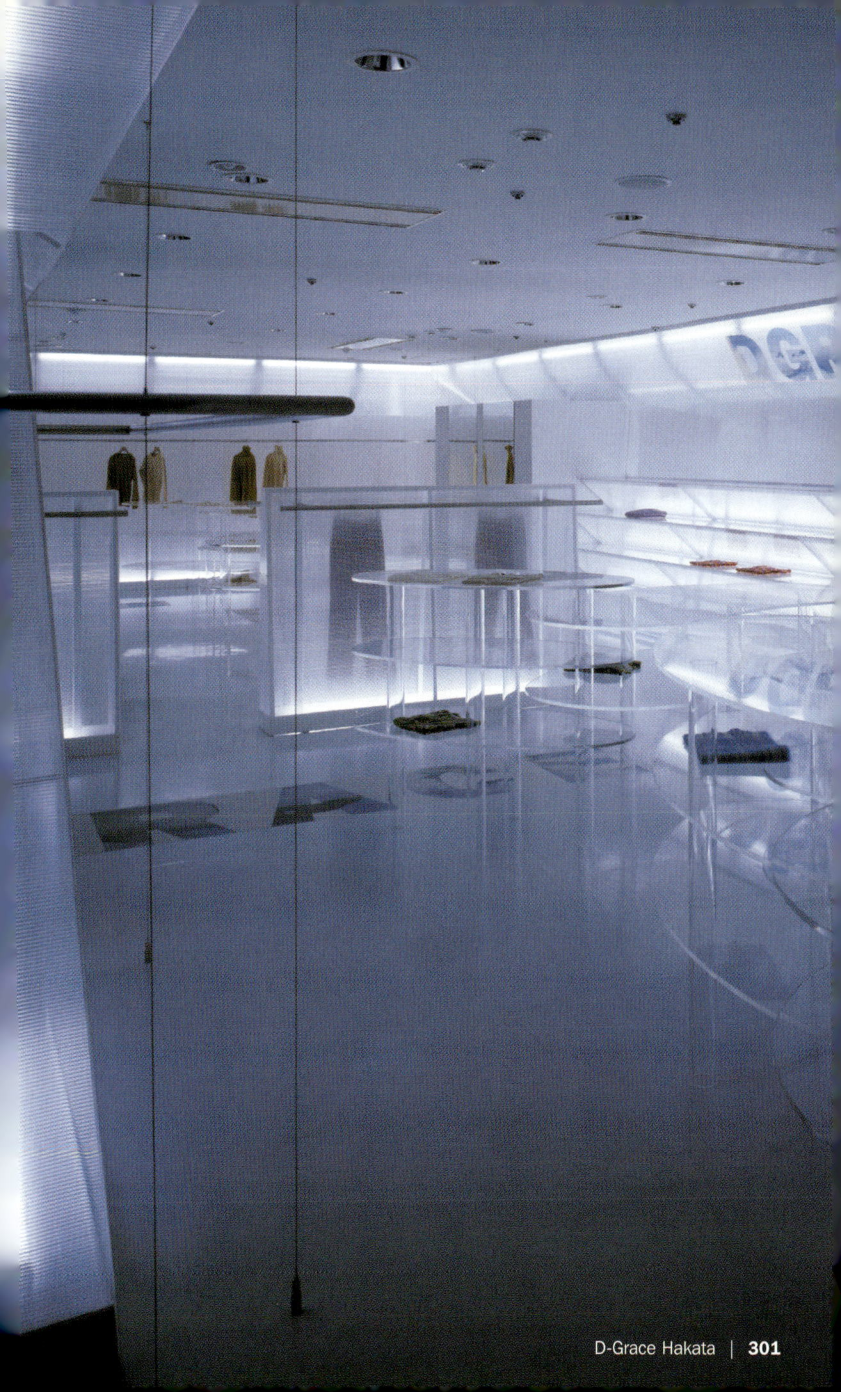

The fashion store, Stand, presents its clothes without central core or fussy decoration. It is reminiscent of a cabin: an architecturally sparse landscape, atmospherically enveloped in a blue ceiling, consisting of a structure made of slats. Simplicity, which focuses on the essential and concentrates on the products.

Entkernt und ohne Schnörkel präsentiert der Fashion-Store von Stand seine Mode. Er erinnert an eine Kabine: eine architektonisch karge Landschaft, atmosphärisch umhüllt von einer blauen Decke, bestehend aus einer Stab-Struktur. Schlichtheit, die die Konzentration auf das Wesentliche lenkt, auf die Produkte.

Le magasin de mode Stand présente sa mode sans noyau central ni fioritures. Il ressemble à une cabine : un paysage à l'architecture dépouillée, enveloppé d'un plafond atmosphérique bleu fait de lattes. Une simplicité qui concentre l'attention sur l'essentiel, les produits.

Sin núcleo y sin ornamentos, esta es la forma en que la tienda de moda de Stand presenta sus prendas. Su diseño interior recuerda al de una cabina: un paisaje arquitectónicamente árido envuelto por un techo azul con estructura de listones. Sencillez que permite concentrarse en lo esencial, los productos.

Sventrato e ricostruito con spiccata tendenza alla riduzione: ecco come il fashion store di Stand si presenta dopo la ristrutturazione. L'effetto cabina bene armonizza con l'ambiente minimalista avvolto da una struttura lamellare blu. Una sintesi sobria che mette in risalto ciò che è veramente essenziale: le creazioni moda.

Suppose Design Office

13-2 Kako-mati Naka-ku
Hiroshima 730-0812
Japan
www.suppose.jp

Photos by Nacása & Partners Inc.

Stand

Nakamati 1
Hiroshima 730-0037
Japan

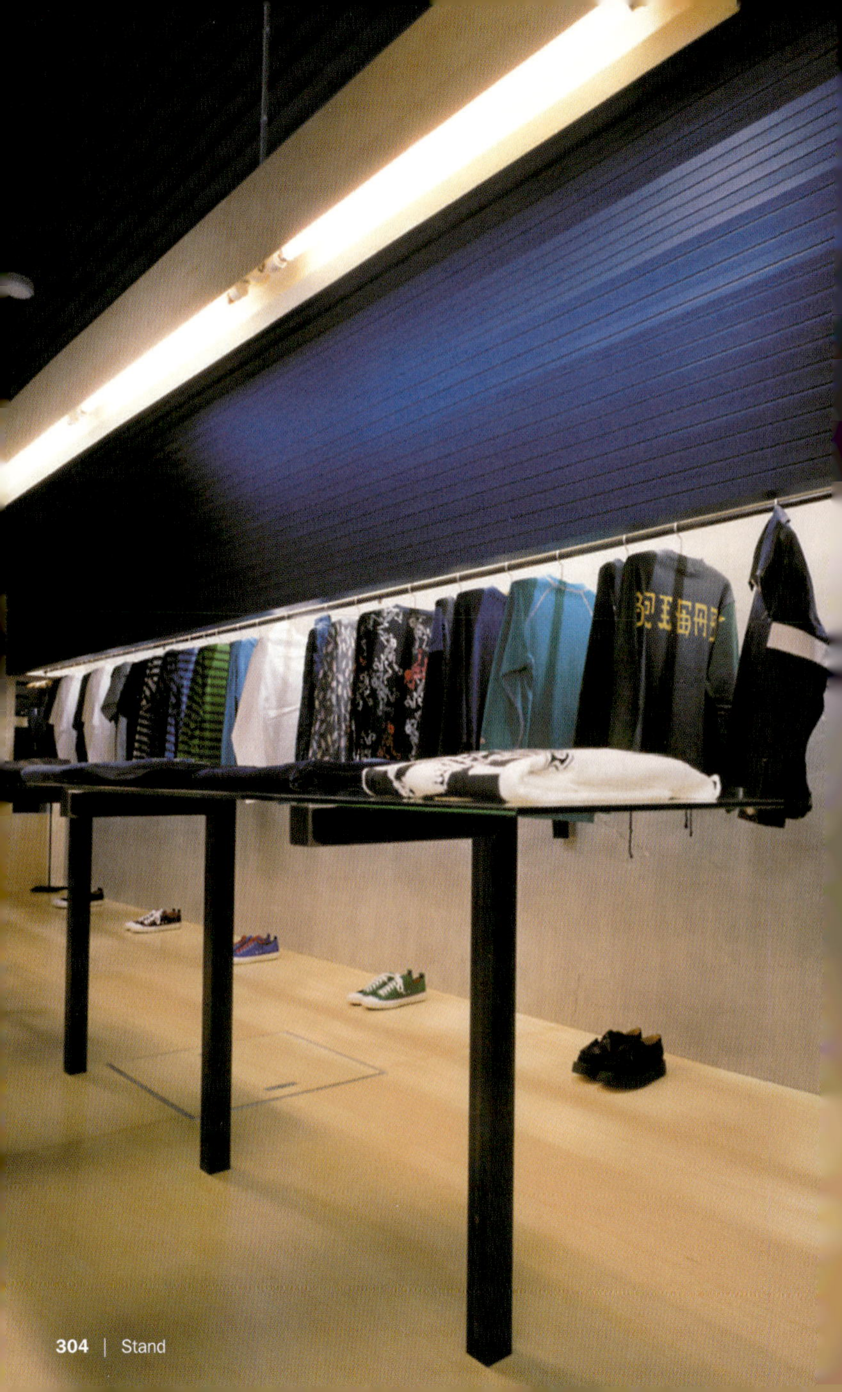

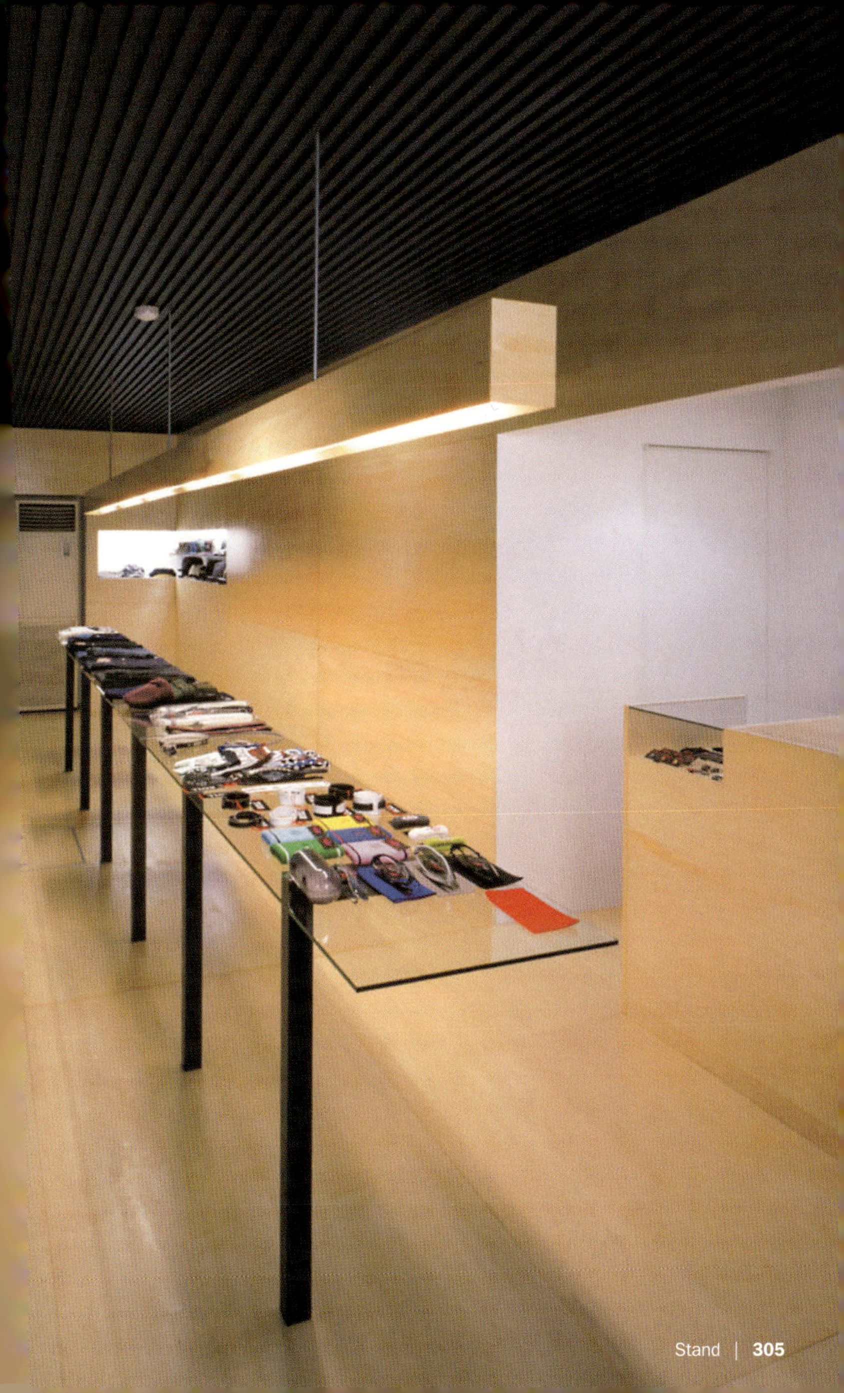

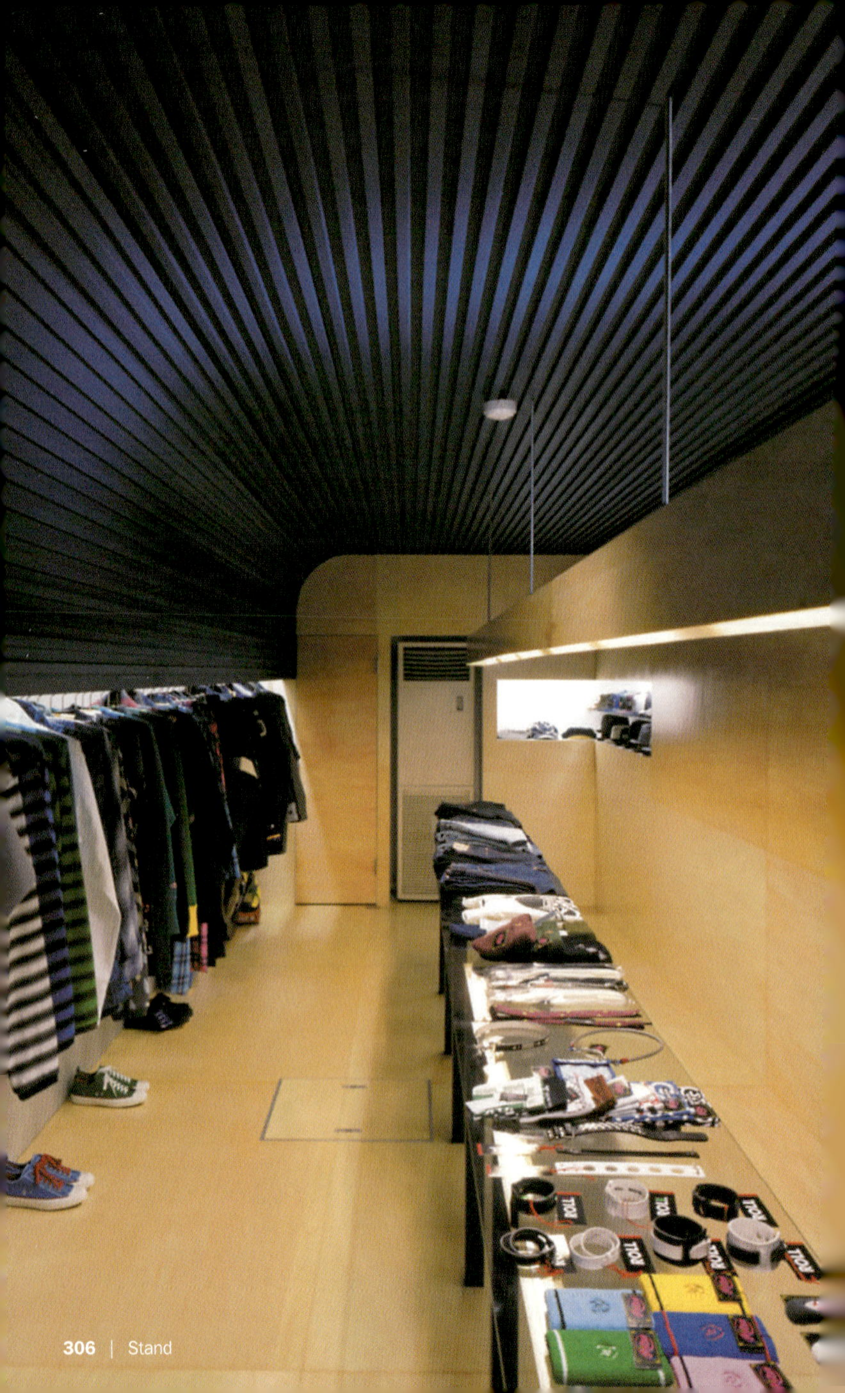

Stand | 307

The color white is predominant in Jayro White's clothing store. However, architect Colucci wants to create atmospheres the same as at sunrise. For this, he uses transparent, sandwich walls, which recreate the color-play of the rising sun. The impact of the staircase is like a stylized gangway—kind of an invitation for lift off.

Im Kleidershop von Jayro White dominiert die Farbe Weiß. Dennoch will Architekt Colucci Stimmungen wie bei einem Sonnenaufgang erzeugen. Dafür verwendet er transparente Sandwich-Wände, die das Farbspiel einer aufgehenden Sonne nachstellen. Die Treppe wirkt wie eine stilisierte Gangway – eine Einladung quasi zum Abheben.

Dans le magasin de vêtements de Jayro White le blanc domine. Pourtant l'architecte Colucci cherche à créer des atmosphères de lever de soleil. Pour cela il fait appel à des cloisons sandwich transparentes qui recréent le jeu des couleurs du soleil levant. L'escalier fait l'effet d'une passerelle stylisée – presque une invitation à décoller.

En la tienda de ropa de Jayro White domina el color blanco. Y sin embargo, el arquitecto Colucci quiere recrear el ambiente de una salida de sol. Para ello emplea tabiques sándwich transparentes que recrean el juego de colores de un amanecer. La escalera se asemeja a una pasarela estilizada que parece invitarnos a despegar.

Nella boutique Jayro White il colore bianco è protagonista assoluto. Tuttavia con il gioco caleidoscopico di effetti colorati sui pannelli sandwich trasparenti l'architetto Colucci intende ricreare le atmosfere del sole nascente all'alba. La scala evoca l'immagine di una passerella d'imbarco stilizzata...un po' come un invito ad alzarsi in volo.

Claudio Colucci Design

4-9-2 Higashi Shibuya-ku
Tokyo 150-0011
Japan
www.colucci-design.com

Photos by Nacása & Partners Inc.

Jayro White

1-6-24 Sannomiya-sho Chuo-ku
Kobe-shi
Kyogo 650-0021
Japan
www.jayrowhite.com

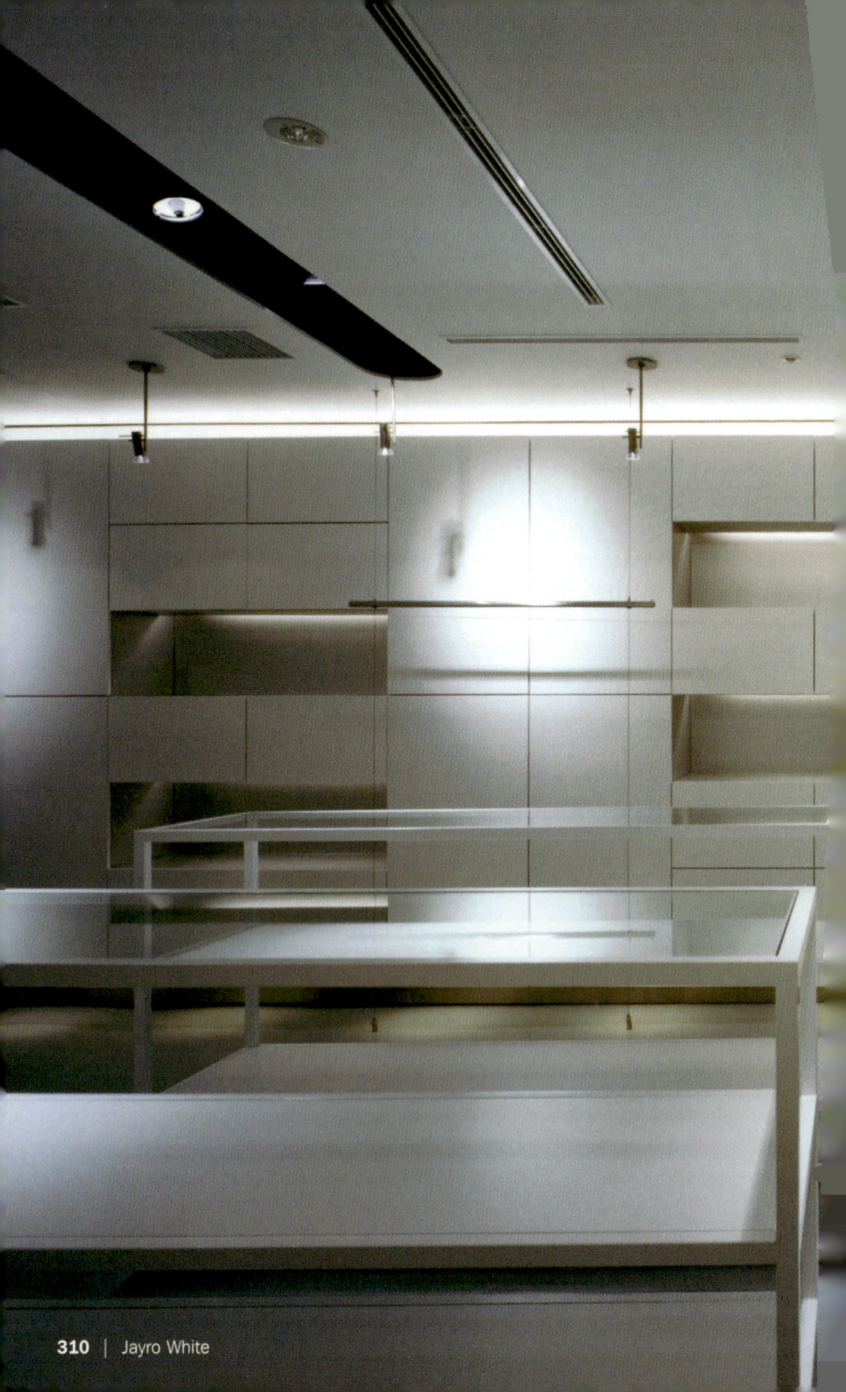

Jayro White | 311

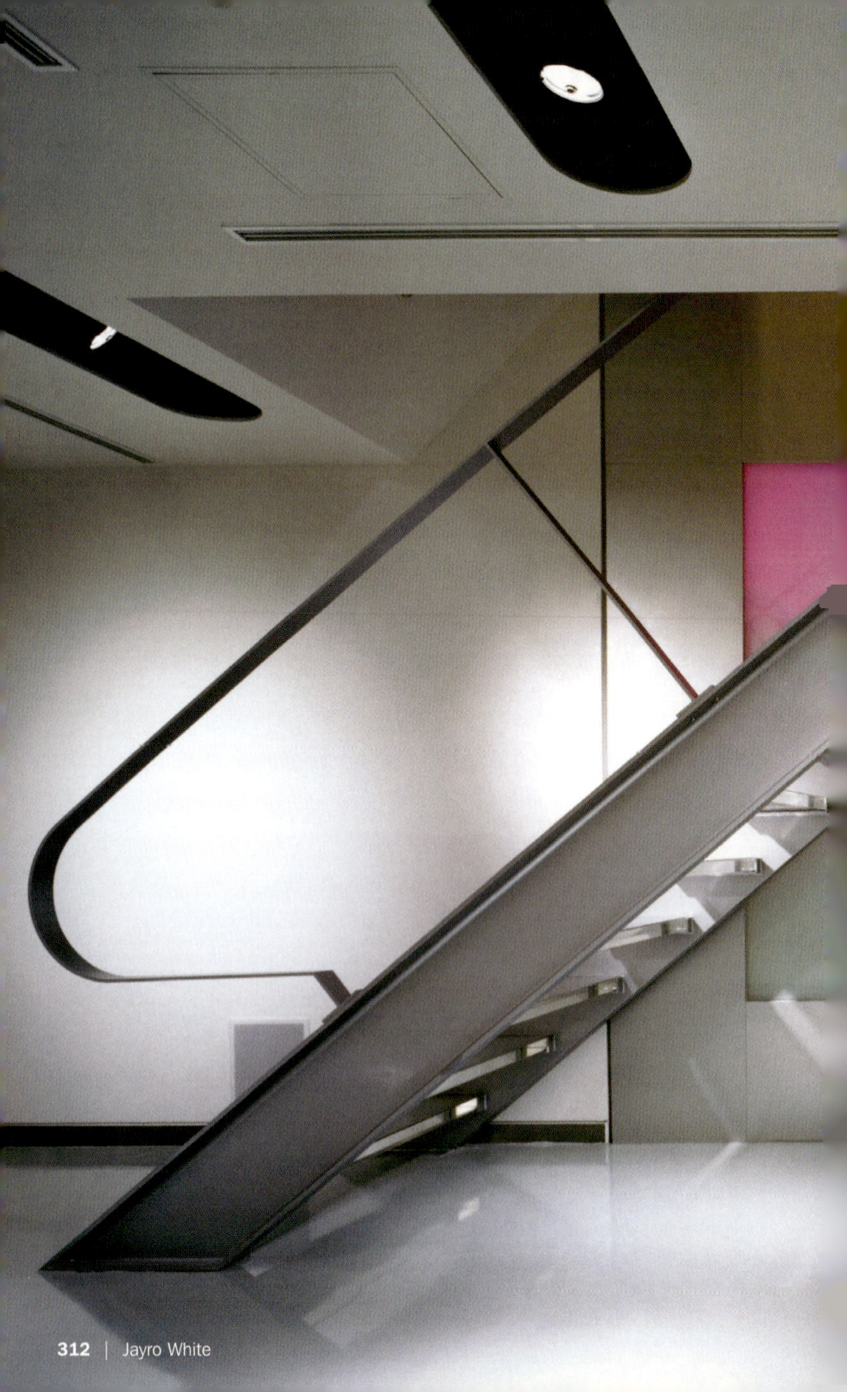

Jayro White

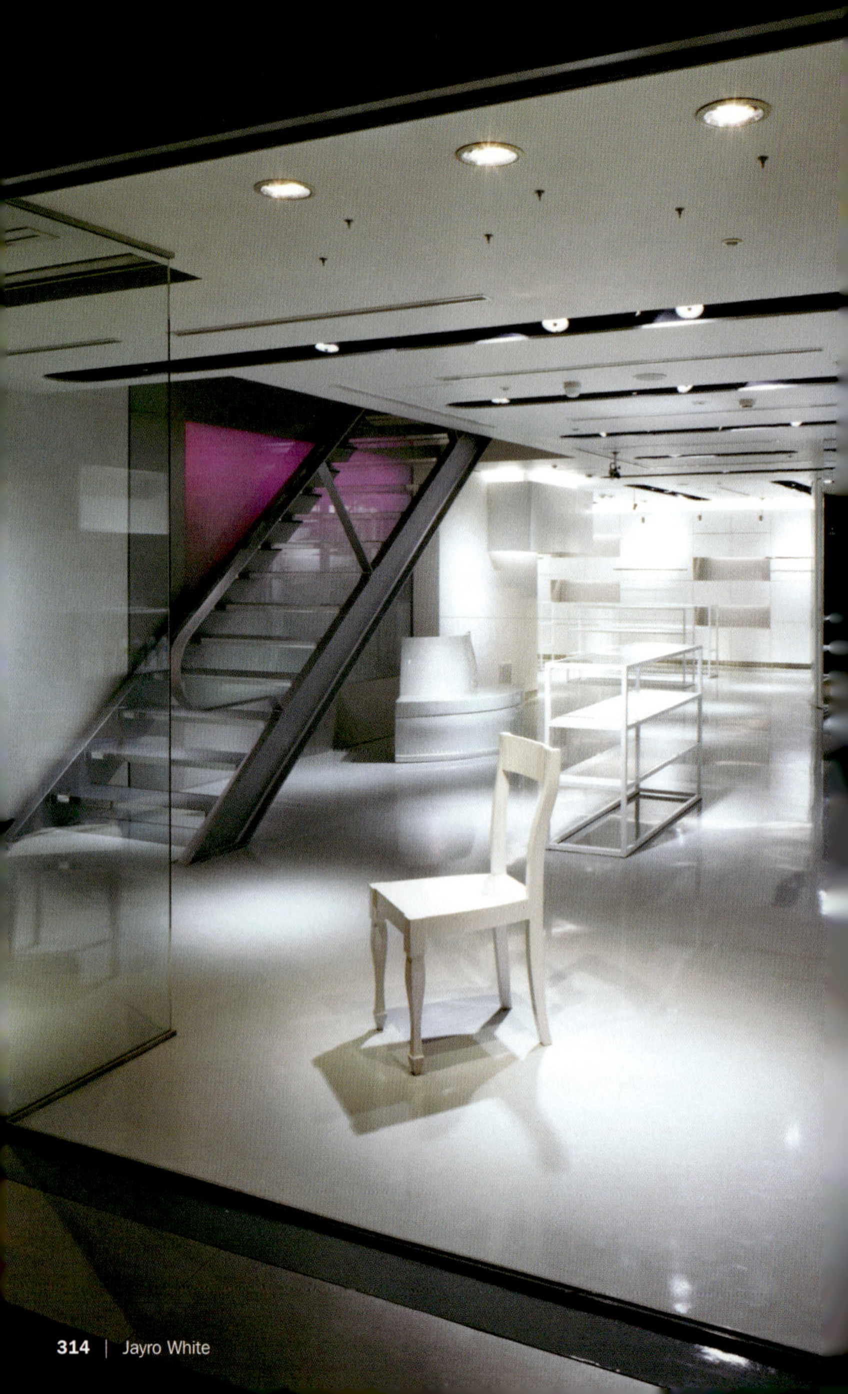

JAYRO white

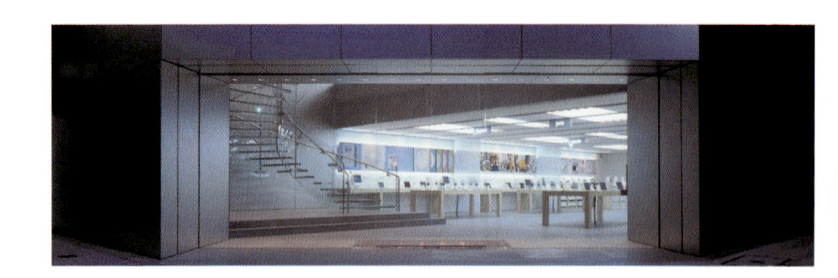

The store's façade is defined by extreme simplicity. The Apple signature that is flaunted is visible from afar. The view to the inside is deliberately directed towards the winding glass staircase. The suspended, light stairway sculpture is the facility's centerpiece. Cool elegance also influences the remainder of the interior.

Die Fassade des Stores ist bestimmt von äußerster Schlichtheit. Weithin sichtbar prangt darauf das Apple-Signet. Der Blick nach innen ist gezielt auf die gewundene Glastreppe ausgerichtet. Die schwebend leichte Stufenskulptur ist das Herzstück des Objekts. Kühle Eleganz prägt auch das übrige Interieur.

La façade du magasin se caractérise par son extrême simplicité. Visible de loin, le logo d'Apple resplendit dessus. Le regard sur l'intérieur est délibérément dirigé vers l'escalier de verre sinueux. La sculpture légère et suspendue des marches est le point central de l'objet. Une élégance froide définit également l'intérieur.

La fachada de esta tienda está caracterizada por una extremada sencillez. Llama la atención el símbolo de Apple, visible desde lejos. La vista hacia el interior es conducida hacia la sinuosa escalera de cristal. La flotante y ligera escultura de peldaños conforma el corazón del espacio. El resto del interior también se caracteriza por una fría elegancia.

L'estrema semplicità è l'elemento determinante della facciata dell'Apple Store Shinsaibashi. Su di essa spicca, ben visibile da lontano, il marchio a forma di mela. Lo scorcio di prospettiva si apre volutamente sulla sinuosa scala in vetro, caratterizzata da una leggerezza come sospesa. La scultura in vetro costituisce il fulcro architettonico degli interni, contraddistinti da sobria eleganza.

Bohlin Cywinski Jackson

49 Geary Street, Suite 300
San Francisco, CA 94108
USA
www.bcj.com

Photos by Koji Okumura

Apple Store Shinsaibashi

1-5-5 Nishi-shinsaibashi
Chuo-ku Osaka-shi
Osaka 542-0086
Japan
www.apple.com

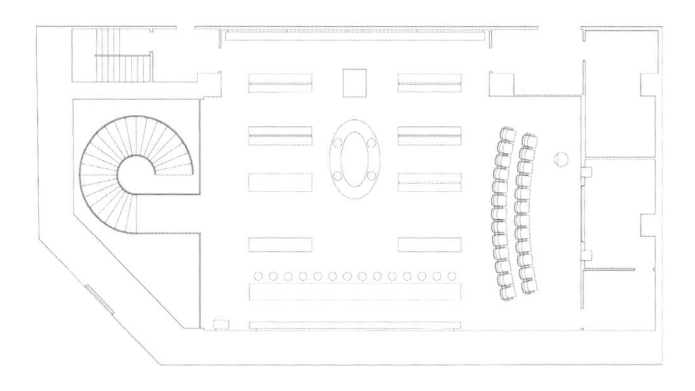

Apple Store Shinsaibashi

Apple Store Shinsaibashi | 219

Apple Store Shinsaibashi

Apple Store Shinsaibashi | 321

The shop design consciously utilizes an unusual type of scenery. An illuminated tent landscape is created out of PVC, from which the storage surfaces and niches develop. The arched mirrors in the entrance lobby have a unique power of attraction.

Das Shop-Design setzt bewusst auf eine Inszenierung von ungewöhnlicher Art. Aus PVC entsteht eine durchleuchtete Zeltlandschaft, aus der sich die Ablagen und Nischen entfalten. Einen eigentümlichen Sog lösen die gewölbten Spiegel im Entree aus.

La conception du magasin joue volontairement sur une mise en scène inhabituelle. Il se crée un paysage illuminé de tentes en PVC, à partir duquel se déploient les étalages et les niches. Les miroirs bombés de l'entrée exercent un pouvoir d'attraction unique.

El diseño de la tienda apuesta conscientemente por una escenificación fuera de lo común. Sus creadores emplean el PVC para recrear el interior de una tienda de campaña iluminada de cuyas paredes surgen las estanterías y los nichos. Los espejos de la entrada desencadenan un remolino con la sinuosidad de sus formas.

Lo shop design punta volutamente ad un insolito impatto scenografico: l'effetto tenda creato dalla struttura retroilluminata in PVC, che col suo movimento fluido delimita nicchie e ripiani espositivi. Di singolare fascino gli specchi curvi all'ingresso.

Acconci Studio

20 Jay Street Suite #215
Brooklyn, NY 11201
USA
www.acconci.com

Photos by Vito Acconci, Sergio Pirrone, courtesy United Bamboo

United Bamboo Store

20-14 Sarugaku-cho
Tokyo 150-0033
Japan
www.unitedbamboo.com

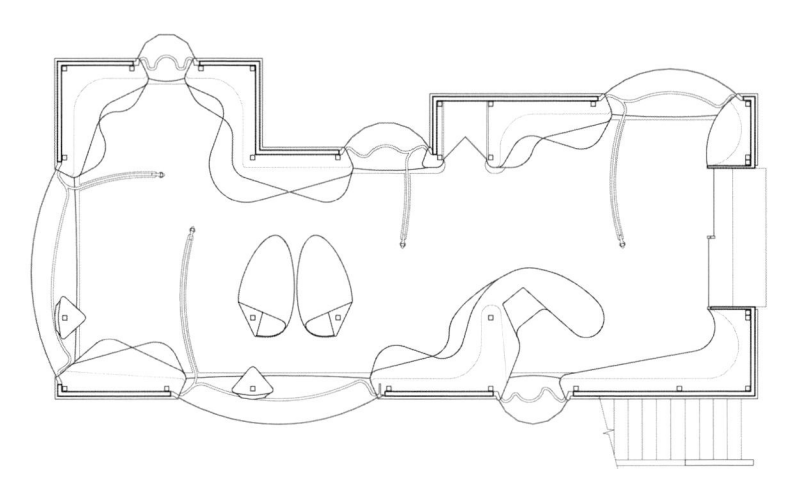

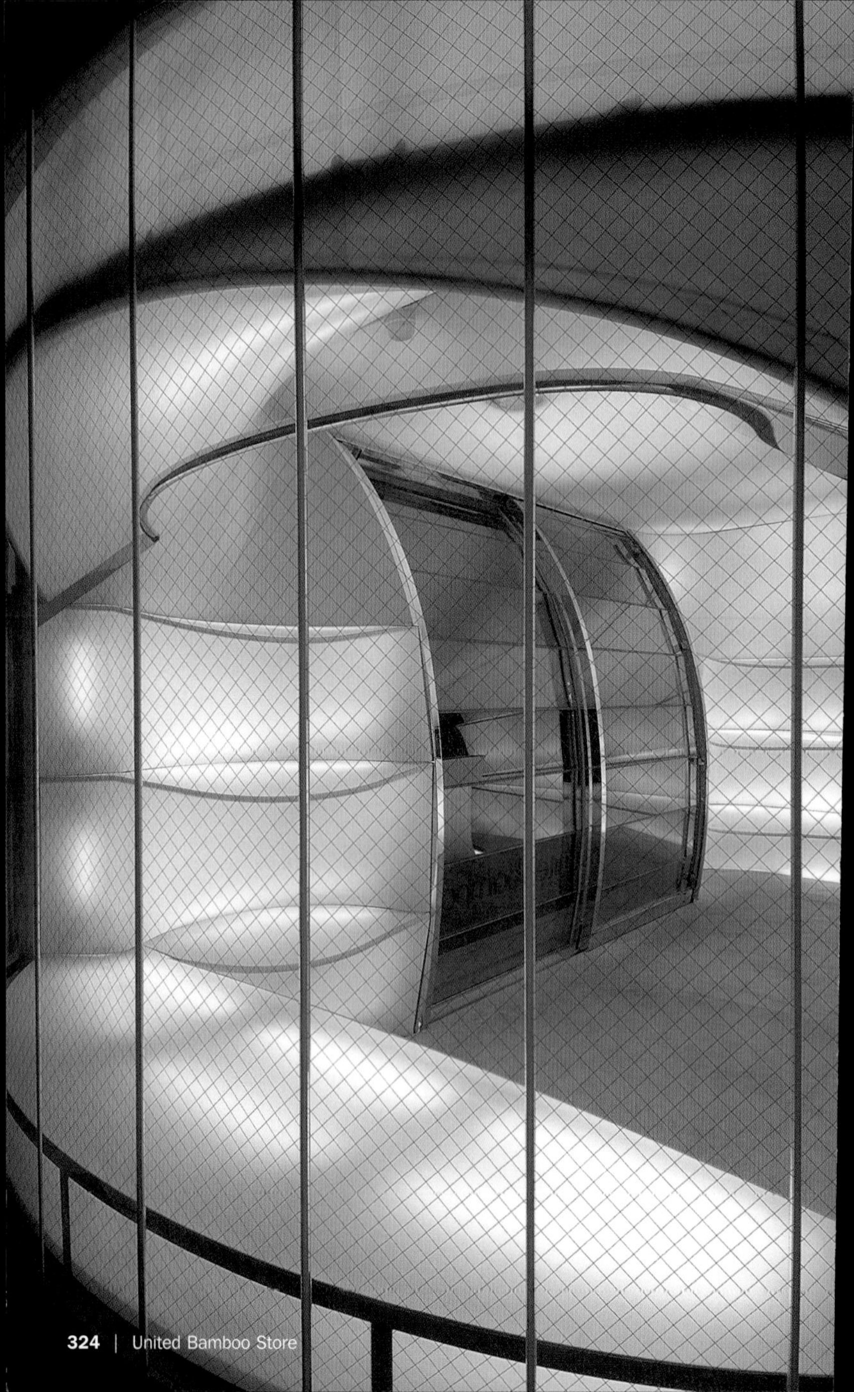

United Bamboo Store | 325

326 | United Bamboo Store

United Bamboo Store | 327

Cultural uprootedness and life as a game are themes for Turkish-Cypriot fashion designer Hussein Chalayan. The backgammon inlays in the floor serve as spatial metaphors to suggest this. Allusions to air travel are visible, for instance, as service trolleys, which act as display elements.

Kulturelle Entwurzelung und das Leben als ein Spiel sind die Themen des türkisch-zypriotischen Modemachers Hussein Chalayan. Als räumliche Metaphern fungieren hierfür die Backgammon-Intarsien im Boden und Anspielungen auf die Luftfahrt. Letztere wird zum Beispiel sichtbar in den Service-Trolleys, die als Auslagen dienen.

Le déracinement culturel et la vie en tant que jeu sont les thèmes du créateur de mode turco-chypriote Hussein Chalayan. Leur expression métaphorique se retrouve dans les incrustations de backgammon sur le sol et les allusions à l'aviation, comme par exemple les chariots de service qui servent de présentoirs.

El desarraigo cultural y la vida como un juego, estos son los temas de la casa de moda turco-chipriota de Hussein Chalayan. El juego backgammon taraceado en el suelo y las referencias a los viajes en avión son metáforas espaciales. La aviación se refleja también en los carritos, que se emplean como estanterías.

Lo sradicamento culturale e l'aspetto ludico della vita sono temi ricorrenti nel lavoro dello stilista turco-cipriota. Nell'Hussein Chalayan Shop essi trovano espressione nelle metafore spaziali rappresentate dagli intarsi del pavimento ispirati al gioco del backgammon e dalle allusioni al mondo aeronautico. Queste ultime si concretizzano per esempio nei carrelli di servizio che fungono da elementi espositivi.

Block Architecture

83a Geffrye Street
London UK-E2 8HX
United Kingdom
www.blockarchitecture.com

Photos by Leon Chew

Hussein Chalayan Shop

1-4-8 Aobadai, Meguro-kuf
153-0042 Tokyo
Japan

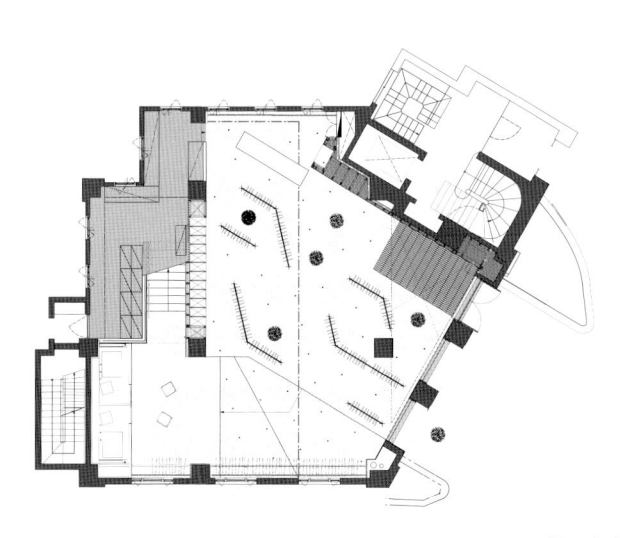

330 | Hussein Chalayan Shop

Hussein Chalayan Shop | 331

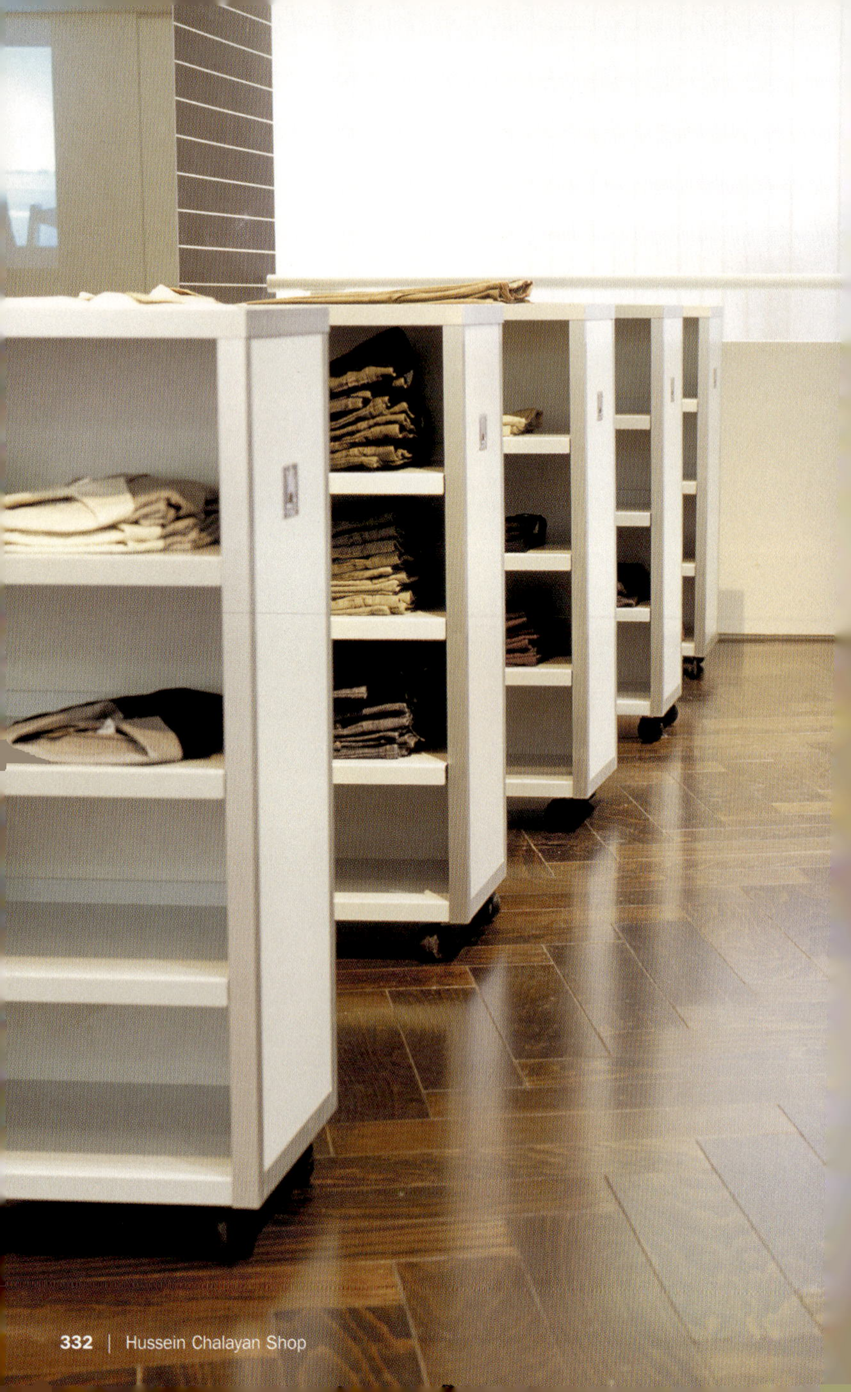

Hussein Chalayan Shop | 333

Le Salon—a name that equates with a program. The Salon stands for luxury, exclusivity and a relaxed atmosphere. Here, Claudio Colucci's design combines the experience of an open space, accessible to everyone, and with interiors that are meant to convey the ease and comfort of an apartment.

Le Salon – ein Name als Programm. Der Salon steht für Luxus, Exklusivität und entspannte Atmosphäre. Claudio Coluccis Design verbindet hier das Erlebnis eines offenen, für jedermann zugänglichen Raums mit einer Einrichtung, die die Behaglichkeit und den Komfort einer Wohnung vermitteln will.

Le Salon – un nom assimilé à un programme. Le Salon est synonyme de luxe, d'exclusivité et d'atmosphère décontractée. Le design de Claudio Colucci combine ici l'expérience d'un espace ouvert, accessible à tous avec un aménagement visant à donner la sensation de bien-être et de confort d'un appartement.

Le Salon – un nombre que lo dice todo. Salón es sinónimo de lujo, exclusividad y atmósfera distendida. El diseño de Claudio Colucci fusiona en esta tienda la experiencia de un espacio abierto y accesible a cualquiera, con un mobiliario que quiere transmitir el confort y la comodidad de una vivienda.

Le Salon: il nome è già un programma. Sinonimo di lusso, esclusività ed atmosfera distesa. L'ambiente creato dal designer Claudio Colucci riesce a trasmettere la sensazione di uno spazio aperto, accessibile a tutti, e al tempo stesso il senso di intimità e di confortevolezza di casa propria.

Claudio Colucci Design

4-9-2 Higashi Shibuya-ku
Tokyo 150-0011
Japan
www.colucci-design.com

Photos by Nacása & Partners Inc.

Le Salon

Tower 1F Hotel New Otani
4-1 Kioi-cho
Chiyoda-ku
Tokyo 102-0094
Japan
www.le-salon.info/english/top.html

Le Salon

Le Salon | **337**

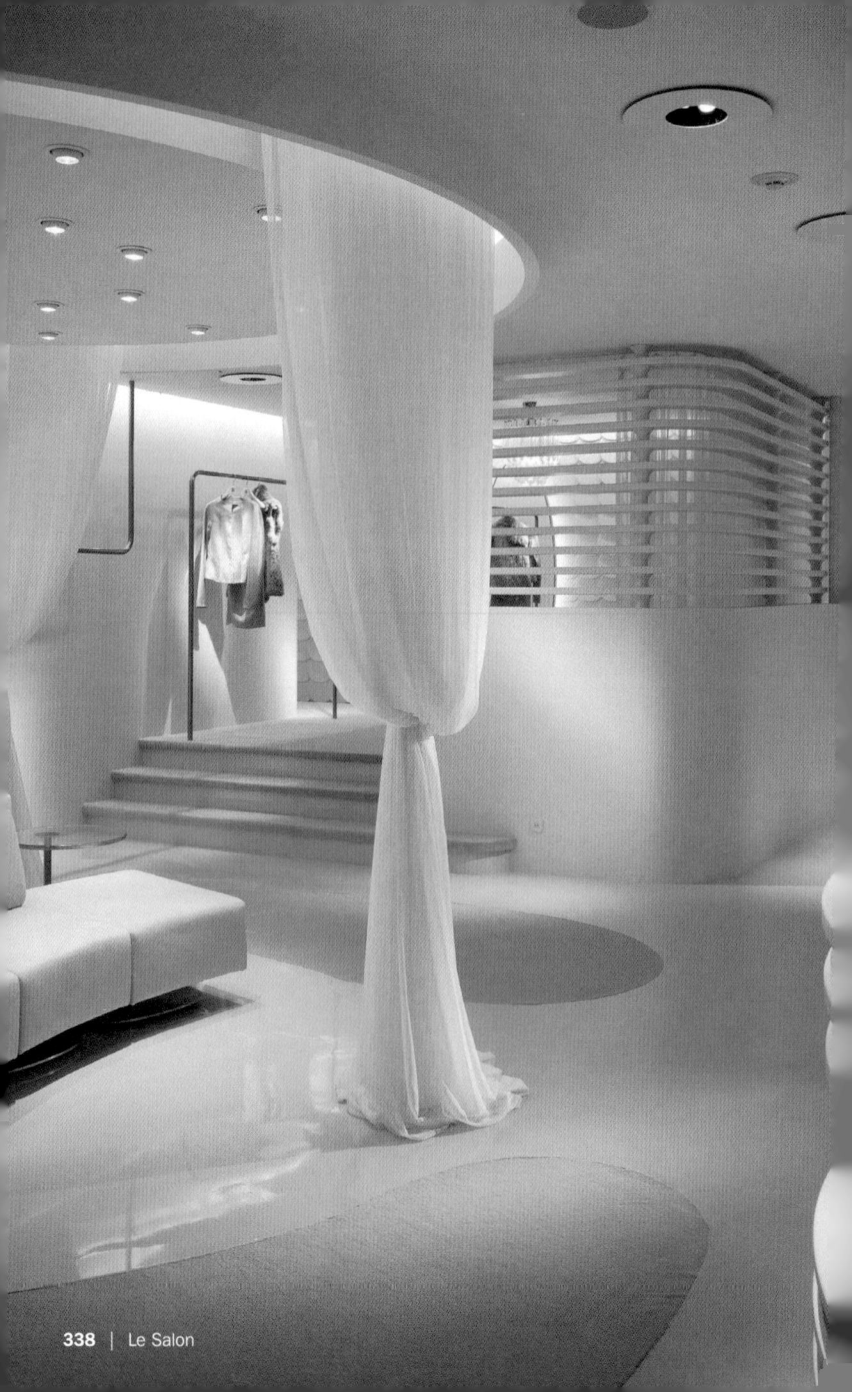

Le Salon | **339**

Le Salon

Le Salon | 341

You feel as though you are transported to a futuristic gallery. Wait a minute: is it because of the flickering light-play? Or do the corrugated roofs and open, vast rolling surfaces create this effect? It is a successful symbiosis of each design element that Yasui Hideo uses to create a galaxy for avant-garde fashion.

Man fühlt sich in eine futuristische Galerie versetzt. Nur: Liegt es am flimmernden Lichtspiel? Oder erzeugen die Welldächer sowie offene, weit geschwungene Flächen diesen Effekt? Es ist die gelungene Symbiose beider Gestaltungselemente, mit der Yasui Hideo eine Galaxie für avantgardistische Mode erschafft.

On se croirait transporté dans une galerie futuriste. Seulement voilà : est-ce dû au scintillement des jeux de lumière ? Ou les plafonds ondulés et les vastes surfaces incurvées créent-ils cet effet ? C'est la symbiose réussie de ces deux éléments de design avec lesquels Yasui Hideo crée une galaxie pour une mode avant-gardiste.

En esta tienda se tiene la sensación de estar en una galería futurista. ¿Se debe al centelleante juego de luz? ¿O son los ondulados techos y las amplias superficies abiertas y sinuosas las que crean este efecto? Es la lograda simbiosis entre ambos elementos con la que Yasui Hideo crea una galaxia para la moda de vanguardia.

È come sentirsi catapultati in una galleria futuristica. Dipende dagli effetti luce di diversa intensità? O sono piuttosto la struttura ondulata o le volte movimentate del soffitto a produrre questa sensazione? È la sintesi ben riuscita tra i due elementi realizzata da Yasui Hideo: il risultato è la cornice spaziale in cui contestualizzare una visione avanguardistica della moda.

Yasui Hideo Atelier

4-3-27 Shibuya
Shibuya-ku
Tokyo 150-0002
Japan
www.yasui-atr.com

Photos by Nacása & Partners Inc.

Advanced Chique

Minami-Aoyama 6-2-11
Minato-ku
Tokyo 107-0062
Japan

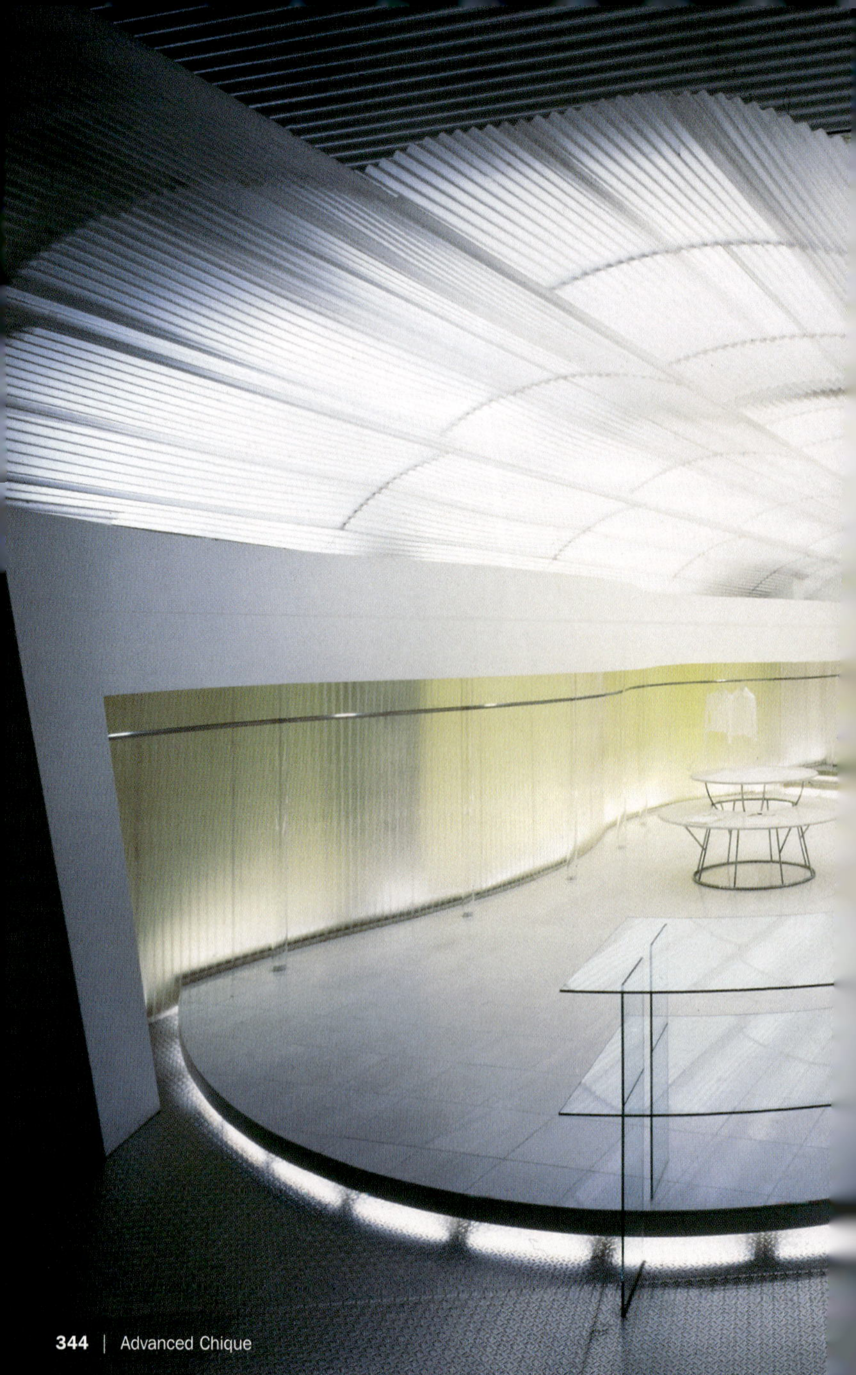

Advanced Chique | 345

346 | Advanced Chique

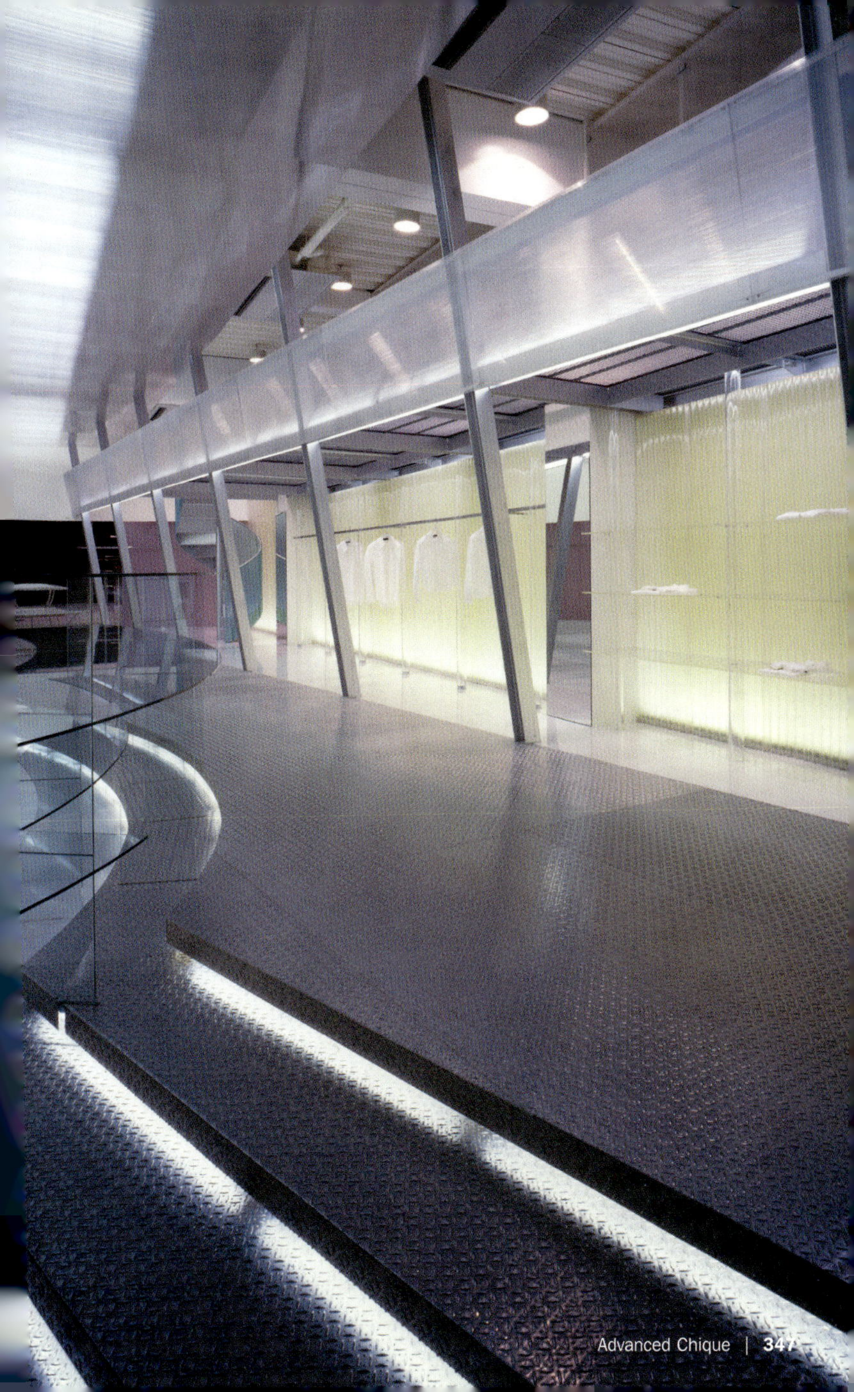

This store wants to make clear that the products on display are the results of a creative process. The design is therefore restricted to few, concentrated display features. Descriptive texts on transparent surfaces also provide explanations of the idea and development of the fashion creations.

Dass die zur Schau gestellten Produkte Ergebnisse eines kreativen Prozesses sind, will dieser Store deutlich machen. Dafür beschränkt sich das Design auf wenige, konzentriert wirkende Auslagen. Beschreibende Texte auf den transparenten Flächen erläutern dazu Idee und Entwicklung der modischen Kreationen.

Ce magasin veut démontrer que les produits exposés sont le résultat d'un processus de création. C'est pourquoi le design se limite à quelques rares étalages concentrés. Des textes descriptifs sur les surfaces transparentes expliquent l'idée et le développement des créations de mode.

Esta tienda quiere dejar claro que los productos expuestos son el resultado de un proceso creativo. Para ello el diseño se limita al uso de un número reducido de estanterías que parecen concentradas. Además, las descripciones escritas en las superficies transparentes explican la idea y el desarrollo de la creación de las prendas.

Presentare le creazioni moda come il risultato finale di un processo creativo: questa è l'idea di fondo che pervade il Gomme Laforet Harajuku store. Lo shop design è ridotto, in cifra minimalista, a pochi elementi espositivi. Sulle superfici trasparenti, brevi formule testuali sintetizzano la concezione e lo sviluppo delle creazioni.

Yasui Hideo Atelier

4-3-27 Shibuya
Shibuya-ku
Tokyo 150-0002
Japan
www.yasui-atr.com

Photos by Nacása & Partners Inc.

Gomme Laforet Harajuku

Jingumae 1-16-6
Sibuya-ku
Tokyo 150-0001
Japan

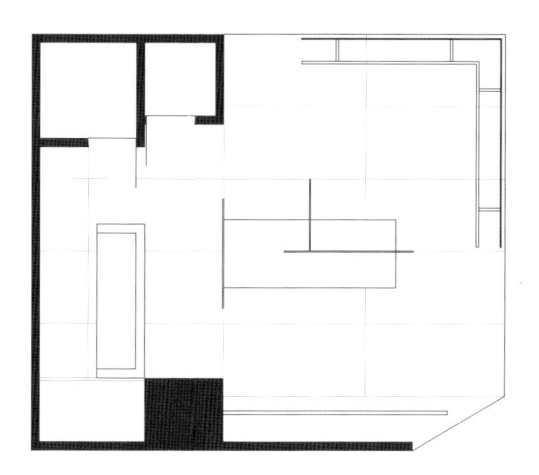

La robe qui paraît recouvrir un corps de
la gomme. des
Ce n'est point un vêtement qui triche sur
L'évolution
un système vivant.
transmuter

évolution de la morphogenèse es
central des travaux de re
en effet, la morphogenèse est un des
phénomènes les plus étonnants qui régiss
ème vivan

gomme
gomme
gomme gomm
des

robe qui paraît recouvrir un cor
la gomme
Ce n'est point un vêtemen
elques choses qui ne vont pas, mais, au contraire, il rehausse, en «ho
Envisageons heu
possible, a transmute
l'on se croit avoir quelques choses d

Gomme Laforet Harajuku | 351

352 | Gomme Laforet Harajuku

Gomme Laforet Harajuku

The plissee works that are so typical of Issey Miyake's fashion could hardly be more distinctively reflected in the room design: primarily, it is the closely ordered, colored nuances of glass surfaces that are reminiscent of the traditional technique of folding pleats. Additionally, the room design appears easy to survey and clear.

Die für Issey Miyakes Mode so typischen Plisseearbeiten könnten kaum markanter im Raum-Design gespiegelt werden: Es sind vor allem die eng gestellten, farblich nuancierten Glasflächen, die an die traditionelle Technik der Faltenwürfe erinnern. Dazu wirkt die Raumgestaltung übersichtlich und klar.

Les travaux de plissé si typiques de la mode d'Issey Miyake ne sauraient être traduits de façon plus signifiante : ce sont avant tout les surfaces de verre placées côte à côte et nuancées dans la couleur qui rappellent la technique traditionnelle de la draperie. De plus, il est aisé d'embrasser du regard l'agencement de la pièce.

Los plisados tan característicos de la creación de Issey Miyake no podrían haber sido reflejados de una forma más clara en el diseño de este espacio: son sobre todo las superficies de cristal dispuestas de forma agrupada y con sus colores armonizados las que evocan la técnica tradicional del plisado. Por lo demás, el diseño del interior transmite una sensación de apertura y claridad.

L'effetto plissé, motivo ricorrente in tante creazioni dello stilista Issey Miyake, non poteva trovare pendant espressivo di più spiccata corrispondenza. Sono soprattutto le superfici in vetro di diverse sfumature cromatiche, disposte l'una accanto all'altra, ad evocare l'immagine della tecnica tradizionale della plissettatura. Un espediente sottolineato dall'ordine sobrio e ben definito dell'ambiente circostante.

Ito Masaru Design Project / Sei

101 Mikawdai Heights
4-3-6 Roppongi Minatoku
Tokyo 106-0032
Japan
www.itomasaru.com

Photos by Nacása & Partners Inc.

Issey Miyake Men

Ginza Matsuya 4F, 3-6-1
Ginza Chuo-ku
Tokyo 103-0000
Japan
www.isseymiyake.com

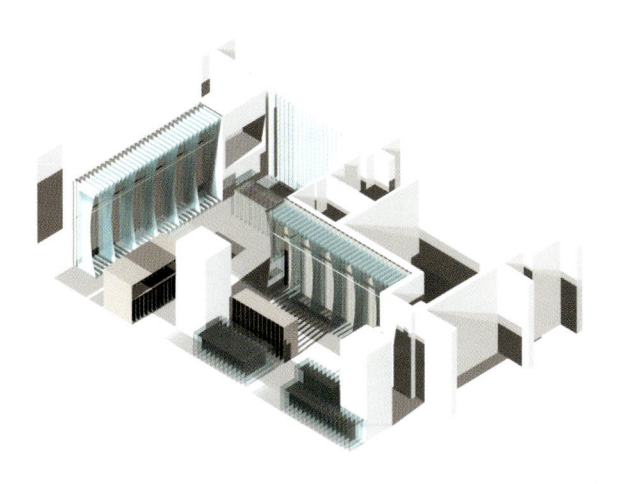

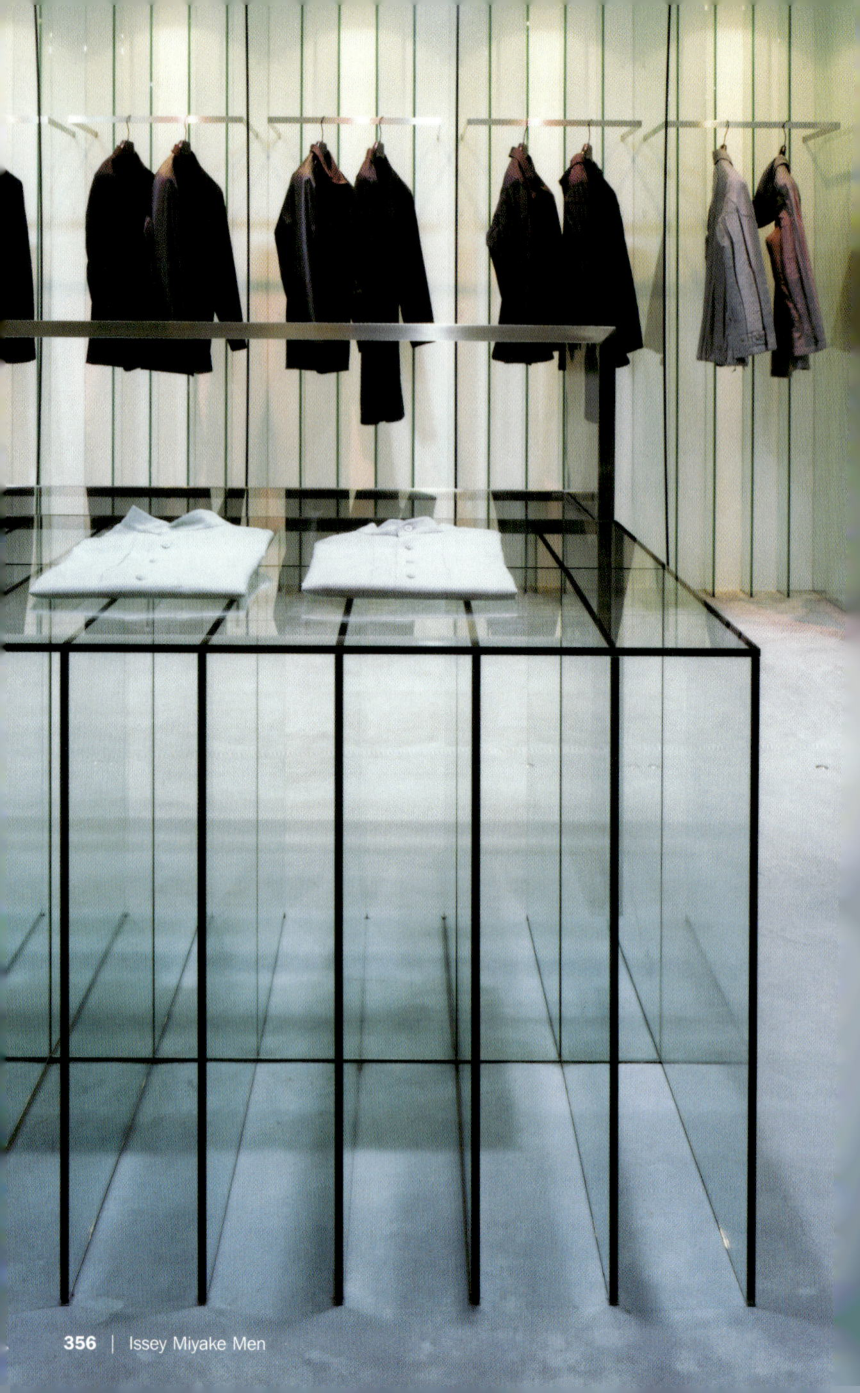

Issey Miyake Men | 357

358 | Issey Miyake Men

Issey Miyake Men | 359

In the world of exclusive consumerism, things should also be "corrupt, erotic and humorous". At least, this is the design intention for this shop. For this purpose, designer Ito Masaru breaks with usual decorative measures. Instead, he creates a murky scenario, which he ironizes with floral animations.

In der Welt des exklusiven Konsums soll es auch „korrupt, erotisch und humorvoll" zugehen. Jedenfalls ist dies die Intention für die Gestaltung dieses Shops. Designer Ito Masaru bricht dafür mit den üblichen Mitteln der Verschönerung. Stattdessen erschafft er ein düsteres Szenario, das er mit Blumenanimationen ironisiert.

Dans le monde de la consommation exclusive il y a aussi des choses « corrompues, érotiques et humoristiques ». C'est du moins ce que le design de ce magasin veut montrer. Le concepteur Ito Masaru rompt ici avec les moyens d'embellissement habituels. A la place, il invente un scénario lugubre, rempli d'ironie par des animations florales.

En el mundo del consumo exclusivo también tiene que existir la "corrupción, el erotismo y el humor". Por lo menos esta es la intención del diseño de esta tienda. Para ello, el creador Ito Masaru rompe con los típicos elementos del embellecimiento para crear un escenario lóbrego que ironiza con las animaciones florales.

Nel mondo del consumo di lusso ci dovrebbe anche essere posto per un'interpretazione "corrotta, erotica e spiritosa". O questa è per lo meno l'intenzione che sottende lo shop design firmato Ito Masaru. Rompendo con il canone estetico tradizionale il designer crea una scenografia cupa, spezzata solo dall'elemento ironizzante costituito dalle animazioni floreali.

Ito Masaru Design Project / Sei

101 Mikawdai Heights
4-3-6 Roppongi Minatoku
Tokyo 106-0032
Japan
www.itomasaru.com

Photos by Kozo Takayama

trois0

5-46-12 Jingumae
Sibuya-ku
Tokyo 150-0001
Japan
www.troiso.jp

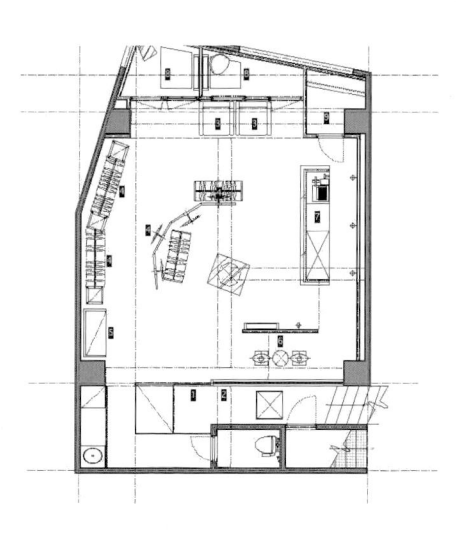

trois0

trois0 | 363

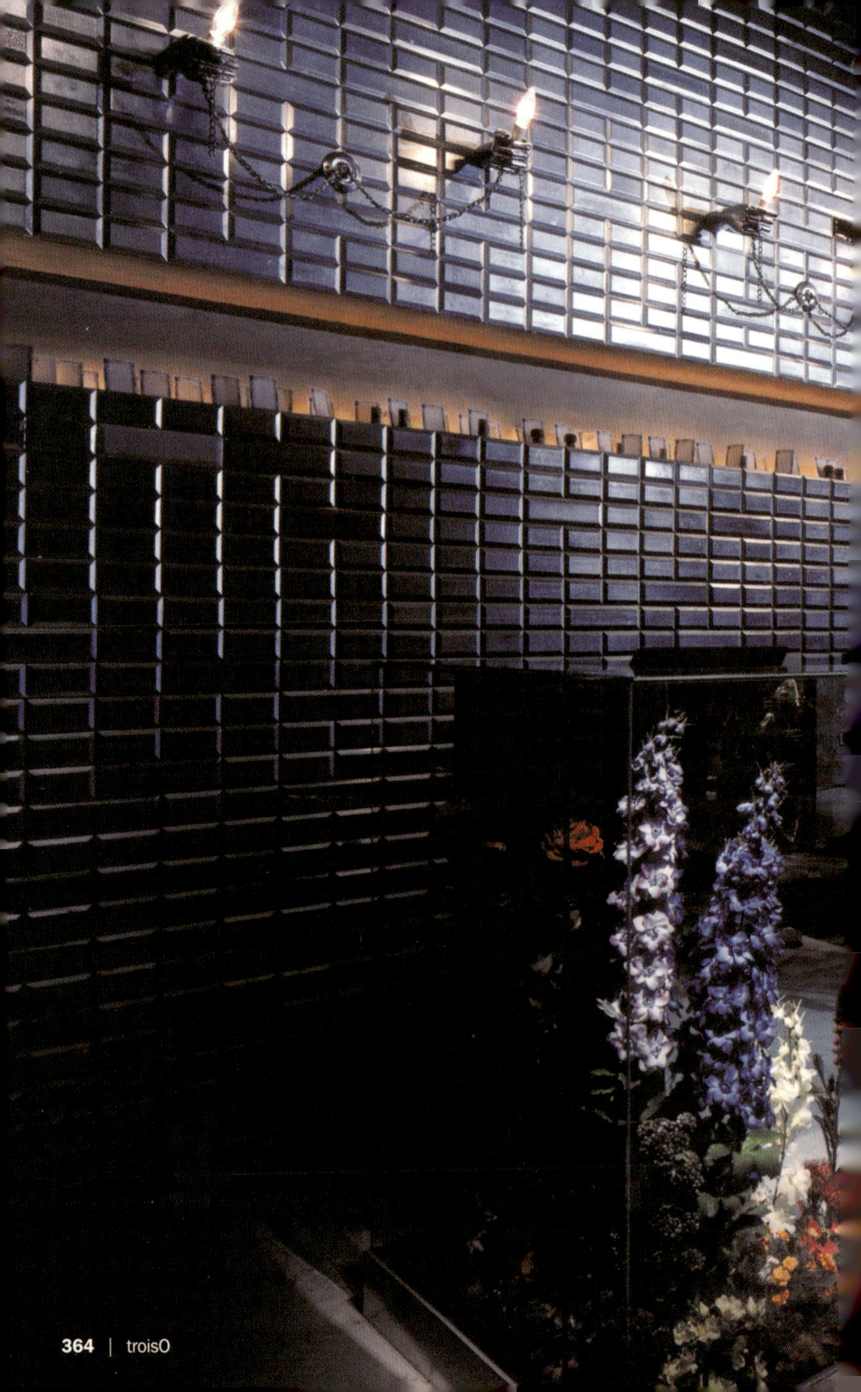

troisO | 365

The shop of fashion designer Martine Sitbon is arranged longways and has an open-access window frontage. The designers of the boutique would like to create an aquarium-like situation. Decorative items such as a shining, flat erratic block or a suspended spindle-reel are placed in distinctive positions.

Der Shop der Modemacherin Martine Sitbon ist länglich angelegt und besitzt eine durchgängige Fensterfront. Die Designer der Boutique möchten damit eine Situation wie in einem Aquarium erzeugen. Dekorationsobjekte wie etwa ein blanker, flacher Findling oder eine schwebende Spindel sind an markanten Stellen platziert.

Le magasin de la créatrice de mode Martine Sitbon est tout en longueur et sa façade en est la vitrine. Les designers de la boutique souhaitent donc procéder comme avec un aquarium. Des objets de décoration tels qu'un bloc erratique poli et plat ou un fuseau suspendu sont placés en évidence.

La tienda de la diseñadora de moda Martine Sitbon tiene una disposición alargada y posee una fachada de cristal continua. Los diseñadores querían crear un interior que evocase a un acuario. Los objetos de la decoración, como la roca lisa y desnuda o el huso colgante, están colocados en lugares destacados.

La boutique della stilista Martine Sitbon è di forma oblunga e termina con una facciata continua vetrata. L'effetto volutamente ricreato dai designer è quello di un acquario. Gli elementi decorativi, come ad esempio il masso lapideo lucido e piatto o il fuso fluttuante, sono posizionati strategicamente.

ga.a architects

891-15 Bangbae-Dong
Seocho Gu
Seoul 137-841
Korea
www.gaa-arch.com

Photos by Jung Sik Moon

Martine Sitbon

135-100 Cheongdamdong
Kangnamgu
Seoul 137-841
Korea

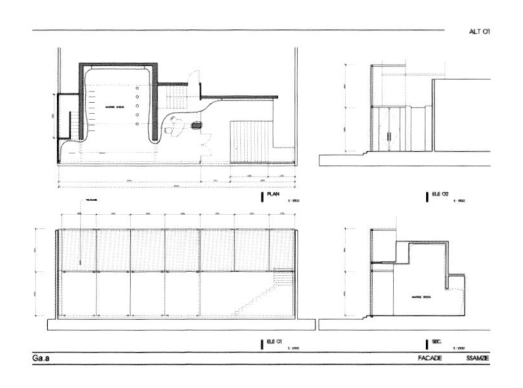

368 | Martine Sitbon

Martine Sitbon | 369

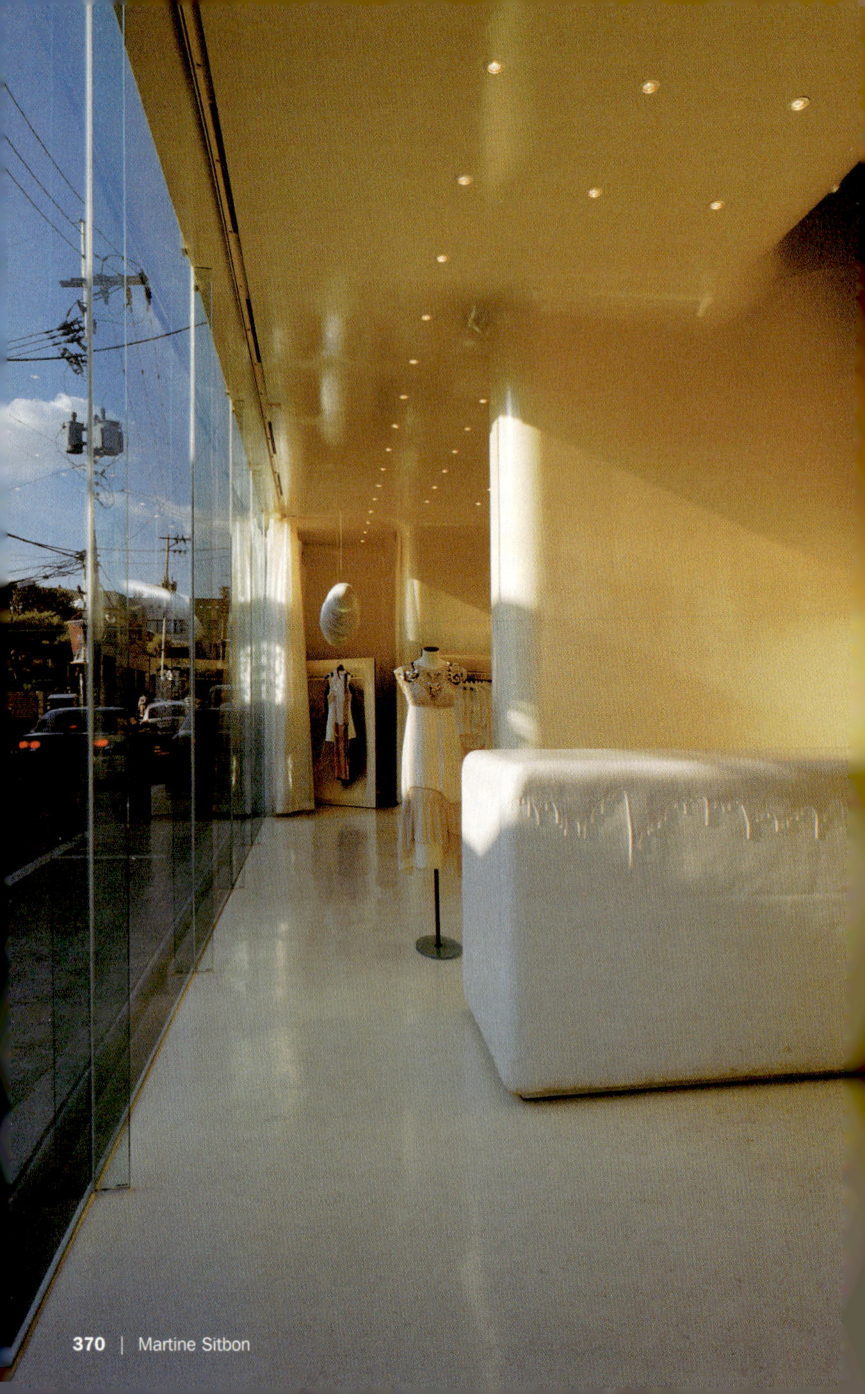

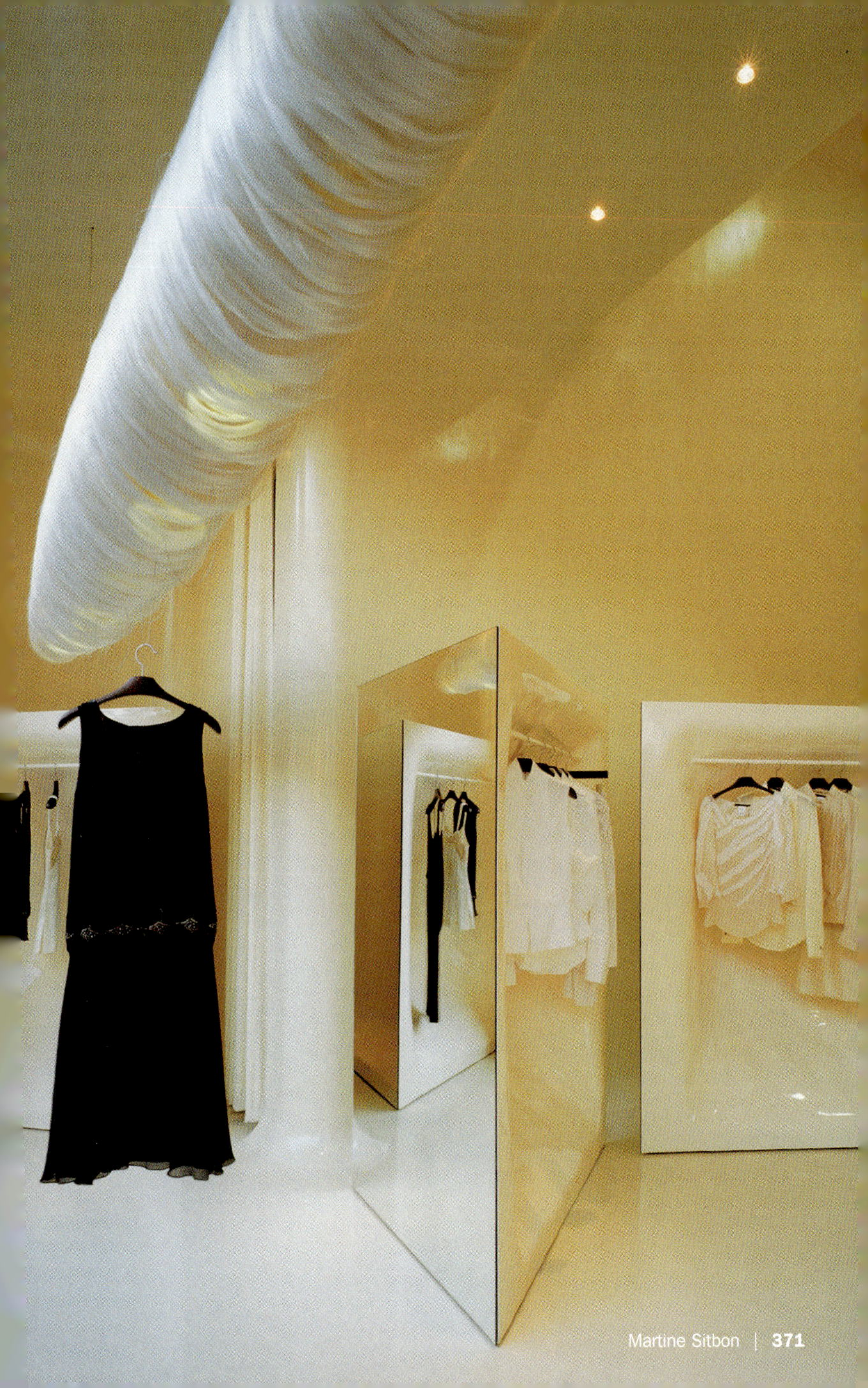

Architects & Designers

Acconci Studio

Actually, Vito Acconci is a poet and artist. He shot films, created installations and appeared in public. But in 1988, the Italian American decided to concentrate exclusively on room design. To achieve this, he surrounded himself with a team of designers and architects. The distinctive principle of the New York studio: total re-design of existing rooms and locations and creating a different landscape idea in the space. Examples of this work are creating an island site in Graz, completing a skater's park in San Juan and designing a fashion shop in Tokyo.

Eigentlich ist Vito Acconci ein Poet und Künstler. Er drehte Filme, kreierte Installationen und trat vor Publikum auf. 1988 jedoch entschied sich der Italoamerikaner, sich ganz auf die Gestaltung von Räumen zu konzentrieren. Dazu versammelte er eine Gruppe von Designern und Architekten um sich. Das markante Prinzip des New Yorker Büros: bestehende Räume und Plätze völlig neu zu erfinden und darin eine andere Idee von einer Landschaft aufgehen zu lassen. Derart wurde z. B. eine Insel in Graz angelegt, ein Skaterpark in San Juan realisiert und ein Fashion-Shop in Tokio gestaltet.

En fait Vito Acconci est artiste et poète. Il a tourné des films, créé des installations et joué en public. Pourtant en 1988 cet américain d'origine italienne a décidé de se consacrer entièrement à l'aménagement d'espaces. Il a donc rassemblé autour de lui un groupe de designers et d'architectes. Le principe déterminant du cabinet de New York : réinventer complètement des pièces et des lieux existants et y faire naître une nouvelle idée de paysage. Ainsi une île a-t-elle été créée à Graz, un parc de skateboard réalisé à San Juan et un magasin de mode aménagé à Tokyo.

En realidad Vito Acconci es un poeta y un artista. Ha producido películas, creado instalaciones y actuado delante del público. En 1988, sin embargo, este italoamericano decidió dedicarse por completo al diseño de los espacios. Además reunió a un grupo de diseñadores y arquitectos a su alrededor. El principio más destacado de este estudio neoyorquino es reinventar los espacios y los lugares ya existentes para crear en ellos escenarios completamente nuevos. Así, por ejemplo, colocaron una isla en Graz, en San Juan realizaron una instalación para practicar el patinaje y en Tokio decoraron una tienda de moda de ropa.

Vito Acconci nasce come poeta ed artista. Dopo aver girato film e creato installazioni nelle quali l'interazione con il pubblico occupa un posto centrale, a partire dal 1988 l'artista italoamericano abbandona la concezione di spazio in relazione alla propria corporeità e si dedica alla progettazione di luoghi pubblici, avvalendosi della collaborazione di un gruppo di designer e architetti. Il principio ispiratore alla base dei lavori dello studio di New York è il seguente: reinventare spazi e siti preesistenti per dare vita ad una nuova idea di contesto. Su questa falsariga sono nati ad esempio: la Mur Island di Graz, lo Skate Park di San Juan e un fashion shop ad Tokio.

Arno Design GmbH

The name Arno Design represents the Munich creative studio run by Mirka Nassiri, Peter Haberlander and Claus Neuleib. The design group was established in 1994 and concentrates on exhibition buildings, showrooms and stores—an area where famous clients can turn to Arno Design. The group achieved international acclaim through their commissions for Fair Trade projects and ecologically conscious companies. Objective clarity, emotional depth and, wherever possible, use of sustainable materials define the Munich team's designs.

Hinter dem Namen Arno Design verbirgt sich das Münchner Kreativbüro von Mirka Nassiri, Peter Haberlander und Claus Neuleib. Die 1994 gegründete Design-Gruppe konzentriert sich auf Messebauten, Showrooms und Stores – einen Bereich, in dem namhafte Auftraggeber auf Arno Design zurückgreifen. Weltweit Ansehen erlangte die Gruppe durch

Arbeiten für Fair-Trade-Konzepte und ökologisch ausgerichtete Unternehmen. Sachliche Klarheit, emotionale Tiefe und die Verwendung möglichst nachhaltiger Materialien bestimmen die Entwürfe der Münchener.

Derrière le nom d'Arno Design se cache l'agence de création munichoise de Mirka Nassiri, Peter Haberlander et Claus Neuleib. Le groupe de design fondé en 1994 se concentre sur les halls de foires expositions, les showrooms et les magasins – un domaine dans lequel de nombreux donneurs d'ordre célèbres font appel à Arno Design. Le groupe a acquis une renommée mondiale en s'engageant pour des concepts de commerce équitable et en travaillant pour des entreprises axées sur l'environnement. Une clarté objective, une profondeur dans l'émotion et le recours à des matériaux si possible durables caractérisent les projets des Munichois.

Detrás del nombre Arno Design se esconde el estudio creativo de Mirka Nassiri, Peter Haberlander y Claus Neuleib. Este grupo dedicado al diseño fue fundado en 1994 y se concentra en obras para los recintos feriales, *showrooms* y tiendas, siendo en estas últimas donde Arno Design recibe encargos de renombradas marcas. El grupo consiguió el reconocimiento mundial con trabajos para los conceptos de *fair trade* (comercio justo) y otras empresas del sector ecológico. La claridad objetiva, la profundidad emocional y el empleo de materiales duraderos determinan los proyectos de estos muniqueses.

Dietro il nome Arno Design si cela lo studio di creative design di Monaco di Baviera creato da Mirka Nassiri, Peter Haberlander e Claus Neuleib. Fondato nel 1994 il gruppo di design si è specializzato nella realizzazione di allestimenti nell'ambito dell'exhibition design, dello shop design e di showroom, attività per le quali committenti rinomati si avvalgono del supporto di Arno Design. Di grande fama internazionale i lavori realizzati all'insegna del mercato equo-solidale e per le aziende a vocazione ambientalista. I progetti dei designer di Monaco si contraddistinguono per funzionale sobrietà, profondità emotiva e per l'utilizzo di materiali il più possibile ecologici.

Asymptote Architecture

Two names are connected to the New York architectural studio Asymptote: Hani Rashid and Lise Anne Couture. Since establishing their studio in 1988, the architectural duo achieved an international reputation. The transitions in their creative output are fluid between architecture, design and art. Asymptote made a name for itself with award-winning commissions, such as the Hydra-Pier (Netherlands) and the new library in Alexandria. They designed the A3 office system for Knoll International. Their installation projects are on show, among others, at New York's MoMA.

Mit dem New Yorker Architekturbüro Asymptote verbinden sich zwei Namen: Hani Rashid und Lise Anne Couture. Seit Gründung des Büros im Jahre 1988 erarbeitete sich das Architektenpaar ein internationales Standing. In ihrem kreativen Schaffen sind die Übergänge von Architektur, Design und Kunst fließend. Bekannt wurde Asymptote mit preisgekrönten Arbeiten wie dem Hydra-Pier (Niederlande) und der neuen Bibliothek in Alexandria. Für Knoll International entwarfen sie das Bürosystem A3. Ihre Installationsarbeiten sind u. a. im MoMA in New York zu sehen.

Deux noms sont associés au cabinet d'architecture new-yorkais Asymptote : Hani Rashid et Lise Anne Couture. Depuis la fondation du cabinet en 1988, ce couple d'architectes s'est taillé une renommée internationale. Dans leur œuvre de création, les transitions entre l'architecture, le design et l'art sont fluides. Asymptote s'est rendu célèbre par plusieurs réalisations couronnées de prix telles que l'Hydra-Pier aux Pays-Bas et la nouvelle bibliothèque d'Alexandrie. Pour Knoll International ils ont conçu le système de meubles de bureau A3. Leurs travaux d'installations sont exposés entre autres au MoMA de New York.

Con el estudio de arquitectura neoyorquino Asymptote se asocian dos nombres: Hani Rashid y Lise Anne Couture. Desde la fundación de este estudio en el año 1988, esta pareja de arquitectos ha logrado el reconocimiento internacional. En su proyección creativa los límites entre la arquitectura, el diseño y el arte fluyen. El grupo Asymptote saltó a la fama al obtener varios premios por sus trabajos, como el Hydra-Pier (Países Bajos) y la nueva biblioteca en Alejandría. Para Knoll International diseñaron el sistema de despachos A3. Sus instalaciones pueden verse en diferentes museos, como en el MoMA de Nueva York.

Sono due i nomi associati allo studio Asymptote di New York: Hani Rashid e Lise Anne Couture. Il sodalizio fra i due architetti, stretto nel 1988 con la fondazione dello studio newyorchese, ha valso loro standing internazionale. I lavori firmati Asymptote sono caratterizzati da una linea di demarcazione fluida fra architettura, design ed arte. La notorietà è giunta con progetti come il pluripremiato Hydra-Pier (Paesi Bassi) e la nuova biblioteca di Alessandria d'Egitto. Su commissione della Knoll International il duo ha progettato il sistema A3 open office. Le loro installazioni sono esposte in diverse collezioni fra cui quella MoMA di New York.

Christian Biecher & Associes

In the nineties, Frenchman Christian Biecher was regarded as a shooting star in the world of architecture and design. As a graduate of the Paris L'Ecole d'Architecture, he owes this not least to his two mentors, Henri Ciriani and Bernard Tschumi. Since 1992, he has worked under his own name for such famous clients as Issey Miyake, Pantone or Lancôme. This traveler between the world of product design and architecture is famous for the Joseph Store on the Parisian Rue Saint-Honoré. In 2002, Biecher was France's "Designer of the Year".

In den neunziger Jahren galt der Franzose Christian Biecher als Shooting-Star in der Welt des Designs und der Architektur. Das verdankt der Absolvent der Pariser L'Ecole d'Architecture nicht zuletzt seinen beiden Mentoren Henri Ciriani und Bernard Tschumi. Seit 1992 arbeitet er unter eigenem Namen für so bekannte Auftraggeber wie Issey Miyake, Pantone oder Lancôme. Bekannt ist der Wandler zwischen den Welten des Produktdesigns und der Architektur für den Joseph Store in der Pariser Rue Saint-Honoré. 2002 wurde Biecher in Frankreich „Designer des Jahres".

Dans les années quatre-vingt-dix, le Français Christian Biecher était considéré comme l'étoile filante du monde du design et de l'architecture. Ce diplômé de l'Ecole d'architecture parisienne le doit surtout à ses deux mentors Henri Ciriani et Bernard Tschumi. Depuis 1992, il travaille sous son propre nom pour des donneurs d'ordre célèbres tels que Issey Miyake, Pantone ou Lancôme. Ce promeneur entre les mondes du design de produit et de l'architecture est connu pour le magasin Joseph de la rue Saint-Honoré à Paris. En 2002 Biecher a été élu « designer de l'année » en France.

En la década de 1990, el antiguo alumno de la parisina L'Ecole d'Architecture, y el francés Christian Biecher, era la estrella en el mundo del diseño y la arquitectura, y esto se lo debía especialmente a sus dos mentores: Henri Ciriani y Bernard Tschumi. Desde 1992 trabaja bajo su propio nombre para conocidos clientes como Issey Miyake, Pantone o Lancôme. Este artista que transita entre los mundos del diseño del producto y de la arquitectura es conocido por la tienda Joseph Store, en la parisina Rue Saint-Honoré. En 2002 Biecher fue reconocido en Francia como el "diseñador del año".

Negli anni novanta il francese Christian Biecher era considerato l'astro nascente nel firmamento del design e dell'architettura. Il laureato dell'Ecole d'Architecture di Parigi deve questa fama non da ultimo ai suoi due mentori, Henri Ciriani e Bernard Tschumi. Dal 1992 lavora a nome proprio per rinomati committenti come le griffe Issey Miyake, Pantone o Lancôme. Talento eclettico perfettamente a suo agio tanto nel mondo del product design quanto dell'architettura, Biecher deve la sua fama allo Joseph Store situato nella lussuosa rue Saint-Honoré di Parigi. Nel 2002 Biecher è stato insignito del riconoscimento francese "designer dell'anno".

Bisazza Design Studio, Carlo Dal Bianco

Italian architect Carlo Dal Bianco developed his unique aesthetic signature through early commissions on historic buildings: in strict succession, he interprets a classic series of aesthetic ideals, with a contemporary touch, injecting an experimental mind-set of modern design. His personality combines a meticulous touch with the avant-garde, virtually making him destined for glass-mosaic pieces, which he designs for Bisazza, earning him international acclaim. Carlo Dal Bianco lives and works in Vicenza.

Der italienische Architekt Carlo Dal Bianco entwickelte durch seine früheren Arbeiten an historischen Gebäuden seine eigene ästhetische Signatur: in strenger Nachfolge klassischer Schönheitsideale, die er in die heutige Zeit überträgt und denen er den experimentellen Geist des modernen Designs verleiht. So vermischt sich in seiner Person Akribie mit Avantgarde, die ihn geradezu prädestiniert für die Glas-Mosaikarbeiten, die er für Bisazza entwirft und denen er seine weltweite Anerkennung verdankt. Carlo Dal Bianco lebt und arbeitet in Vicenza.

L'architecte italien Carlo Dal Bianco a développé à travers ses précédents travaux sur des bâtiments historiques sa propre signature esthétique : dans le strict héritage des idéaux de la beauté classique qu'il transpose dans le monde contemporain et auxquels il prête l'approche expérimentale du design moderne. Ainsi se fondent en lui méticulosité et avant-garde, qui le prédestinent incontestablement aux travaux de mosaïque de verre qu'il dessine pour Bisazza et à qui il doit sa reconnaissance internationale. Carlo Dal Bianco vit et travaille à Vicenza.

El arquitecto italiano Carlo Dal Bianco desarrolló su propia firma estética a través de sus primeros trabajos en edificios históricos: en una estricta sucesión de ideales clásicos de la belleza que traslada al tiempo ideal y a los que dota del espíritu experimental del diseño moderno. Así, en su misma persona se mezcla la precisión con la vanguardia, fusión que le predestina para las obras de mosaico de cristal que diseña para Bisazza y a las que debe su reconocimiento mundial. Carlo Dal Bianco vive y trabaja en Vicenza.

L'architetto italiano Carlo Dal Bianco ha creato la sua cifra estetica misurandosi nei suoi primi lavori con la tipologia degli edifici storici: rigorosamente fedele agli ideali di bellezza classica che traspone in epoca contemporanea interpretandoli in chiave sperimentale all'insegna del design moderno. Allo stesso modo nella sua persona si mescolano meticolosità ed avanguardia, che fuse insieme lo rendono l'artista predestinato a realizzare per Bisazza i mosaici in vetro che gli hanno valso stima internazionale. Carlo Dal Bianco vive e lavora a Vicenza.

Block Architecture

Block Architecture belongs to the cream of British design talents, recently collecting an award in 2005 at the Blueprint Session for interior design. The works of Londoners Greame Williamson and Zoe Smith often appear eclectic and blend futurist approaches with playful irony. Such approaches float free of ideology between the worlds of commerce and art. Their installations are frequently to be spotted in contemporary exhibitions. Architectural projects were already completed in Tokyo, New York, Stockholm and Dubai.

Block Architecture gehört in die vorderste Reihe der britischen Design-Talente, zuletzt 2005 ausgezeichnet bei der Blueprint Session für einen Interieurentwurf. In den oft eklektisch wirkenden Arbeiten der Londoner Greame Williamson und Zoe Smith mischen sich futuristische Ansätze mit spielerischer Ironie. Dergleichen wandeln sie frei von Ideologie zwischen den Welten des Kommerzes und der Kunst. Installationen von ihnen finden sich häufiger in zeitgenössischen Ausstellungen. Architekturprojekte wurden bereits in Tokio, New York, Stockholm und Dubai realisiert.

Block Architecture se place au tout premier rang des talents britanniques du design, récompensé en dernier lieu en 2005 lors de la Blueprint Session pour un projet d'intérieur. Dans les travaux paraissant souvent éclectiques des Londoniens Greame Williamson et Zoe Smith se mélangent une approche futuriste et une ironie ludique. Ils naviguent pareillement libres de toute idéologie entre les mondes du commerce et de l'art. On découvre plus souvent leurs installations artistiques dans des expositions contemporaines. Ils ont déjà réalisé des projets architecturaux à Tokyo, New York, Stockholm et Dubai.

Block Architecture es uno grupo de talento que se sitúa entre los diseñadores de primera fila británicos. En 2005 fue reconocido por el diseño de un interior durante la Blueprint Session. En las obras, a menudo eclécticas, de los londinenses Greame Williamson y Zoe Smith se mezclan los principios futuristas con la ironía caprichosa. De igual forma oscilan libres de ideologías entre los mundos del comercio y del arte. Sus instalaciones se encuentran a menudo en exposiciones modernas. Algunos de sus proyectos arquitectónicos se han realizado en Tokio, Nueva York, Estocolmo y Dubai.

Nel panorama britannico del design d'autore, gli architetti londinesi Greame Williamson e Zoe Smith occupano un posto di assoluta preminenza, come è stato attestato loro anche dall'ultimo riconoscimento ottenuto nel 2005 dalla rivista Blueprint con la nomina "migliori progettisti di interni". Nei loro lavori, dal taglio spesso decisamente eclettico, l'approccio futuristico si mescola a leggiadra ironia. Ugualmente fluido e scevro da connotazioni ideologiche è il passaggio fra il mondo commerciale e quello artistico. Le loro installazioni sono spesso esposte in mostre contemporanee. Esempi di progettazioni che portano la loro firma si possono già vedere a Tokio, New York, Stoccolma e Dubai.

Bohlin Cywinski Jackson

Some may have heard of Bohlin, Cywinski and Jackson from numerous feature articles circulating about them in internationally relevant journals. Others may recall their distinction as studio of the year, awarded by the American Institute for Architecture (1994). The Americans can cite over 300 awards on their reference list. But the ultimate recommendation is their designs: their signature is always high precision and an individual contextualization of the project. The impact is as sensitive as it is properly thought through.

Die einen mögen Bohlin, Cywinski und Jackson aus vielen Beiträgen kennen, die über sie weltweit in einschlägigen Journalen kursieren. Die anderen erinnern sich derweil an ihre Auszeichnung als Büro des Jahres durch das amerikanische Institut für Architektur (1994). Insgesamt über 300 Awards können die Amerikaner auf ihrer Referenzliste vorweisen. Doch letztlich zeichnen sie sich durch ihre Entwürfe aus: Immer belegen sie in der Handschrift eine hohe Präzision, die sich individuell in das Umfeld des Objektes einfügt. Das wirkt genauso einfühlsam wie durchdacht.

Certains connaissent Bohlin, Cywinski et Jackson par les nombreuses chroniques publiées sur eux de par le monde dans les journaux spécialisés. Les autres se rappellent plutôt la distinction de Cabinet de

l'Année décernée par l'Institut américain pour l'Architecture (1994). Ces Américains peuvent se glorifier de plus de 300 prix dans leur liste de références : ils font preuve, dans leur signature, d'une grande précision qui s'intègre individuellement dans l'environnement de l'objet. L'impact est aussi empathique que raisonné.

Algunos conocerán a Bohlin, Cywinski y Jackson a través de los numerosos artículos que sobre ellos se publican por todo el mundo en revistas de primer orden. Otros se acordarán de su reconocimiento como "estudio del año" por el Instituto de Arquitectura americano (1994). En total estos americanos acumulan en su lista de referencias más de 300 premios. Pero lo más destacado en ellos son, sobre todo, sus proyectos: muestran siempre una elevada precisión que encaja de forma individual en el entorno de cada objeto. Esto transmite tanto comprensión como reflexión.

A qualcuno i nomi Bohlin, Cywinski e Jackson sono forse noti dai numerosi articoli apparsi su di loro nella stampa specialistica internazionale. Qualcun altro forse li associa al riconoscimento ottenuto dall'Istituto Americano di Architettura come "miglior studio dell'anno" (1994). Complessivamente sono ben 300 i riconoscimenti che i tre professionisti americani possono esibire come referenze. Ma alla fin fine sono i loro progetti a sintetizzare al meglio il loro stile, caratterizzato da un'elevata precisione, di volta in volta perfettamente adattata al contesto, dal forte impatto razionale ed emozionale.

Giorgio Borruso Design

Giorgio Borruso first drew attention to himself in 1995 when he introduced an innovative design for a laptop. With this success, the young Italian made the breakthrough in Los Angeles. He opened his own architectural studio in L.A., specializing in industrial design, buildings and interior design. Borruso's most famous project is the Miss Sixty store in South Coast Plaza, for which he was inundated with international awards. Other award-winning shop designs followed. In 2005, Display and Design Ideas nominated him as "Designer of the Year".

Giorgio Borruso machte 1995 zum ersten Mal auf sich aufmerksam, als er ein innovatives Design für einen Laptop vorstellte. Ein Erfolg, mit dem der junge Italiener den Sprung nach Los Angeles schaffte. Dort eröffnete er ein eigenes Architekturbüro, das sich auf Industriedesign, Gebäude und Raumgestaltung spezialisiert hat. Borrusos bekanntestes Projekt ist der Store Miss Sixty im South Coast Plaza, für den er mit internationalen Awards überhäuft wurde. Weitere preisgekrönte Shopdesigns folgten. 2005 kürte ihn Display and Design Ideas zum „Designer des Jahres".

Giorgio Borruso a fait parler de lui pour la première fois en 1995 quand il a présenté un design innovant pour un ordinateur portable. Un succès qui a permis au jeune Italien de sauter le pas vers Los Angeles. Il y a ouvert son propre cabinet d'architecture qui s'est spécialisé dans le design industriel, les bâtiments et l'aménagement d'espaces. Le projet de Borruso le plus connu est le magasin Miss Sixty dans le South Coast Plaza pour lequel il a été submergé de distinctions internationales. Suivirent d'autres designs de magasin également couronnés de prix. En 2005, Display and Design Ideas l'a élu « Designer de l'Année ».

Giorgio Borruso llamó por primera vez la atención en 1995 cuando presentó un innovador diseño para un ordenador portátil. Un éxito que permitió a este joven italiano dar el salto hasta Los Ángeles. En esta ciudad abrió su propio estudio de arquitectura especializado en el diseño industrial, en los edificios y en la decoración de los espacios. El proyecto más conocido de Borruso es la tienda Miss Sixty en South Coast Plaza, ganador de numerosos premios internacionales. Este diseño fue seguido por otros también reconocidos con premios. En 2005 Display and Design Ideas le eligió como "diseñador del año".

Dopo aver guadagnato per la prima volta le luci della ribalta con il design innovativo di un laptop, il giovane designer italiano Giorgio Borruso ha saputo sfruttare appieno questo successo facendone un trampolino di lancio verso il mercato d'oltreoceano. A Los Angeles ha aperto un suo studio di architettura, specializzandosi via via in disegno industriale, progettazione architettonica e di interni. Il suo progetto più rinomato è senz'altro il plurimpremiato Miss Sixty, il monomarca ubicato nel prestigioso mall South Coast Plaza, cui hanno fatto seguito altri numerosi riconoscimenti per il migliore shop design. Nel 2005 è stato incoronato "designer dell'anno" dalla rivista Display and Design Ideas.

Buratti + Battiston Architects

A trio works together at the Buratti + Battiston Architects Milan studio: two architects, Gabriele and Oscar Buratti, and the engineer Ivano Battiston. Battiston already designed in the 1970's for gas and electrical goods manufacturer, Zanussi. After the group's formation, from 1992 onwards, numerous international commissions followed for industry and trade. In addition, diverse projects emerged for private buildings. The group earned its unique reputation for the renovation of historic sites (including the Chiesa Valmalenco).

Im Mailänder Büro Buratti + Battiston Architects arbeitet ein Trio zusammen: die beiden Architekten Gabriele und Oscar Buratti sowie der Ingenieur Ivano Battiston. Letzterer entwarf bereits in den siebziger Jahren für den Gas- und Elektrogerätehersteller Zanussi. Aus dem Zusammenschluss als Gruppe ergaben sich ab 1992 eine Vielzahl auch internationaler Aufträge für Industrie und Handel. Hinzu kamen diverse private Bauten. Mit der Renovierung von historischen Objekten (u. a. Chiesa Valmalenco) erwarb sich die Gruppe einen ganz eigenen Ruf.

C'est un trio qui travaille dans le cabinet milanais Buratti + Battiston Architects : les deux architectes Gabriele et Oscar Buratti ainsi que l'ingenieur Ivano Battiston. Ce dernier a déjà réalisé des designs dans les années soixante-dix pour Zanussi, fabricant d'appareils électroménagers fonctionnant à l'électricité et au gaz. Leur regroupement à partir de 1992 a débouché sur de nombreux projets internationaux pour l'industrie et le commerce. Auxquels se sont ajoutés diverses constructions privées. La rénovation d'édifices historiques (dont la Chiesa Valmalenco) leur vaut une réputation particulière.

En el estudio milanés Buratti + Battiston Architects trabaja un trío: los arquitectos Gabriele y Oscar Buratti y el ingeniero Ivano Battiston. Este último realizó varios diseños

Shop Design | 377

en la década de 1970 para la empresa fabricante de gas y electrodomésticos Zanussi. A partir de la unión del grupo en 1992 recibieron un gran número de encargos internacionales para la industria y el comercio. A estos se le añadieron algunos proyectos privados. El grupo se hizo con un reconocimiento muy propio a través de la renovación de objetos históricos (como Chiesa Valmalenco).

Nello studio milanese Buratti + Battiston Architects è all'opera un trio di professionisti: i due architetti Gabriele e Oscar Buratti e l'ingegnere Ivano Battiston, che già negli anni settanta svolgeva attività di ricerca nel settore dell'industrializzazione edilizia alla Zanussi, azienda produttrice di cucine a gas ed elettriche. Dal sodalizio dei tre deriva, a partire dal 1992, tutta una serie di progetti internazionali in ambito commerciale, industriale nonché residenziale. Fama tutta particolare hanno valso allo studio gli interventi di ristrutturazione in complessi edilizi storici (fra cui Chiesa Valmalenco).

burdifilek

The Toronto design studio burdifilek combines the creative brains of Diego Burdi and business partner Paul Filek. Filek sees his role as the management driving force. Together, over the last decade, the duo has defined their unmistakable style in interior design of shops, restaurants and spas: a crossover of sensual appeal and visible elegance. In Canada, they are among the stars of the design scene (with over 40 awards). Meanwhile, international commissions are rolling in (such as: Brown Thomas, JOOP!).

Das Designbüro burdifilek aus Toronto setzt sich aus dem kreativen Kopf Diego Burdi und Kompagnon Paul Filek zusammen. Letzterer versteht sich eher als treibende Kraft des Managements. Zusammen haben die Zwei in den letzten zehn Jahren zu einem unverkennbaren Stil in der Interieurausstattung von Shops, Restaurants und Spas gefunden: Ein Crossover von sinnlicher Ansprache und sichtbarer Eleganz. In Kanada zählen sie zu den Stars in der Gestalterszene (über 40 Auszeichnungen). Indessen mehren sich die internationalen Aufträge (u. a.: Brown Thomas, JOOP!).

L'agence de design burdifilek de Toronto est constituée d'une tête créatrice, Diego Burdi, et de son compagnon Paul Filek. Ce dernier joue davantage le rôle de locomotive au plan du management. Ces dix dernières années, ces deux créateurs ont développé un style caractéristique dans le domaine de la décoration intérieure de magasins, restaurants et spas : un croisement de sensualité suggérée et d'élégance ostensible. Au Canada ils font partie des stars de la scène des concepteurs (plus de 40 distinctions reçues). En attendant, les commandes internationales se multiplient (par ex.: Brown Thomas, JOOP!).

El estudio de diseño burdifilek, de Toronto, está formado por el creativo Diego Burdi y su compañero Paul Filek. Este último se ve más a sí mismo como la fuerza impulsora de la gestión. Juntos han encontrado en los últimos diez años un inconfundible estilo en el diseño de interiores de tiendas, restaurantes y spas: una mezcla de un discurso sensual y una elegancia manifiesta. En Canadá están considerados como estrellas dentro del mundo del diseño (más de 40 galardones). En la actualidad aumentan los encargos internacionales (p.ej., Brown Thomas, JOOP!).

Lo studio di design burdifilek di Toronto si compone (anche nel nome) di una mente creativa (Diego Burdi) e del suo socio (Paul Filek), forza trainante nella gestione degli affari. Insieme, negli ultimi dieci anni, il duo ha sperimentato diversi itinerari fino ad approdare ad uno stile inconfondibile che contraddistingue gli arredamenti di interni di boutique, ristoranti e SPA che portano la loro firma: un'insolita mescolanza fra l'approccio polisensoriale e l'eleganza concreta. Con oltre 40 riconoscimenti sono fra gli architetti-star più promettenti del firmamento del design d'interni d'autore in Canada ed oltre. Anche i progetti internazionali (ad es. Brown Thomas, JOOP!) si stanno infatti moltiplicando.

David Chipperfield Architects

The architect David Chipperfield was born in London in 1953. In 1978, he completed his diploma at the London Architectural Association. After initially joining the studios of Douglas Stephen, Richard Rogers and Norman Foster, in 1984, he established his own studio (in London and Berlin). Chipperfield has plenty of international commissions: for instance, the Villaverde project in Madrid, the art museum in Davenport, USA, and the Courts of Justice in Salerno. His most famous project is the current remodeling of the Neues Museum at Berlin's Museum Island.

Der Architekt David Chipperfield wurde 1953 in London geboren. Dort erwarb er 1978 sein Diplom bei der Architectural Association. Nachdem er zunächst in den Büros von Douglas Stephen, Richard Rogers und Norman Foster mitwirkte, gründete er 1984 sein eigenes Büro (London und Berlin). Chipperfield weist eine Fülle internationaler Aufträge vor: etwa das Villaverde Projekt in Madrid, das Kunstmuseum in Davenport, USA, und der Justizpalast in Salerno. Sein renommiertestes Projekt ist der derzeitige Umbau des Neuen Museums auf der Berliner Museumsinsel.

L'architecte David Chipperfield est né en 1953 à Londres. Là, il a obtenu en 1978 son diplôme de l'Architectural Association. Après avoir tout d'abord collaboré dans les cabinets de Douglas Stephen, Richard Rogers et Norman Foster, il a fondé son propre cabinet (Londres et Berlin) en 1984. Chipperfield affiche une longue liste de commandes internationales telles que le projet Villaverde à Madrid, le Musée d'Art à Davenport, Etats-Unis, et le Palais de Justice à Salerno. Son projet le plus célèbre est l'actuelle transformation du Nouveau Musée de la Museumsinsel à Berlin.

El arquitecto David Chipperfield nació en 1953 en Londres. Allí se licenció en 1978 en la Architectural Association. Después de trabajar en los estudios de Douglas Stephen, Richard Rogers y Norman Foster, fundó en 1984 su propio estudio (Londres y Berlín). Chipperfield ha llevado a cabo un gran número de encargos internacionales como, por ejemplo, el proyecto de Villaverde en Madrid, el museo del arte en Davenport, EEUU, y el palacio de Justicia en Salerno. Su proyecto más aclamado es la reforma actual del Nuevo Museo en la Isla de los Museos berlinesa.

Nato a Londra nel 1953, David Chipperfield consegue la laurea presso l'Architectural Association nel 1978. Dopo aver collaborato negli studi di Douglas Stephen, Richard Rogers e Norman Foster, si mette in proprio dando vita nel 1984 allo studio David Chipperfield Architects (con sedi a Londra e Berlino), che ha al suo attivo un numero cospicuo di progetti internazionali: il complesso condominiale Villaverde a Madrid, il Museum of Art di Davenport (USA) e il Palazzo di Giustizia di Salerno. Fra i lavori più prestigiosi merita particolare rilievo la ricostruzione del Neues Museum dell'Isola dei musei di Berlino (in corso di realizzazione).

Claudio Colucci Design

In his fledgling career, the native of Swiss Locarno, Claudio Colucci, can already cite work with top architects and designers. He designed projects in cooperation with Ron Arad, Nigel Coates and Philippe Starck (including: Thompson Multimedia). He established his own studio from 2002 onwards in Tokyo and Paris. His focus includes product design and interior architecture. As well as several acclaimed exhibitions, he was twice awarded "Best Designer of the Year" (Salon du Meuble de Paris and Elle Deco, France).

Der im schweizerischen Locarno geborene Claudio Colucci kann in seiner jungen Karriere bereits auf die Zusammenarbeit mit namhaften Architekten und Designern verweisen. So gestaltete er Projekte in Kooperation mit Ron Arad, Nigel Coates und Philippe Starck (u. a.: Thompson Multimedia). Mit seinem eigenen Büro ist er seit 2002 in Tokio und Paris präsent. Zu seinen Schwerpunkten gehören Produktdesign und Innenarchitektur. Neben mehreren renommierten Ausstellungen erhielt er zweimal die Auszeichnung „Bester Designer des Jahres" (Salon du Meuble de Paris und Elle Deco, Frankreich).

Claudio Colucci, né à Locarno en Suisse, peut s'enorgueillir dans sa jeune carrière d'une collaboration avec des architectes et designers célèbres. Ainsi a-t-il réalisé des projets en coopération avec Ron Arad, Nigel Coates et Philippe Starck (entre autres : Thompson Multimedia). Depuis 2002 il est présent avec sa propre agence à Tokyo et Paris. Ses points forts sont le design de produit et l'architecture intérieure. Parallèlement à de nombreuses expositions renommées, il s'est vu attribuer par deux fois le titre de « Meilleur Designer de l'Année » (Salon du Meuble de Paris et Elle Deco en France).

Claudio Colucci, nacido en el suizo Locarno, ya ha trabajado en su corta carrera con arquitectos y diseñadores de renombre. Ha realizado proyectos en cooperación con Ron Arad, Nigel Coates y Philippe Starck (entre otros Thompson Multimedia). Desde 2002 está presente en Tokio y en París con su propio estudio. Su trabajo se concentra en el diseño de productos y en la arquitectura de interiores. Además de varias exposiciones célebres, ha obtenido dos veces la distinción de "mejor diseñador del año" (Salon du Meuble de París y Elle Deco, Francia).

Nonostante la giovane carriera il giovane designer svizzero nativo di Locarno può vantare la collaborazione con architetti e designer blasonati quali Ron Arad, Nigel Coates e Philippe Starck (ad es. per Thompson Multimedia). Dal 2002 è titolare dello studio Claudio Colucci Design con sedi a Tokio e Parigi, specializzato in product design e architettura di interni. Oltre ad aver esposto in numerose mostre rinomate ha ottenuto due volte il riconoscimento "miglior designer dell'anno" (Salon du Meuble di Parigi e Elle Deco, Francia).

NMDA, Inc., Neil M. Denari Architects

NMDA, a Los Angeles based architecture firm, has made an international name for itself under the directorship of Neil M. Denari: it represents innovative solutions for complex questions, relating to modern and contemporary urban design. Neil M. Denari looks for answers that are just as functional as provocative. For that reason, not every project turns out exactly as it is expected from him. This has not influenced his success: not only the shop I.a. Eyeworks won awards, but also the finished Mitsubishi Bank building in Tokyo.

Das Architekturbüro NMDA in Los Angeles hat sich unter der Führung von Neil M. Denari international einen Namen gemacht: Es steht für innovative Lösungen für komplexe Fragestellungen, die ein modernes wie zeitgemäßes urbanes Design betreffen. Neil M. Denari sucht darauf genauso funktionelle wie provozierende Antworten. So fällt nicht jeder Entwurf so aus, wie es von ihm erwartet wurde.

Seinem Erfolg hat es keinen Abbruch getan: Nicht nur der Shop I.a. Eyeworks erhielt Auszeichnungen, sondern auch das realisierte Gebäude der Mitsubishi Bank in Tokio.

Le cabinet d'architecture NMDA à Los Angeles s'est fait un nom au niveau international sous la direction de Neil M. Denari : celui-ci est synonyme de solutions innovantes à des problèmes complexes concernant un design urbain moderne et aussi contemporain. Neil M. Denari leur cherche des réponses à la fois fonctionnelles et provocatrices. Le résultat de ses projets n'est pas toujours ce qu'on attend de lui. Cela n'a aucunement nui à son succès : non seulement le magasin I.a. Eyeworks mais aussi la réalisation du bâtiment de la Banque Mitsubishi à Tokyo ont été récompensés.

El estudio de arquitectura NMDA en Los Ángeles ha conseguido el reconocimiento internacional bajo la dirección de Neil M. Denari. Es sinónimo de soluciones innovadoras para cuestiones complejas referentes a un diseño urbano moderno y actual. En este sentido, Neil M. Denari busca respuestas tanto funcionales como provocadoras. Esto hace que cada proyecto pueda ser diferente a lo esperado. Pero su éxito no se ha visto afectado; la tienda I.a. Eyeworks no ha sido su único proyecto premiado, también el edificio del Mitsubishi Bank en Tokio.

Lo studio di architettura NMDA di Los Angeles si è conquistato fama internazionale grazie alla direzione di Neil M. Denari, distinguendosi nella ricerca di soluzioni innovative di design urbano volte a conciliare esigenze complesse di modernità e di funzionalità senza per questo voler rinunciare alla provocazione. Al punto che nemmeno un risultato discordante dalle aspettative può scalfire il suo successo. Anzi: la boutique I.a. Eyeworks nonché l'edificio realizzato come sede della Mitsubishi Bank a Tokio sono stati entrambi premiati.

Sean Dix

Sean Dix was born in Kansas City and grew up in the Fiji Islands, in Micronesia and on the Philippines. He studied industrial design, interior architecture and sculpture at the School of Art

Institute in Chicago. After working in Europe for such reputable designers as Tom Dixon, James Irvine and Ettore Sottsass, he founded his own Milan design studio in 2000. Dix' designs cover a broad spectrum. But his shops and furniture designs enjoy the highest international acclaim.

Sean Dix wurde in Kansas City geboren und wuchs auf den Fidschi-Inseln, in Mikronesien und auf den Philippinen auf. Er studierte Industriedesign, Innenarchitektur und Skulptur an der School of Art Institute in Chicago. Nachdem er in Europa für so namhafte Designer wie Tom Dixon, James Irvine und Ettore Sottsass arbeitete, gründete er im Jahre 2000 sein eigenes Designstudio in Mailand. Dix' Entwürfe decken ein breites Spektrum ab. Die größte internationale Aufmerksamkeit erzielen indes die von ihm gestalteten Shops und Möbelstücke.

Sean Dix est né à Kansas City mais a grandi sur les îles Fidji, à la Micronésie et aux Philippines. Il a fait des études de design industriel, d'architecture intérieure et de sculpture à la « School of Art Institute » de Chicago. Après avoir travaillé en Europe pour des designers aussi célèbres que Tom Dixon, James Irvine et Ettore Sottsass, il a fondé en 2000 sa propre agence de design à Milan. Les projets de Dix couvrent un large spectre. Toutefois, l'attention internationale se porte essentiellement sur les magasins et le mobilier qu'il dessine.

Sean Dix nació en Kansas City y creció en las islas Fidji, en Micronesia y en Filipinas. Estudió diseño industrial, arquitectura de interiores y escultura en la School of Art Institute de Chicago. Después de trabajar en Europa para diseñadores tan conocidos como Tom Dixon, James Irvine y Ettore Sottsass, fundó en 2000 su propio estudio de diseño en Milán. Los proyectos de Dix abarcan un amplio espectro. Por el momento son las tiendas y el mobiliario diseñados por él los que mayor reconocimiento internacional han obtenido.

Nato a Kansas City e cresciuto alle isole Figi, in Micronesia e nelle Filippine, Sean Dix ha studiato disegno industriale, architettura di interni e scultura alla School of Art Institute di Chicago. Nel 2000, dopo aver lavorato per famosi designer quali Tom Dixon, James Irvine ed Ettore Sottsass, apre a Milano uno studio di design di cui è titolare.

I suoi progetti coprono un ampio spettro, anche se sono soprattutto le realizzazioni nel campo dello shop design ed i mobili di design ad essersi imposti all'attenzione internazionale.

Emmanuelle Duplay

Emmanuelle Duplay, a French national, studied architecture at the Paris L'Ecole d'Architecture. She rapidly found her own niche in interior and set design, the latter especially for exhibitions, film sets and new product launches. This is how she worked for Wim Wenders' cinema epic "To the Ends of the Earth". At Kenzo product launches, she frequently took over the launch-design. Her projects are influenced by sensitive material selection. Additionally, Duplay loves toying with contradictions.

Die Französin Emmanuelle Duplay studierte Architektur an der Pariser L'Ecole d'Architecture. Sehr bald fand sie ihre eigene Nische im Interieur- und Set-Design, letzteres vor allem für Ausstellungen, Filmkulissen und die Präsentationen von neuen Produkten. So arbeitete sie für Wim Wenders' Kinoepos „Bis ans Ende der Welt". Bei Produkteinführungen von Kenzo übernahm sie häufiger die Gestaltung des Launch-Designs. Ihre Projekte sind geprägt von einer sensitiven Materialauswahl. Zudem liebt Duplay das Spiel mit Widersprüchen.

La française Emmanuelle Duplay a fait ses études d'architecture à l'Ecole d'Architecture de Paris. Elle s'est très rapidement trouvé une niche dans le design intérieur et le set-design, celui-ci essentiellement pour des expositions, des décors de film et des présentations de nouveaux produits. Ainsi a-t-elle travaillé pour l'épopée cinématographique de Wim Wenders « Jusqu'au bout du monde ». Lors du lancement de produits de Kenzo elle a souvent été chargée de la conception du design de lancement. Ses projets se caractérisent par un choix très sensitif des matériaux. De plus, Duplay aime jouer avec les contradictions.

La francesa Emmanuelle Duplay estudió arquitectura en el parisino L'Ecole d'Architecture. Pronto encontró su hueco en el diseño de interiores y de escenarios, especialmente para exposiciones, películas y la presentación de nuevos productos. Así, por ejemplo, trabajó para la epopeya fílmica de Wim Wenders "Hasta el fin del mundo".

También se ha hecho cargo de la creación del diseño del lanzamiento de productos de Kenzo. Sus proyectos están caracterizados por la sensibilidad en la elección de los materiales. Además a Dupley le fascina el juego con las contradicciones.

Dopo aver studiato architettura all'Ecole d'Architecture di Parigi, l'architetto francese Emmanuelle Duplay ha trovato ben presto la sua strada specializzandosi in interior e set design, in particolare nella presentazione di nuovi prodotti sul mercato, nella progettazione di esposizioni e scenografie. È in questo contesto che nasce la sua collaborazione alla realizzazione dell'epos cinematografico di Wim Wenders "Fino alla fine del mondo". Inoltre ha spesso curato le attività di contestualizzazione legate al lancio dei nuovi prodotti della griffe Kenzo. I suoi progetti si contraddistinguono per la scelta estremamente sensibile dei materiali e per l'ironia dei contrasti.

Enzenauer Architekturmanagement

Architect Gisbert Enzenauer graduated in engineering from 1970 to 1975 at Cassel Polytechnic. He gained early career experience by joining the studios of Prof. Dr. G. Grzimek and Prof. M. Einsele. In 1979, he launched his own studio in Düsseldorf. With his team of employees, he specialized in the planning and design of homes and gardens. At the same time, he furnishes private residences like commercial offices. His background is revealed in his design style, which is influenced by a high standard of cultural sophistication and an appreciation of discreet luxury. Among other projects, he completed the park facility at Glücksburg Castle in Holstein and the E.ON subsidiary in Paris.

Der Architekt Gisbert Enzenauer absolvierte von 1970 bis 1975 ein Ingenieurstudium an der Gesamthochschule Kassel. Erste berufliche Erfahrungen sammelte er in den Büros von Prof. Dr. G. Grzimek und Prof. M. Einsele. 1979 gründete er sein eigenes Büro in Düsseldorf. Mit seinen Mitarbeitern hat er sich auf die Planung und Gestaltung von Häusern und Gärten spezialisiert. Zugleich stattet er private wie geschäftliche Räume aus. Seine Herkunft zeigt sich in seinem Gestaltungsstil, der geprägt ist von hohem kulturellem Anspruch und Sinn für dezenten Luxus. Unter anderem realisierte er die Parkanlage des Schloss Glücksburg in Holstein und die Niederlassung von E.ON in Paris.

L'architecte Gisbert Enzenauer a fait des études d'ingénieur de 1970 à 1975 à L'École Polyvalente de Kassel. Il a fait ses premières expériences professionnelles dans les cabinets du Prof. Dr. G. Grzimek et du Prof. M. Einsele. Il a fondé son propre cabinet à Düsseldorf en 1979. Ses collaborateurs et lui se sont spécialisés dans la conception et le design de maisons et jardins. Parallèlement il aménage des espaces privés et commerciaux. Ses origines transparaissent dans son style de design emprunt d'une haute exigence culturelle et d'un sens inné pour un luxe discret. Il a réalisé entre autres les jardins du château de Glücksburg dans le Holstein et la filiale de E.ON à Paris.

El arquitecto Gisbert Enzenauer cursó entre 1970 y 1975 sus estudios de ingeniería en la universidad integrada de Kassel. Adquirió sus primeras experiencias profesionales en el estudio del Cat. Dr. G. Grzimek y del Cat. M. Einsele. En 1979 fundó su propio estudio en Dusseldorf. Con sus trabajadores se ha especializado en la planificación y el diseño de casas y jardines. También decora espacios privados y comerciales. Su origen se refleja en el estilo de su diseño, marcado por una elevada pretensión cultural y un sentido para el lujo discreto. Entre sus proyectos se cuenta la realización del jardín del palacio Glücksburg en Holstein y la sede de E.ON en París.

Dopo aver studiato ingegneria alla Gesamthochschule Kassel fra il 1970 e il 1975, l'architetto Gisbert Enzenauer matura le prime esperienze lavorative al fianco di professori come Prof. Dr. G. Grzimek e Prof. M. Einsele. Nel 1979 crea a Düsseldorf l'Enzenauer Architekturmanagement. Supportato da un valido staff di collaboratori, lo studio va via via specializzandosi nella progettazione architettonica, di interni e paesaggistica in ambito residenziale e commerciale. La matrice culturale di Enzenauer si riflette nello stile che contraddistingue i suoi progetti, caratterizzato dall'esigenza di un'interpretazione intellettualmente impegnativa e da una cifra estetica ispirata ad un sobrio lusso. Fra le opere realizzate meritano menzione il parco del castello Glücksburg dello Holstein e la sede di E.ON a Parigi.

Massimiliano Fuksas, Doriana O. Mandrelli

Massimiliano Fuksas is Lithuanian. But he was born and raised in Rome, where he graduated in architecture from the La Sapienza Universitas. Over four decades, Fuksas earned a leading international reputation, with studios in Rome, Paris, Vienna and Frankfurt. He lectures as a guest professor at European and American universities and is also a member of numerous academies for architecture. Amongst the long list of his completed projects is, most recently, the national archive in Paris, the concert hall in Strasbourg, or even the new Ferrari headquarters. He has been working together with Doriana O. Mandrelli since 1985.

Massimiliano Fuksas ist Litauer. Doch geboren und aufgewachsen ist er in Rom, wo er auch sein Architekturstudium an der La Sapienza Universitas absolvierte. Fuksas erwarb sich in vier Jahrzehnten ein hervorragendes Renommee weltweit, mit Büros in Rom, Paris, Wien und Frankfurt. Er lehrt als Gastprofessor an Universitäten in Europa und Amerika und ist überdies Mitglied zahlreicher Akademien für Architektur. Zu der langen Liste seiner Referenzobjekte sind zuletzt das Nationalarchiv in Paris, die Konzerthalle in Straßburg oder auch das neue Headquarter von Ferrari hinzugekommen. Er arbeitet seit 1985 mit Doriana O. Mandrelli zusammen.

Massimiliano Fuksas est Lituanien. Mais il est né et a grandi à Rome où il a également obtenu son diplôme d'architecture à la Sapienza Universitas. En l'espace de quatre décennies Fuksas a conquis une renommée mondiale exceptionnelle avec des cabinets à Rome, Paris, Vienne et Francfort. Il enseigne comme professeur invité dans des universités en Europe et en Amérique. De plus, il est membre de nombreuses académies d'architecture. A la longue liste de ses projets de référence se sont ajoutés dernièrement les Archives Nationales à Paris, la Salle de Concert de Strasbourg ou encore le nouveau siège de Ferrari. Il travaille avec Doriana O. Mandrelli depuis 1985.

Massimiliano Fuksas es lituano aunque creció en Roma, donde finalizó sus estudios de arquitectura en La Sapienza Universitas. Durante cuatro décadas Fuksas obtuvo un extraordinario reconocimiento mundial, con estudios en Roma, París, Viena y Fráncfort. Es catedrático visitante en universidades europeas y americanas, además de miembro de numerosas academias de arquitectura. A su vasta lista de proyectos se le han añadido en los últimos tiempos el Archivo Nacional de París, la sala de conciertos en Estrasburgo y la nueva sede principal de Ferrari. Trabaja con Doriana O. Mandrelli desde 1985.

Pur essendo di origine lituana, Massimiliano Fuksas è nato e cresciuto a Roma dove ha conseguito la laurea in architettura all'università La Sapienza. In quasi quarant'anni Fuksas ha acquisito una straordinaria notorietà, assicurandosi grande visibilità grazie agli studi aperti a Roma, Parigi, Vienna e Francoforte. Oltre ad insegnare in qualità di visiting professor in diverse università europee ed americane, è membro di numerose Accademie d'architettura. Alla lunga lista di opere realizzate si sono aggiunti di recente l'Archivio centrale di Stato di Parigi, la sala concerti di Strasburgo e ancora il nuovo quartier generale della Ferrari. Dal 1985 collabora con Doriana O. Mandrelli.

ga.a architects

Moongyu Choi was born in 1961. The Korean graduated in architecture at his local Yonsei University and from Columbia University in New York. After graduation, he worked for international architectural studios in Tokyo and Korea. In 1999, he founded his own studio in Seoul. Choi already achieved various international awards for his works, such as the New York AIA Award in 2004. ga.a architects is especially well known in Asia, among other things, due to the Cheong Hansook Memorial and the Dalki theme park.

Moongyu Choi wurde 1961 geboren. Der Koreaner absolvierte sein Studium der Architektur an der einheimischen Yonsei University und der Columbia University in New York. Nach dem Studium arbeitete er für international tätige Architekturbüros in Tokio und Korea. 1999 gründete er sein eigenes Büro in Seoul. Mit seinen Arbeiten konnte Choi bereits diverse internationale Awards gewinnen, so etwa den New Yorker AIA-Award 2004. Bekannt ist ga.a architects vor allem in Asien, u. a. durch das Cheong Hansook Memorial und den Dalki Themenpark.

Moongyu Choi est né en 1961. Le Coréen a effectué ses études d'architecture à l'Université Yonsei dans son pays et à l'Université Columbia à New York. A l'issue de ses études, il a travaillé pour des cabinets d'architecture opérant au plan international à Tokyo et en Corée. En 1999 il a fondé son propre cabinet à Séoul. Ses travaux lui ont déjà valu diverses distinctions internationales, comme par exemple le AIA Award 2004 de New York. ga.a architects est surtout connu en Asie, par ex. grâce au Mémorial Cheong Hansook et au parc à thème Dalki.

Moongyu Choi nació en 1961. Este coreano finalizó sus estudios de arquitectura en la Yonsei University, en Corea, y en la Columbia University, en Nueva York. Después de su carrera trabajó para estudios de arquitectura con presencia internacional en Tokio y en Corea. En 1999 fundó su propio estudio en Seúl. Con sus proyectos, Choi ha podido ganar varios premios internacionales, como el AIA Award 2004 neoyorquino. ga.a architects es conocido, sobre todo, en Asia por proyectos como el Cheong Hansook Memorial y el parque temático Dalki.

Nato nel 1961, l'architetto coreano Moongyu Choi compie gli studi universitari alla facoltà di architettura presso l'università locale Yonsei University e la Columbia University di New York. Dopo aver maturato le prime esperienze di lavoro in studi di architettura di caratura internazionale a Tokio e in Corea, nel 1999 fonda un suo studio a Seoul. I suoi lavori sono già stati insigniti di ambiti riconoscimenti internazionali, come ad esempio il New York AIA Award 2004. Lo studio ga.a architects gode di grande notorietà soprattutto in Asia, dove fra le opere realizzate meritano particolare menzione il Cheong Hansook Memorial e il Dalki Theme Park.

Sophie Hicks, S. H. Architects Limited

Sophie Hicks lives and works as a freelance architect in London. As well as commissions for private homes, which she has completed, Hicks has earned a reputation as an exhibition and shop designer. She already worked on various projects for the Royal Academy of Arts (including a Picasso exhibition). Additionally, she is responsible for the flagship store concept both of Chloe and Paul Smith. Whether in London, Milan, Paris, Tokyo or even Hong Kong, these shops show her feminine and clear signature everywhere.

Sophie Hicks lebt und arbeitet in London als freie Architektin. Neben privaten Residenzen, die sie realisierte, hat sich Hicks einen Namen als Ausstellungs- und Shop-Designerin gemacht. Sie arbeitete schon verschiedentlich für die Royal Academy of Arts (u. a. für eine Picasso-Ausstellung). Daneben ist sie verantwortlich für das Flagshipstore-Konzept sowohl von Chloe als auch Paul Smith. Ob in London, Mailand, Paris, Tokio oder etwa Hongkong, überall tragen diese Shops ihre feminine wie klare Handschrift.

Sophie Hicks vit et travaille à Londres comme architecte libérale. Outre les résidences privées qu'elle a réalisées, Hicks s'est fait un nom comme créatrice d'expositions et de magasins. Elle a déjà travaillé à plusieurs reprises pour la Royal Academy of Arts (entre autres pour une exposition Picasso). Elle est en outre responsable du concept de magasin étendard de Chloe mais aussi de Paul Smith. Que ce soit à Londres, Milan, Paris, Tokyo ou bien Hong Kong, ces magasins portent partout sa signature claire et féminine.

Sophie Hicks vive y trabaja en Londres como arquitecta autónoma. Hicks se ha hecho un nombre especialmente como diseñadora de exposiciones y de tiendas, además de residencias privadas. También ha trabajado varias veces para la Royal Academy of Arts (para una exposición de Picasso, entre otras). Además es responsable del concepto de la tienda insigne de Chloe y de Paul Smith. Tanto en Londres, en Milán, en París, Tokio o Hong Kong, todas estas tiendas llevan su firma clara y femenina.

Sophie Hicks vive e lavora come libero professionista a Londra. Oltre che per la progettazione di residenze esclusive si è imposta all'attenzione del pubblico per le opere realizzate nel campo dello shop design nonché dell'exhibition design. In questa veste ha già curato diverse esposizioni della Royal Academy of Arts (fra cui la mostra dedicata a Picasso). Inoltre è responsabile del flagship store concept delle griffe Chloe e Paul Smith. Poco importa se a Londra, Milano, Parigi, Tokio o ancora Hong Kong: le boutique firmate Sophie Hicks si contraddistinguono ovunque per la spiccata femminilità e la coerenza dello stile.

Yasui Hideo Atelier

Yasui Hideo counts among those Japanese architects, who know how to decorate a strictly traditional Asian room structure with a futuristic touch. Hideo was born in Shizuoka. He studied architecture at the Aichi Institute of Technology. Until 1985, he was partner at the Kitaoka Design Studio. Afterwards, he launched his own studio, which meanwhile has several subsidiaries in Japan. His extensive work includes museums, hospitals, city halls, boutiques and restaurants, which ensure recognition beyond Asia's borders.

Yasui Hideo gehört zu jenen japanischen Architekten, die es verstehen, ein strenges traditionell asiatisches Raumgefüge mit einem futuristischen Hauch zu versehen. Geboren wurde Hideo in Shizuoka. Danach studierte er Architektur am Aichi Institute of Technology. Bis 1985 war er Partner des Kitaoka Design Studios. Anschließend eröffnete er sein eigenes Studio, mit inzwischen mehreren Dependancen in Japan. Seine umfangreiche Arbeit umfasst Museen, Hospitäler, Stadthallen, Boutiquen und Restaurants, die über Asiens Grenzen hinaus für Aufmerksamkeit sorgen.

Yasui Hideo fait partie de ces architectes japonais qui savent apporter une touche futuriste à la stricte structure asiatique traditionnelle de l'espace. Hideo est né à Shizuoka. Puis il a étudié l'architecture au Aichi Institute of Technology. Jusqu'en 1985 il a été partenaire du cabinet Kitaoka Design. Il a ensuite ouvert son propre cabinet qui compte entre temps plusieurs agences au Japon. Ses activités s'étendent à des musées, des hôpitaux, des salles polyvalentes, des boutiques et des restaurants qui attirent l'attention bien au-delà des frontières de l'Asie.

Yasui Hideo pertenece a ese grupo de arquitectos japoneses que saben cómo dotar a la estricta estructura tradicionalmente asiática de un toque futurista. Hideo nació en Shizuoka. Después estudió arquitectura en el Aichi Institute of Technology. Hasta 1985 fue socio del Kitaoka Design Studio. Después abrió su propio estudio que, en la actualidad, cuenta con varios despachos en Japón. Su vasto trabajo incluye museos, hospitales, pabellones municipales, tiendas y restaurantes que despiertan el interés más allá de las fronteras de Asia.

Yasui Hideo è fra gli architetti giapponesi dotati del talento di saper conciliare una concezione spaziale ispirata al rigore della tradizione asiatica con atmosfere vagamente futuristiche. Nato a Shizuoka, Hideo ha studiato architettura presso l'Aichi Institute of Technology. Dopo aver collaborato come partner nel Kitaoka Design Studio, nel 1985 crea lo Yasui Hideo Atelier, che può ormai avvalersi del supporto di diverse sedi in Giappone. Le opere realizzate spaziano da contesti quali musei, ospedali, strutture per manifestazioni culturali a boutique e ristoranti, amplificando la notorietà di Hideo ben oltre i confini asiatici.

ippolito fleitz group, identity architects

The ippolito fleitz group is an international design studio operating from Stuttgart, directed by Peter Ippolito and Gunter Fleitz. Whilst Ippolito worked at Daniel Libeskind's studio, Fleitz can cite project management on the construction of the Leipzig Federal Courts of Justice. The duo Ippolito and Fleitz stand for a wide spectrum of works: from landscape architecture to multimedia projects, to furniture and lighting design. Their international standing is shown by projects such as the Rose Garden Villa in Chongping, China, and the Leitz Bathing House in India.

Die ippolito fleitz group ist ein international tätiges Designstudio aus Stuttgart, geführt von Peter Ippolito und Gunter Fleitz. Während Ippolito im Studio von Daniel Libeskind mitarbeitete, kann Fleitz auf die Projektleitung beim Leipziger Bau des Bundesgerichtshofes verweisen. Das Duo Ippolito Fleitz steht für ein breites Spektrum an Arbeiten: von der Landschaftsarchitektur bis hin zu Multimedia-Projekten und Möbel- und Leuchtendesign. Ihre internationale Bedeutung belegen Projekte wie die Rose Garden Villa in Chongping, China, und das Badehaus Leitz in Indien.

Shop Design | **385**

L'ippolito fleitz group est une agence de design basée à Stuttgart, opérant au plan international et dirigé par Peter Ippolito et Gunter Fleitz. Tandis qu'Ippolito a collaboré avec l'agence de Daniel Libeskind, Fleitz a pour référence la direction de projet pour la construction de la Cour de Cassation Allemande à Leipzig. Le duo Ippolito Fleitz est l'artisan de travaux d'une grande diversité : de l'architecture paysagère à des projets multimédias et au design de meubles et d'éclairages. Leur importance mondiale est attestée par des projets tels que la Rose Garden Villa à Chongping en Chine et les Thermes Leitz en Inde.

El ippolito fleitz group es un estudio de diseño de Stuttgart con presencia internacional que está dirigido por Peter Ippolito y Gunter Fleitz. Mientras que Ippolito ha trabajado en el estudio de Daniel Libeskind, Fleitz ha dirigido el proyecto de la construcción en Leipzig del Tribunal Federal Supremo. Los trabajos del dúo Ippolito Fleitz abarcan un amplio espectro: desde la arquitectura de paisajes hasta proyectos multimedia y diseño de muebles e iluminación. Su relevancia internacional viene avalada por proyectos como la Rose Garden Villa en Chongping, China, y la casa de baños Leitz en India.

L'ippolito fleitz group è uno studio di design con spiccata vocazione internazionale con sede a Stoccarda gestito da Peter Ippolito e Gunter Fleitz. Il duo può vantare prestigiosi antecedenti, fra i quali la collaborazione di Ippolito nello studio di Daniel Libeskind e la direzione del progetto di costruzione della Corte federale di giustizia di Lipsia da parte di Fleitz. L'ampio portfolio delle opere realizzate rispecchia un approccio multidisciplinare: dall'architettura dei paesaggi fino alla progettazione di mobili di design e all'architettura della luce attraverso il design multimediale. Di caratura internazionale i progetti Rose Garden Villa a Chongping (Cina) e Bagni Termali Leitz (India).

Craig Konyk / konyk

Craig Konyk lives and works as an architect in Brooklyn. Being on New York's architectural circuit earned him a professorship at Columbia State University. Besides, he is also a member of a whole series of respected societies, (Architectural League of New York). Konyk's designs include (at the invitation of "dwell magazine") the living design for the "UP!House" and the "GLAD" residential tower in New York. His designs of showrooms (Tuttle Street ONE in Miami) also earned international recognition.

Craig Konyk lebt und arbeitet als Architekt in Brooklyn. Seine Präsenz in der New Yorker Architekturlandschaft brachte ihm eine Professur an der Columbia State University ein. Außerdem ist er Mitglied in einer ganzen Reihe von angesehenen Vereinigungen (Architectural League of New York). Konyk gestaltete unter anderem (auf Einladung des dwell magazine) das Wohndesign für das UP!House und den Wohntower GLAD in New York. Auch seine Entwürfe von Showrooms (Tuttle Street ONE in Miami) stoßen weltweit auf Resonanz.

Craig Konyk vit et travaille comme architecte à Brooklyn. Sa présence dans le paysage new-yorkais de l'architecture lui a valu une chaire de professeur à la Columbia State University. De plus, il est membre d'un grand nombre d'associations prestigieuses (Architectural League of New York). A l'invitation du dwell magazine, Konyk a conçu entre autres le design d'habitation pour la UP!House et l'immeuble résidentiel GLAD à New York. De même, ses projets de showrooms (Tuttle Street ONE à Miami) ont un énorme succès dans le monde entier.

Craig Konyk vive y trabaja como arquitecto en Brooklyn. Su presencia en el mundo de la arquitectura neoyorquina le proporcionó su cargo catedrático en la Columbia State University. Además es miembro de toda una serie de renombradas asociaciones (Architectural League of New York). Konyk ha diseñado, entre otros, el interior de la vivienda UP!House por encargo de la revista dwell magazine, y la torre de viviendas GLAD en Nueva York. Sus proyectos para diferentes showrooms (Tuttle Street ONE en Miami) han tenido también resonancia internacional.

Craig Konyk vive e lavora come professionista a Brooklyn. L'essersi affermato nel panorama architettonico newyorchese gli ha valso la cattedra alla Columbia State University. È inoltre membro di svariate associazioni prestigiose fra cui L'Architectural League di New York. Fra le opere realizzate da Konyk vanno ricordate le progettazioni degli interni della UP!House (su invito della rivista dwell magazine) e del grattacielo residenziale GLAD a New York. Forte risonanza internazionale ha riscontrato anche l'edificio adibito a showroom creato per il Design District di Miami (Tuttle Street ONE Miami).

Lynch / Eisinger / Design

Both partners Christian Lynch and Simon Eisinger have known each other since they studied together at Columbia University in New York. Further stages in Lynch's fledgling career led him to Stanley Saitowitz and Franklin D. Israel. Eisinger fine-tuned his architectural profile with Günter Behnisch and I. M. Pei. Lynch and Eisinger's clear and nuanced style is a result of these influences. From 1997 onwards, they are working together at their studio in New York, trading under the name of Lynch / Eisinger / Design.

Die beiden Partner Christian Lynch und Simon Eisinger kennen sich seit ihrem gemeinsamen Studium an der Columbia University in New York. Lynchs weitere Stationen in seiner noch jungen Karriere führten ihn zu Stanley Saitowitz und Franklin D. Israel. Eisinger schärfte sein architektonisches Profil bei Günter Behnisch und I. M. Pei. Lynchs und Eisingers klarer wie pointierter Stil resultiert aus diesen Einflüssen. Seit 1997 arbeiten sie in ihrem Büro in New York zusammen und firmieren unter Lynch / Eisinger / Design.

Les deux associés Christian Lynch et Simon Eisinger se connaissent depuis leurs études communes à la Columbia University de New York. D'autres étapes dans la carrière encore jeune de Lynch l'ont conduit vers Stanley Saitowitz et Franklin D. Israel. Eisinger a affûté son profil architectural auprès de Günter Behnisch et I. M. Pei. Le style clair et précis de Lynch et Eisinger résulte de ces influences. Depuis 1997 ils travaillent ensemble dans leur cabinet new yorkais, leur société portant le nom de Lynch / Eisinger / Design.

Los dos socios Christian Lynch y Simon Eisinger se conocieron cursando sus estudios en la Columbia University en Nueva York. Los primeros destinos profesionales de Lynch le llevaron a Stanley Saitowitz y Franklin D. Israel. Eisinger dio forma a su perfil arquitectónico trabajando con Günter Behnisch y I. M. Pei. El estilo claro y conceptuoso de Lynch y Eisinger es el resultado de estas influencias. Desde 1997 trabajan juntos en su propio estudio en Nueva York y firman sus proyectos como Lynch / Eisinger / Design.

I due partner Christian Lynch e Simon Eisinger si conoscono dai tempi degli studi universitari compiuti insieme alla Columbia University di New York. Durante le tappe successive della sua pur giovane carriera, Lynch è approdato negli studi di architettura Stanley Saitowitz e Franklin D. Israel. Al profilo professionale di Eisinger invece hanno dato spessore le esperienze maturate al fianco di Günter Behnisch e I. M. Pei. Entrambi gli influssi sono confluiti nello stile preciso e definito che contraddistingue i lavori dei due soci, che dal 1997 collaborano nello studio di New York apponendo ai loro progetti la firma Lynch / Eisinger / Design.

Peter Marino Architects and Eric Carlson, Carbondale

Peter Marino, an American architect of Italian descent, had I. M. Pei, and others, as master architect. His own studio, established in 1978, operates on an international basis. The list of his clients includes many famous fashion labels, cultural institutions (Dresden's Zwinger) and artists.
After graduation, the American Eric Carlson initially worked for industry greats such as Mark Mack and Rem Koolhaas, before he built up his own department for architecture at Louis Vuitton in 1997. Here, he significantly influenced the new image for the spatial appearance at LV.

Peter Marino, amerikanischer Architekt italienischer Abstammung, hatte u. a. I. M. Pei als Lehrmeister. Sein eigenes Büro, 1978 gegründet, ist weltweit tätig. In der Liste seiner Auftraggeber finden sich viele berühmte Modemarken, Kulturinstitutionen (Dresdner Zwinger) und Künstler.

Shop Design | **387**

Der Amerikaner Eric Carlson arbeitete nach seinem Diplom zunächst bei solchen Branchengrößen wie Mark Mack und Rem Koolhaas, bevor er 1997 die eigene Abteilung für Architektur von Louis Vuitton aufbaute. Dort prägte er maßgeblich das neue Erscheinungsbild für den räumlichen Auftritt von LV.

Peter Marino, architecte américain d'origine italienne, a eu entre autres I. M. Pei pour maître. Son propre cabinet fondé en 1978 travaille au plan international. La liste de ses donneurs d'ordre compte de nombreuses marques de mode célèbres, des institutions culturelles (Dresdner Zwinger) et des artistes.
L'Américain Eric Carlson a travaillé, après son diplôme, avec de grandes pointures de l'architecture telles que Mark Mack et Rem Koolhaas avant de mettre sur pied en 1997 la section architecture de la maison Louis Vuitton. Il y influença de façon déterminante la nouvelle présentation des magasins LV.

Peter Marino, arquitecto americano de origen italiano, tuvo, entre otros maestros, a I. M. Pei. Su estudio, fundado en 1978, realiza proyectos en todo el mundo. En la lista de sus clientes se encuentran muchas marcas famosas de moda, instituciones culturales (Dresdner Zwinger) y artistas.
El americano Eric Carlson trabajó al finalizar sus estudios con grandes nombres del sector como Mark Mack y Rem Koolhaas, antes de crear el propio departamento de arquitectura de Louis Vuitton en 1997. Aquí caracterizó de forma determinante la nueva imagen de los interiores de LV.

L'architetto americano di origine italiana Peter Marino annovera fra i suoi maestri I. M. Pei. Lo studio omonimo di cui è titolare e che ha fondato nel 1978 opera a livello internazionale. Fra i suoi prestigiosi committenti figurano numerose griffe della moda, istituzioni culturali (Dresdner Zwinger) ed artisti.
Dopo la laurea l'americano Eric Carlson si è formato al seguito di matite celebratissime del panorama architettonico internazionale quali Mark Mack e Rem Koolhaas prima di essere chiamato a creare, nel 1997, lo studio di progettazione interno della Louis Vuitton. Ed è qui che svolge il ruolo determinante di gestire la nuova immagine della maison curando tutti i dettagli della contestualizzazione architettonica del monogramma LV.

Ito Masaru Design Project / Sei

Ito Masaru is mainly known in Asia, so his shop projects are primarily located in Japan. Nevertheless, sales floors designed by Ito Masaru are frequently atomized by a staged magic. For that reason, Issey Miyake has, for a long while, put faith in his designs. The Japanese designer, born in 1961 in Osaka, and a graduate of the Tokyo Zokei University, knows how to inject unusual humor into commercial sites. The fashion shop troisO is one example of this, Citrus Note in Roppongi is another.

Ito Masaru ist hauptsächlich im asiatischen Raum bekannt, so findet man seine Shop-Projekte überwiegend in Japan. Nichtsdestotrotz: Die von Ito Masaru gestalteten Verkaufsräume sprühen oft vor inszenierter Magie. Issey Miyake vertraut deswegen schon länger auf seine Entwürfe. Der japanische Designer, der 1961 in Osaka geboren wurde und die Tokioter Zokei Universität absolvierte, versteht es, ungewöhnlichen Witz in kommerzielle Objekte zu legen. Der Fashionshop troisO ist ein Beispiel dafür, Citrus Note in Roppongi ein anderes.

Ito Masaru est principalement connu du côté de l'Asie si bien qu'on trouve ses projets de magasins en majorité au Japon. Néanmoins, les espaces de vente conçus par Ito Masaru étincellent souvent de magie mise en scène. C'est pourquoi Issey Miyake table depuis longtemps sur ses projets. Le designer japonais, né à Osaka en 1961 et diplômé de l'Université Zokei de Tokyo, possède l'art inattendu de mettre de l'esprit dans des objets commerciaux. La boutique de mode troisO est un exemple, Citrus Note à Roppongi un autre.

Ito Masaru es conocido sobre todo en los países asiáticos y sus proyectos para tiendas se encuentran principalmente en Japón. Esto no impide, sin embargo, que los interiores de las tiendas diseñados por Ito Masaru emanen a menudo una magia escenificada. Por eso Issey Miyake confía desde hace mucho tiempo en sus proyectos. El diseñador japonés, que nació en Osaka en 1961 y cursó sus estudios en la universidad Zokei de Tokio, sabe cómo introducir una nota de insólito ingenio en los espacios comerciales. Ejemplo de ello son las *boutiques* de ropa troisO o del Citrus Note a Roppongi.

Benché Ito Masaru sia conosciuto soprattutto nella regione asiatica, dove la sua notorietà è amplificata dai progetti di shop design realizzati per lo più in Giappone, i suoi allestimenti sono pervasi da un fascino scenografico che va oltre i confini geografici. È questo il motivo per cui Issey Miyake confida già da tempo nell'istinto del designer giapponese. Nato nel 1961 ad Osaka e laureatosi all'università Zokei di Tokio, Masaru ha il particolare talento di saper contestualizzare un umorismo insolito in un formato commerciale, come dimostrano le formule del troisO o del Citrus Note a Roppongi.

Patrick E. Naggar Architect

Patrick E. Naggar was born in 1947 in Egypt, his parents spoke French and held an Italian passport. The Parisian architect's multicultural roots, which oscillate around the part-European, part-Arabian Mediterranean, distinguish his works. Many classical and mythological elements are reflected in his furniture, houses and room designs. At the same time, the designs follow the industrial logic of functional aesthetics. But Naggar also paints and sketches as an artist, who loves to weave stories into his projects.

Patrick E. Naggar wurde 1947 in Ägypten geboren und hatte Französisch sprechende Eltern mit italienischem Pass. Diese multikulturellen Wurzeln des Pariser Architekten, die sich um das halb europäische, halb arabische Mittelmeer bewegen, zeichnen seine Arbeiten aus. In seinen Möbeln, Häusern und Raumgestaltungen finden sich viele klassische und mythologische Elemente wieder. Zugleich folgen die Entwürfe der industriellen Logik funktionaler Ästhetik. Dabei ist Naggar ein malender und zeichnender Künstler, der es liebt, seinen Objekten Geschichten einzuweben.

Patrick E. Naggar, né en Egypte en 1947, avait des parents parlant français et détenant un passeport italien. Les racines multiculturelles de cet architecte parisien qui plongent dans la Méditerranée mi-européenne et mi-arabe, caractérisent ses travaux. On retrouve dans ses meubles, maisons et intérieurs de nombreux éléments classiques et mythologiques. Pourtant ses projets répondent à la logique industrielle de l'esthétique fonctionnelle. Ce faisant, Naggar est un artiste peintre et dessinateur qui aime à tisser des histoires dans ses objets.

Patrick E. Naggar nació en 1947 en Egipto y sus padres eran franco parlantes con pasaporte italiano. Estas raíces multiculturales del arquitecto parisino, que se extienden por casi la mitad de Europa y del Mediterráneo árabe, caracterizan sus trabajos. En el mobiliario, las casas y los espacios diseñados por él pueden encontrarse numerosos elementos clásicos y mitológicos, al mismo tiempo que sus proyectos siguen la lógica industrial de la estética funcional. Naggar es un artista que pinta y dibuja y al que le gusta entretejer sus proyectos con historias.

Patrick E. Naggar nasce nel 1947 in Egitto da genitori francofoni con passaporto italiano. L'identità multiculturale, sottesa fra le due sponde del Mediterraneo, segna profondamente i lavori dell'architetto parigino. Nella progettazione architettonica, arredi e design d'interni sono ricorrenti numerosi elementi classici e mitologici ma traspare allo stesso tempo la logica industriale dell'estetica funzionale. In tutto ciò Naggar rimane pittore e disegnatore, con una particolare predilezione per le storie che ama intessere attorno alle sue creazioni.

Palazzo Gianfranco Ferré

Italian fashion creator Gianfranco Ferré is internationally among the most successful fashion designers. He transferred from architecture to the fashion industry, developing his own label under his own name. He creates women's, men's and children's fashion. A highlight of his career was from 1989 to 1996 when he worked as creative director for Christian Dior. Until the end of his time at Dior, he developed women's haute couture fashion.

Der italienische Modemacher Gianfranco Ferré gehört zu den international erfolgreichen Modedesignern. Er wechselte als Architekt in die Fashionbranche und entwickelte dort seine eigene Linie, die unter seinem Namen auftritt. Er entwirft Damen-, Herren- und Kindermode. Ein Höhepunkt seiner Karriere stellte von 1989 bis 1996 die Tätigkeit als Kreativdirektor von Christian Dior dar. Dort entwickelte er bis zum Ende seiner Dior-Zeit die Haute Couture der Damenmode.

Le créateur de mode italien Gianfranco Ferré fait partie des designers de mode qui jouissent d'un succès international. Il est passé comme architecte au monde de la mode et y a développé sa propre ligne de produits qui porte son nom. Il dessine de la mode féminine, masculine et enfantine. Sa carrière a connu son apogée de 1989 à 1996 alors qu'il était directeur de la création chez Christian Dior. Jusqu'à la fin de sa période chez Dior, il y a développé la Haute Couture de la mode féminine.

El modista italiano Gianfranco Ferré pertenece al grupo de los diseñadores con éxito internacional. Originariamente arquitecto, se pasó al sector de la moda donde desarrolló su propia línea que presenta bajo su nombre. Diseña ropa para señora, caballero y niños. El cenit de su carrera lo alcanzó entre 1989 y 1996 como director creativo de Christian Dior. En esta casa desarrolló hasta el final de su era Dior la *haute couture* de la moda femenina.

Lo stilista italiano Gianfranco Ferré è uno dei nomi più affermati nel mondo internazionale della moda. Dopo aver conseguito la laurea in architettura decide di intraprendere una nuova strada, proponendosi all'Olimpo della moda con una linea che porta il suo nome. Disegna creazioni per uomo, donna e bambino. Un momento culminante della sua carriera è rappresentato dalla sua attività in veste di direttore creativo di Christian Dior fra il 1989 e il 1996, periodo in cui disegnò la Haute Couture femminile della maison.

PURPUR. ARCHITEKTUR
Toedtling, Laengauer, Boric und Loebell

At the architects' group PURPUR, the name is a program for the hedonistic approach to designing rooms: it is just full of passion and open for different perspectives. The Graz studio, with subsidiary in Vienna, has traded since 1999 and involves four individuals: Christian Toedtling, Thomas Laengauer, Alfred Boric and Alexander Loebell. Urban planning strategies are included in the quartet's portfolio, as well as art projects, interior and product design.

Bei der Architektengruppe PURPUR ist der Name Programm für das hedonistische Herangehen an die Gestaltung von Räumen: eben lustvoll und offen für verschiedene Perspektiven. Das Grazer Büro mit Wiener Dependance besteht seit 1999 und setzt sich aus vier Köpfen zusammen: Christian Toedtling, Thomas Laengauer, Alfred Boric und Alexander Loebell. Städtebauliche Strategien werden von dem Quartett genauso abgedeckt wie Kunstprojekte, Interior- und Produktdesign.

Dans le cas du groupe d'architectes PURPUR, leur nom révèle leur approche hédoniste de l'aménagement des pièces : voluptueuse donc et ouverte sur divers horizons. Le cabinet de Graz qui possède une agence à Vienne existe depuis 1999 et se compose de quatre membres : Christian Toedtling, Thomas Laengauer, Alfred Boric et Alexander Loebell. Le quatuor traite aussi bien les stratégies d'urbanisme que les projets artistiques et le design d'intérieur et de produit.

El nombre del grupo de arquitectos PURPUR refleja su acercamiento hedonista en la decoración de los espacios, es decir, con deleite y abiertos a nuevas perspectivas. Este estudio de Graz con despacho también en Viena existe desde 1999 y está compuesto por cuatro personas: Christian Toedtling, Thomas Laengauer, Alfred Boric y Alexander Loebell. El cuarteto realiza proyectos urbanísticos y artísticos además de diseños para interiores y para productos.

PURPUR. ARCHITEKTUR: il nome è già un programma. Come se bastasse pronunciarlo per capire che ciò che caratterizza i lavori del gruppo di progettazione austriaco è un approccio edonistico al design d'interni, tutto incentrato sulla ricerca del piacere estetico e proiettato verso nuove dimensioni prospettiche. Fondato nel 1999, lo studio con sede a Graz e Vienna è costituito da quattro menti creative: Christian Toedtling, Thomas Laengauer, Alfred Boric e Alexander Loebell. Un quartetto capace di spaziare dalle strategie urbanistiche all'interior e al product design passando attraverso i progetti artistici.

studio aisslinger

Werner Aisslinger, born in 1964, lives in Berlin. He graduated in design at the University of Berlin, HdK. Before launching the aisslinger studio in 1993, he worked for Jasper Morrison and Ron Arad and for the de Lucchi Milan studio. His studio specializes in product design, design concepts and brand architectures. Aisslinger achieved widespread acclaim for his furniture designs for Cappellini, Zanotta and also Interlübke. He was awarded many prizes (e.g.: Compasso d'Oro) and lectures as Professor at the Staatliche Hochschule für Gestaltung (College for Design in Karlsruhe).

Werner Aisslinger, geboren 1964, lebt in Berlin. Sein Designstudium absolvierte er an der Berliner Hochschule der Künste, HdK. Bevor er 1993 das studio aisslinger gründete, arbeitete er für Jasper Morrison und Ron Arad bzw. für das Mailänder Studio de Lucchi. Sein Büro ist auf Produktdesign, Designkonzepte und Markenarchitekturen spezialisiert. Weithin bekannt wurde Aisslinger durch seine Möbelentwürfe für Cappellini, Zanotta und auch Interlübke. Er erhielt viele Preise (z. B.: Compasso d'Oro) und lehrt als Professor an der Staatlichen Hochschule für Gestaltung in Karlsruhe.

Werner Aisslinger, né en 1964, vit à Berlin. Il détient un diplôme de design de l'Université des Arts de Berlin (HdK). Avant de fonder en 1993 le studio aisslinger, il a collaboré avec Jasper Morrison et Ron Arad, précisément avec le cabinet milanais de Lucchi. Son agence est spécialisée dans le design de produit, les concepts de design et les architectures de marques. Aisslinger s'est largement fait connaître grâce à ces créations de meubles pour Cappellini, Zanotta ainsi que pour Interlübke. Lauréat de nombreux prix (par ex. le Compasso d'Oro), il enseigne comme professeur à la Staatliche Hochschule für Gestaltung de Karlsruhe.

Werner Aisslinger, nacido en 1964, vive en Berlín. Cursó sus estudios de diseño en la berlinesa Universidad de las Artes, HdK. Antes de fundar el studio aisslinger en 1993 trabajó bajo la dirección de Jasper Morrison y Ron Arad, además de en el estudio milanés de Lucchi. Su estudio se ha especializado en el diseño de productos, conceptos de diseños y arquitecturas de marca. Aisslinger ha obtenido el reconocimiento por sus proyectos de muebles para Cappellini, Zanotta y también Interlübke. Ha recibido numerosos premios (p.ej. Compasso d'Oro) e imparte clases como catedrático en la Staatliche Hochschule für Gestaltung (Escuela Superior de Diseño) en Karlsruhe.

Nato nel 1964, Werner Aisslinger vive a Berlino dove ha studiato design alla Hochschule der Künste–Hdk. Collabora con professionisti quali Jasper Morrison e Ron Arad nonché Studio de Lucchi a Milano prima di aprire nel 1993 lo studio aisslinger, specializzato in product design, industrial design e corporate brand management. La progettazione di mobili di design per Cappellini, Zanotta e Interlübke gli ha valso grande notorietà. È vincitore di diversi premi (ad es. il Compasso d'Oro) e titolare della cattedra di product design alla Staatliche Hochschule für Gestaltung di Karlsruhe.

Studio Sofield Inc.

Interior designer William Sofield was born in 1961 in New Jersey and studied architecture and urban planning at Princeton. He made the breakthrough onto the international scene in cooperation with Ralph Lauren. Today, his studio's name in L. A. represents a modern interpretation of glamour. His most famous project is the new design of the Gucci shops worldwide. But Sofield also completed offices (including for the Walt Disney Company), bars and restaurants (Ken Aretsky), and last not least, the award-winning interior of the Soho Grand Hotel in New York.

Interiordesigner William Sofield wurde 1961 in New Jersey geboren und studierte Architektur und Stadtplanung in Princeton. Seinen internationalen Durchbruch schaffte er in der Zusammenarbeit mit Ralph Lauren. Heute steht der Name seines Büros in L. A. für eine moderne Interpretation des Glamours. Sein berühmtestes Projekt ist die Neugestaltung der Gucci-Shops weltweit. Doch Sofield realisierte daneben Büroräume (u. a. für die Walt Disney Company), Bars und Restaurants (Ken Aretsky) sowie nicht zuletzt das preisgekrönte Interieur des Soho Grand Hotel in New York.

Le designer d'intérieur William Sofield est né en 1961 dans le New Jersey et a fait des études d'architecture et d'urbanisme à Princeton. Il a fait une percée internationale grâce à sa collaboration avec Ralph Lauren. Aujourd'hui le nom de son agence à L. A. est synonyme d'interprétation moderne du glamour. Son projet le plus connu est le remodelage des magasins Gucci dans le monde entier. Parallèlement Sofield a également réalisé des espaces de bureaux (par ex. pour la Compagnie Walt Disney), des bars et restaurants (Ken Aretsky) ainsi que dernièrement l'intérieur du Soho Grand Hotel à New York, récompensé par un prix.

El diseñador de interiores William Sofield nació en 1961 en Nueva Jersey y estudió arquitectura y planificación urbanística en Princeton. El éxito internacional lo consiguió a través de su colaboración con Ralph Lauren. Hoy, el nombre de su estudio en L. A. es sinónimo de una moderna interpretación del *glamour*. Su proyecto más famoso a nivel mundial es la redecoración de la tienda de Gucci. Sofield ha diseñado también despachos (entre otros para la Walt Disney Company), bares, restaurantes (Ken Aretsky) y el premiado interior del Soho Grand Hotel en Nueva York.

L'interior designer William Sofield nasce nel 1961 nel New Jersey e studia architettura e pianificazione urbanistica a Princeton. Impostosi all'attenzione internazionale grazie alla collaborazione con Ralph Lauren, è tutt'oggi sulla cresta dell'onda: Studio Sofield Inc. a L. A. è sinonimo di interpretazione moderna di glamour. Se il restyling delle boutique monomarca Gucci ha consacrato il suo nome in tutto il mondo, esso non è certamente l'unico progetto di grande risonanza all'attivo dello studio, specializzato oltre che in shop design anche nella progettazione di uffici (ad es. per la Walt Disney Company), bar e ristoranti (Ken Aretsky) e non da ultimo degli interni, attività premiata con il riconoscimento assegnato all'interior design del Soho Grand Hotel di New York.

Studio X Design Group

Architects Lara Rettondini and Oscar Brito established the Studio X Design Group. Previously, both had cooperated on numerous projects. Located in London and Treviso, their joint studio has been in operation since 2000. It specializes in architecture, design and communication. In addition to designs for gastronomic sites, STX achieved international distinction for the "MANDARING" concept for Mandarina Duck, for which it won several awards.

Die Studio X Design Group wurde von den beiden Architekten Lara Rettondini und Oscar Brito ins Leben gerufen. Die beiden hatten davor schon bei etlichen Projekten zusammen gearbeitet. Ihr gemeinsames Büro besteht seit 2000 und hat seinen Sitz in London und Treviso. Es ist spezialisiert auf Architektur, Design und Kommunikation. Neben den Entwürfen für gastronomische Objekte konnte sich STX international auszeichnen durch das „MANDARING"-Konzept für Mandarina Duck, für das sie mehrere Awards erhielten.

Les deux architectes Lara Rettondini et Oscar Brito ont donné naissance au Studio X Design Group. Auparavant ils avaient tous deux collaboré à un grand nombre de projets. Le siège de leur cabinet d'associés, fondé en 2000, se trouve à Londres et Trévise. Il est spécialisé dans l'architecture, le design et la communication. Outre des projets pour des objets gastronomiques, STX s'est distingué au plan international par le concept « MANDARING » pour Mandarina Duck, couronné de plusieurs prix.

El Studio X Design Group fue fundado por los arquitectos Lara Rettondini y Oscar Brito. Anteriormente habían colaborado ya en otros proyectos. Su estudio existe desde 2000 y tiene su sede en Londres y Treviso. Se han especializado en arquitectura, diseño y comunicación. Además de los proyectos para restaurantes, STX ha obtenido el reconocimiento internacional en forma de varios premios por el concepto "MANDARING" para Mandarina Duck.

Studio X Design Group è stato creato dagli architetti Lara Rettondini e Oscar Brito. Il loro è un sodalizio collaudato già precedentemente attraverso la collaborazione a diversi progetti. Nel 2000 costituiscono a Londra e Treviso uno studio comune specializzato in progettazione architettonica, design e comunicazione. Oltre che con i progetti realizzati in ambito gastronomico il duo ha conquistato le luci della ribalta internazionale con il pluripremiato MANDARING, un sistema modulare creato appositamente per Mandarina Duck.

Suppose Design Office

Makoto Tanijiri is the founding director of Suppose Design Office in Hiroshima. The 32-year-old designer previously worked from 1994 to 2000 at Motokane Architects and at HAL Architects. From 2000 onwards, Tanijiri built up his own studio, which succeeded in establishing itself as a small, but top-class creative studio in Japan. The works of the Suppose Design Office have already won awards several times, including for instance the "Urban Design Award Hiroshima" and the "JCD Design Award". Currently, several projects in Japan are undergoing completion.

Chef und Gründer des Suppose Design Office in Hiroshima ist Makoto Tanijiri. Der 32-jährige Designer arbeitete zuvor von 1994 bis 2000 bei Motokane Architects bzw. bei HAL Architects. Ab dem Jahre 2000 baute Tanijiri sein eigenes Büro auf, das sich als kleines, aber feines Kreativstudio in Japan etablieren konnte. Die Arbeiten von Suppose Design Office sind bereits mehrfach mit Preisen bedacht worden, so u. a. mit dem „Urban Design Award Hiroshima" und „JCD-Design Award". Aktuell werden mehrere Projekte in Japan realisiert.

Le chef et fondateur de Suppose Design Office à Hiroshima est Makoto Tanijiri. Ce designer de 32 ans a auparavant travaillé de 1994 à 2000 chez Motokane Architects, précisément chez HAL Architects. A partir de 2000 Tanijiri a monté sa propre agence désormais établie au Japon comme studio de création modeste mais raffiné. A plusieurs reprises, les travaux de Suppose Design Office ont été récompensés de prix tels que, entre autres, le « Urban Design Award Hiroshima » et le « JCD Design Award ». De nombreux projets sont actuellement réalisés au Japon.

Makoto Tanijiri es el director y el fundador de la Suppose Design Office en Hiroshima. Este diseñador de 32 años trabajó anteriormente, entre 1994 y 2000, en los estudios Motokane Architects y HAL Architects. A partir de 2000, Tanijiri formó su propio estudio que pudo establecerse en Japón como un pequeño pero excelente estudio creativo. Los trabajos de Suppose Design Office han sido reconocidos en varias ocasiones con premios, entre estos, el "Urban Design Award Hiroshima" y el "JCD Design Award". En la actualidad se encarga de la realización de varios proyectos en Japón.

Titolare e fondatore dello studio Suppose Design Office di Hiroshima è Makoto Tanijiri, trentaduenne designer che dal 1994 al 2000 ha maturato le prime esperienze lavorative presso Motokane Architects e HAL Architects. Nel 2000 Tanijiri costituisce un suo studio di design creativo di piccolo dimensioni ma ben posizionato sul mercato giapponese. I progetti realizzati da Suppose Design Office hanno già vinto diversi premi fra cui i riconoscimenti "Urban Design Award Hiroshima" e "JCD Design Award". Numerose le opere in corso di realizzazione in Giappone.

Sybarite

The 34-year-old Briton, Simon Mitchell, is partner to Torquil McIntosh. In 2002, together they founded the London Design- and Architecture Studio known as Sybarite. Their unmistakable style is also emphasized by the studio's name: they want to break out of the boundaries between art, sculpture and architecture. In this sense, organic forms predominate in their designs—ultimately, the expression of sensually inspired luxury, which seeks to integrate into its environment. Totally untouched by this ambition, technical design also flows into their rooms and sites.

Der 34-jährige Brite Simon Mitchell ist Partner von Torquil McIntosh. Zusammen begründeten sie 2002 das Londoner Design- und Architekturstudio Sybarite. Ihren unverkennbaren Stil unterstreicht auch der Name des Studios: Sie wollen die Grenzen sprengen zwischen Kunst, Skulptur und Architektur. Dergestalt herrschen organische Formen in ihren Entwürfen vor — letztlich der Ausdruck von sinnlich inspiriertem Luxus, der sich in sein Umfeld einzufügen sucht. Davon unberührt fließt genauso technisches Design in ihre Räume und Objekte ein.

Le Britannique Simon Mitchell, âgé de 34 ans, est associé avec Torquil McIntosh. Ensemble, ils ont fondé en 2002 l'agence londonienne de design et d'architecture Sybarite. Le nom de leur agence souligne leur style si reconnaissable : ils souhaitent dynamiter les frontières entre l'art, la sculpture et l'architecture. C'est ainsi que dominent les formes organiques dans leurs projets — finalement l'expression d'un luxe d'inspiration sensuelle cherchant à se fondre dans son environnement. Ce qui n'empêche pas l'intégration d'un design technique dans leurs espaces et leurs objets.

El británico Simon Mitchell, de 34 años, es socio de Torquil McIntosh. Juntos fundaron en 2002 el estudio londinés de diseño y arquitectura Sybarite. Su inconfundible estilo recalca el nombre del estudio: quieren eliminar los límites entre el arte, la escultura y la arquitectura. Por eso en sus proyectos dominan las formas orgánicas, expresión última del lujo inspirado en los sentidos y que busca integrarse en su entorno. Esta característica no afecta al diseño técnico que fluye en sus espacios y objetos.

Il 34enne designer britannico Simon Mitchell ha fondato insieme al socio Torquil McIntosh lo studio di design e di architettura Sybarite di Londra nel 2002. La scelta del nome sottolinea già di per sé lo stile inconfondibile dello studio, che traduce in approccio multidisciplinare l'intenzione di rendere fluidi i confini fra arte, scultura ed architettura. È così che nei loro progetti prevalgono le forme organiche, espressione di un lusso di ispirazione sensoriale alla ricerca di una simbiosi con l'ambiente circostante. Senza rinunciare al design tecnico, che si fonde perfettamente con le atmosfere e le ambientazioni realizzate.

SZI Design

The SZI Design group, under managing director Sherrie Zwail, formed in 1990 in Amsterdam. Its focus is on consultancy, planning and design of rooms in the commercial as well as private sector. Clients include internationally respected brands and banks. In addition to room design, the international team also creates its own lighting systems, furniture and graphics. With the "topsy-turvy" shop design at Viktor & Rolf, SZI once again recently attracted international publicity.

Die Gruppe SZI Design um Geschäftsführerin Sherrie Zwail hat sich 1990 in Amsterdam zusammengeschlossen. Ihr Fokus richtet sich auf die Beratung, Planung und Gestaltung von Räumen im kommerziellen wie privaten Sektor. Zu ihren Kunden gehören weltweit angesehene Marken und Banken. Neben der Raumgestaltung entwirft das internationale Team auch eigene Lichtsysteme, Möbel und Grafiken. Mit dem „verdrehten" Shop-Design von Viktor & Rolf verschaffte sich SZI unlängst wieder weltweit große Aufmerksamkeit.

Le groupe SZI Design s'est regroupé en 1990 à Amsterdam autour de la PDG Sherrie Zwail. Son champ d'action se concentre sur le conseil, la planification et l'aménagement de pièces dans le secteur commercial et privé. De par le monde, ses clients sont des marques et des banques réputées. Cette équipe internationale crée des décorations intérieures mais aussi des systèmes d'éclairage, des meubles et des graphiques. Avec le design « inversé » du magasin de Viktor & Rolf, SZI a de nouveau fait récemment sensation dans le monde entier.

El grupo SZI Design, en Ámsterdam, se formó en 1990 alrededor de su gerente Sherrie Zwail. Este grupo se ha especializado, sobre todo, en el asesoramiento, la planificación y la decoración de los espacios en los sectores comercial y privado. Ente sus clientes se encuentran marcas y bancos de prestigio internacional. Además del diseño de interiores, este equipo internacional crea también sus propios sistemas de iluminación, muebles y gráficos. Con el "diseño del revés" de la tienda Viktor & Rolf, SZI volvió a despertar recientemente un gran interés mundial.

Il gruppo SZI Design consolidatosi attorno alla figura di Sherrie Zwail (che ne è alla guida) si è costituito ad Amsterdam nel 1990, dando vita ad uno studio con focus particolare sulle attività di consulenza, progettazione e realizzazione di spazi destinati ad uso privato o commerciale. Fra i clienti dello studio figurano griffe e banche di caratura internazionale. Oltre all'architettura d'interni sono firmati dallo staff internazionale di SZI Design anche sistemi variabili di luce, mobili e progetti grafici. Con lo shop design della boutique "upsidedown" di Viktor & Rolf lo studio è tornato di recente alla ribalta internazionale.

Matteo Thun

Big names accompany the fortunes of the Italian designer. The aspiring architect studied with Oskar Kokoschka in Salzburg. After graduating in Florence, together with Ettore Sottsass, he founded the group Memphis, well known for its new design style. From 1984 onwards, Thun has been working under his own name at his own studio in Milan. His list of references reads like an international "Who is Who": Artemide, Bulgari, Illy, Swatch, Stoll, Villeroy & Boch, Rosenthal, etc. In 2004, Thun was nominated for the "Interior Design Hall of Fame" in New York.

Den Werdegang des italienischen Designers begleiten große Namen. So studierte der angehende Architekt bei Oskar Kokoschka in Salzburg. Nach Abschluss in Florenz gründete er mit Ettore Sottsass die Gruppe Memphis, bekannt für ihren neuen Stil im Design. Seit 1984 arbeitet Thun unter eigenem Namen und mit eigenem Büro in Mailand. Dessen Referenzliste liest sich wie ein internationales Who is Who: Artemide, Bulgari, Illy, Swatch, Stoll, Villeroy & Boch, Rosenthal, usw. 2004 wurde Thun für die „Interior Design Hall of Fame" in New York nominiert.

De grands noms jalonnent la carrière du designer italien. Ainsi l'architecte débutant a-t-il étudié chez Oskar Kokoschka à Salzbourg. A l'issue de ses études à Florence il a fondé avec Ettore Sottsass le groupe Memphis, bien connu pour son style innovant dans le design. Depuis 1984, Thun travaille sous son propre nom et dans sa propre agence à Milan. Sa liste de références ressemble à un Who is Who international : Artemide, Bulgari, Illy, Swatch, Stoll, Villeroy & Boch, Rosenthal, etc. En 2004, Thun a été nominé pour l'« Interior Design Hall of Fame » à New York.

La carrera profesional de este diseñador italiano está acompañada por grandes nombres. Realizó sus estudios con Oskar Kokoschka en Salzburgo. A su finalización en Florencia fundó con Ettore Sottsass el grupo Memphis, conocido por el novedoso estilo de su diseño. Desde 1984, Thun trabaja bajo su propio nombre y en su propio estudio en Milán. Su lista de referencias puede leerse como un "Quién es quién" internacional: Artemide, Bulgari, Illy, Swatch, Stoll, Villeroy & Boch, Rosenthal, etc. En 2004 Thun fue nominado para el "Interior Design Hall of Fame" (salón de la fama del diseño de interiores) en Nueva York.

L'evoluzione professionale del designer italiano è stata supportata dagli incontri con i grandi nomi dello star system del panorama artistico ed architettonico. L'aspirante architetto compie gli studi universitari a Salisburgo al seguito di Oskar Kokoschka. Dopo aver conseguito la laurea a Firenze, fonda con Ettore Sottsass il leggendario gruppo Memphis, noto per aver stravolto il mondo del design con l'introduzione di uno stile tutto nuovo. Dal 1984 Thun lavora a nome proprio nello studio con sede a Milano. La lista delle referenze assomiglia ad un internazionale Who is Who: Artemide, Bulgari, Illy, Swatch, Stoll, Villeroy & Boch, Rosenthal, ecc. Nel 2004 ha ricevuto la nomina per l'inserimento nella "Interior Design Hall of Fame".

tredup | hamann

Ulrich Tredup worked, among others, at Jacques Grange & Didier Aaron, Cie. in Paris, as well as at Mathias Thörner Design in Munich. In July 2000, the interior architect formed a partnership known as tredup hamann with architect, Bettina Hamann. In their Munich studio, they develop the design of interiors for retail outlets, offices, health-care practices, restaurants, cafés and private homes both at home and abroad. This includes design of exclusive furniture items as well as planning new and remodeled buildings, including listed buildings.

Ulrich Tredup arbeitete u. a. bei Jacques Grange & Didier Aaron, Cie. in Paris sowie bei Mathias Thörner Design in München. Der Interior Designer schloss sich im Juli 2000 mit der Architektin Bettina Hamann zur Partnerschaft tredup hamann zusammen. In ihrem Münchener Büro entwickeln sie die Gestaltung von Innenräumen für Geschäfte, Büros, Praxen, Restaurants, Cafés und Privathäuser im In- und Ausland. Dazu gehört der Entwurf von exklusiven Möbelstücken ebenso wie die Planung von Neu- und Umbauten, u. a. bei denkmalgeschützten Objekten.

Shop Design | 395

Ulrich Tredup a travaillé entre autres auprès de Jacques Grange & Didier Aaron, Cie à Paris ainsi que chez Mathias Thörner Design à Munich. En juillet 2000, cet architecte d'intérieur s'est associé avec l'architecte Bettina Hamann pour créer tredup hamann. Dans leur cabinet munichois ils conçoivent l'aménagement d'intérieurs de magasins, bureaux, cabinets médicaux, restaurants, cafés et résidences privées en Allemagne et à l'étranger. Leur travail porte aussi sur la création de meubles exclusifs et la planification de constructions neuves et de transformations, comme dans le cas de bâtiments classés monuments historiques.

Ulrich Tredup trabajo, entre otros, con Jacques Grange & Didier Aaron, Cie. en París y con Mathias Thörner Design en Munich. Este arquitecto de interiores se unió profesionalmente a la arquitecta Bettina Hamann en julio de 2000 y formaron el grupo tredup hamann. En su estudio muniqués desarrollaron la decoración de interiores de tiendas, despachos, consultas médicas, restaurantes, cafeterías y casas privadas dentro del ámbito nacional e internacional. A estos proyectos se les añade el diseño de exclusivos muebles y la planificación de edificios nuevos y reformados, entre ellos construcciones declaradas monumentos nacionales.

L'architetto d'interni Ulrich Tredup collabora dapprima presso diversi studi e gallerie, fra cui Jacques Grange & Didier Aaron, Cie. (Parigi) e Mathias Thörner Design (Monaco di Baviera). Dall'incontro con l'architetto Bettina Hamann nasce un sodalizio consolidato nello studio di Monaco di Baviera tredup hamann specializzato nella progettazione di interni per retail, uffici, ambulatori, ristoranti, caffè e residenze private, su scala nazionale ed internazionale. Completano il portfolio dello studio l'ideazione e la progettazione di mobili esclusivi nonché la progettazione architettonica di edifici nuovi e ristrutturati, con particolare attenzione agli immobili posti sotto la tutela dei beni culturali.

Universal Design Studio Ltd.

Edward Barber, Jay Osgerby and Jonathan Clarke direct the Universal Design Studio. The studio was launched in 2001 and includes a team of architects from interdisciplinary fields, interior specialists as well as product and graphic designers. In addition to large private estates completed in Spain, such as for Damien Hirst, other works include commissions for internationally respected brands and labels: shop designs for Paul Smith and Stella McCartney, as well as product designs for Authentics, Cappellini and Valli & Valli.

Das Universal Design Studio wird von Edward Barber, Jay Osgerby und Jonathan Clarke geführt. In dem 2001 gegründeten Studio versammeln sich interdisziplinär Architekten, Interieurspezialisten sowie Produkt- und Grafikdesigner. Zu großen privaten Residenzen, die in Spanien realisiert wurden, etwa für Damien Hirst, kommen weitere Arbeiten für weltweit angesehene Marken und Labels: Shopdesigns für Paul Smith und Stella McCartney, aber auch Produktgestaltungen für Authentics, Cappellini und Valli & Valli.

L'Universal Design Studio est dirigé par Edward Barber, Jay Osgerby et Jonathan Clarke. Dans ce cabinet fondé en 2001 se sont regroupés pour une pratique multidisciplinaire des architectes, des spécialistes d'intérieur et des designers de produits et de graphiques. Aux grandes résidences privées réalisées en Espagne, pour Damien Hirst par ex., s'ajoutent d'autres travaux pour des marques et des enseignes de réputation mondiale : designs de magasin pour Paul Smith et Stella McCartney mais aussi conceptions de produits pour Authentics, Cappellini et Valli & Valli.

El Universal Design Studio está dirigido por Edward Barber, Jay Osgerby y Jonathan Clarke. Fundado en 2001, en este estudio trabajan arquitectos interdisciplinarios, especialistas de interiores y diseñadores de productos y gráficos. A las grandes residencias privadas construidas en España, como por ejemplo para Damien Hirst, se les unen proyectos para marcas y tiendas de reconocimiento mundial: decoraciones para tiendas de Paul Smith y Stella McCartney y diseños de productos para Authentics, Cappellini y Valli & Valli.

Lo Universal Design Studio viene guidato da Edward Barber, Jay Osgerby e Jonathan Clarke. In virtù dell'approccio interdisciplinare a cui si ispira lo studio, fondato nel 2001, riunisce architetti, specialisti dell'architettura d'interni nonché product designer e designer grafici. Accanto alle grandi residenze private realizzate per esempio in Spagna per Damien Hirst figurano fra i progetti numerosi lavori svolti su commissione di prestigiosi marchi e griffe internazionali: progettazioni di shop design per Paul Smith e Stella McCartney ma anche di prodotti disegnati per Authentics, Cappellini e Valli & Valli.

Vincent Van Duysen Architects

The Belgian architect Vincent Van Duysen obtained his diploma in 1985 at the Higher Institute of Architecture in Ghent. From 1986 to 1987 he was assistant to Aldo Cibic at the Milan studio of Ettore Sottsass. In 1987, he launched Van Duysen as an independent architect and in 1990 he founded his own studio in Antwerp. Over the years, Van Duysen's style has become increasingly pronounced: simple forms and a sensual appeal, which are tangible both in his completed bank buildings as well as busy commercial rooms and private residences.

Der belgische Architekt Vincent Van Duysen erwarb sein Diplom 1985 an dem Higher Institute of Architecture in Gent. Von 1986 bis 1987 war er Assistent von Aldo Cibic im Mailänder Studio von Ettore Sottsass. 1987 startete Van Duysen als unabhängiger Architekt und gründete 1990 in Antwerpen ein eigenes Büro. Im Verlauf der Jahre bildete sich Van Duysens Stil zunehmend deutlicher heraus: einfache Formen und eine sensuelle Ansprache – spürbar sowohl in realisierten Bank- und Wohngebäuden als auch in vielfach frequentierten kommerziellen Räumen.

L'architecte belge Vincent Van Duysen a obtenu son diplôme en 1985 à l'Institut Supérieur d'Architecture de Gand. De 1986 à 1987 il a été l'assistant d'Aldo Cibic dans le cabinet milanais d'Ettore Sottsass. Il s'est lancé comme architecte libéral en 1987 et a créé son propre cabinet en 1990 à Anvers. Au fil des ans, le style de Van Duysen s'est de plus en plus affirmé : des formes simples et une approche sensuelle – sensibles tant dans les immeubles bancaires qu'il a réalisés que dans des espaces commerciaux très fréquentés et les résidences privées.

El arquitecto belga Vincent Van Duysen se licenció en 1985 en el Higher Institute of Architecture, en Gante. Entre 1986 y 1987 fue asistente de Aldo Cibic en el estudio milanés de Ettore Sottsass. En 1987, Van Duysen inició su actividad como arquitecto independiente y fundó su propio despacho en 1990 en Amberes. A lo largo de los años se fue perfilando el estilo Van Duysen: líneas sencillas y un lenguaje sensual, características ambas patentes tanto en los edificios de bancos que ha realizado como en los diversos espacios comerciales ampliamente frecuentados y residenciales.

L'architetto belga Vincent Van Duysen ha conseguito la laurea in architettura presso lo Higher Institute of Architecture di Gent nel 1985. Dal 1986 al 1987 è stato assistente di Aldo Cibic nello studio milanese di Ettore Sottsass. Nel 1987 ha iniziato la sua attività da libero professionista e nel 1990 ha creato un suo studio ad Antwerpen. Nel corso degli anni lo stile di Van Duysen è andato profilandosi con sempre maggior chiarezza: forme semplici ed un approccio sensuale, concreto tanto nella realizzazione di istituti bancari quanto dei più esposti spazi commerciali e residenziali.

Kelly Wearstler

American, Kelly Wearstler, and her design studio KWID count among the international leading designers of hotels, resorts, restaurants and boutiques. She has developed her unique style that is described as "Modern Glamour"—an aesthetic comprised of historically inspired room fittings, graphic patterns and textures. Her projects are illustrated in all the top international magazines on lifestyle and travel, as for example, recommended viewing at Hillcrest Estate, or the boutique-hotel Tides South Beach in Miami, Florida.

Shop Design | **397**

Die Amerikanerin Kelly Wearstler gehört mit ihrem Designstudio KWID zu den weltweit führenden Designern von Hotels, Resorts, Restaurants und Boutiquen. Dabei hat sie einen eigenen Stil geprägt, der als „Modern Glamour" bezeichnet wird – eine Ästhetik, die sich aus historisch inspirierten Raumausstattungen und graphischen Mustern und Texturen zusammensetzt. Ihre Projekte werden in allen international führenden Magazinen über Lifestyle und Reisen abgebildet, so zum Beispiel das sehenswerte Hillcrest Estate oder das Boutique-Hotel Tides South Beach in Miami, Florida.

Avec son agence de design KWID, l'Américaine Kelly Wearstler fait partie des plus grands designers au monde d'hôtels, de resorts, de restaurants et de magasins. Elle a imposé un style qui lui est propre, qualifié de « Glamour Moderne » – une esthétique qui allie des aménagements intérieurs d'inspiration historique et des textures et motifs graphiques. Ses projets sont reproduits dans tous les grands magazines spécialisés de Lifestyle et de voyages, comme par ex. le remarquable Hillcrest Estate ou l'hôtel Tides South Beach à Miami en Floride.

La americana Kelly Wearstler se encuentra, con su estudio de diseño KWID, entre los diseñadores más prestigiosos a nivel mundial de hoteles, *resorts*, restaurantes y tiendas. Es la creadora de su propio estilo denominado "glamour moderno"; una estética que se compone de diseños de espacios con inspiraciones históricas y dibujos y texturas gráficas. Sus proyectos aparecen en todas las revistas líderes internacionales sobre estilo de vida y viajes, como por ejemplo el notable Hillcrest Estate o el hotel boutique Tides South Beach en Miami, Florida.

L'americana Kelly Wearstler e il suo studio di design KWID occupano una posizione leader su scala internazionale nella progettazione di hotel, resort, ristoranti e boutique. Lo stile andatosi via via affermando si può definire "modern glamour": un senso estetico nato dalla sintesi fra le contestualizzazioni di ispirazione storica e tessuti e motivi grafici. Le opere realizzate trovano ampio spazio nella stampa specialistica internazionale nelle rubriche lifestyle e viaggi, come ad esempio i progetti Hillcrest Estate e il boutique-hotel Tides South Beach a Miami in Florida.

Isay Weinfeld

Isay Weinfeld, born in 1952 in São Paulo, graduated from Mackenzie University School of Architecture. After graduation, he continued to develop and extend his professional designs to furnishing and sets. He created stage sets for plays and musicals, writing and shooting several films himself. This love of complete sets is the trademark of his architecture. Isay Weinfeld has won many national awards. At the VI. Bienal de Design de Arquitetura de São Paulo, he finally made the breakthrough to the international scene.

Isay Weinfeld, 1952 in São Paulo geboren, absolvierte an der Mackenzie University die School of Architecture. Nach dem Studium folgten Jahre der Entwicklung, in denen er seine professionellen Entwürfe auf Möbel und Kulissen ausdehnte. Er entwarf Bühnenbilder für Theaterstücke und Musicals, schrieb und drehte selbst mehrere Filme. Diese Neigung zu kompletten Szenerien ist Markenzeichen seiner Architektur. National errang Isay Weinfeld damit viele Preise. Bei der VI. Bienal de Design de Arquitetura de São Paulo setzte er sich schließlich auch international durch.

Isay Weinfeld, né en 1952 à São Paulo, a effectué ses études au sein de l'Université Mackenzie à l'Ecole d'Architecture. Ont suivi ensuite quelques années de perfectionnement durant lesquelles ses projets professionnels ont porté sur les meubles et des décors. Il a conçu des décors de théâtre pour des pièces de théâtre et des comédies musicales, et a écrit et tourné lui-même plusieurs films. Cette attirance vers les scénarios complets est la griffe de son architecture. Cela a valu à Isay Weinfeld de nombreux prix dans son pays. Lors de la VI. Bienal de Design de Arquitectura de São Paulo il s'est finalement imposé au niveau international.

Isay Weinfeld, nacida en 1952 en San Paulo, realizó sus estudios de School of Architecture en la Mackenzie University. Después de su carrera siguieron años de desarrollo en los que amplió sus diseños a

398 | Shop Design

los muebles y los escenarios. Realizó proyectos escenográficos para obras de teatro y musicales, y escribió y rodó varias películas. Esta inclinación a la escenificación completa es característica de su arquitectura. Con este estilo Isay Weinfeld ha conseguido muchos premios nacionales. En la VI. Bienal de Design de Arquitetura de São Paulo obtuvo también el reconocimiento internacional.

Isay Weinfeld, nato nel 1952 a San Paolo, ha compiuto gli studi universitari alla School of Architecture della Mackenzie University. Negli anni successivi alla laurea è seguita la sperimentazione in cui la vocazione architettonica si è estesa alla progettazione professionale di mobili e contesti scenografici. È autore di scenografie per pièce teatrali e musical nonché autore e regista di numerosi film. La tendenza all'ideazione, progettazione e realizzazione dei contesti scenografici è il vero marchio di fabbrica dei progetti architettonici che portano il suo nome. Su scala nazionale essi gli hanno valso numerosi premi. Durante la sesta Bienal de Design de Arquitetura de São Paulo si è saputo imporre all'attenzione del pubblico internazionale sbaragliando la concorrenza.

Other Designpocket titles by teNeues:

African Interior Design 3-8238-4563-2
Airline Design 3-8327-9055-1
Asian Interior Design 3-8238-4527-6
Bathroom Design 3-8238-4523-3
Beach Hotels 3-8238-4566-7
Berlin Apartments 3-8238-5596-4
Boat Design 3-8327-9054-3
Café & Restaurant Design 3-8327-9017-9
Car Design 3-8238-4561-6
Cool Hotels Second Edition 3-8327-9105-1
Cool Hotels Africa/Middle East 3-8327-9051-9
Cool Hotels America 3-8238-4565-9
Cool Hotels Asia/Pacific 3-8238-4581-0
Cool Hotels Cool Prices 3-8327-9134-5
Cool Hotels Ecological 3-8327-9135-3
Cool Hotels Europe 3-8238-4582-9
Cool Hotels Romantic Hideaways 3-8327-9136-1
Cosmopolitan Hotels 3-8238-4546-2
Country Hotels 3-8238-5574-3
Food Design 3-8327-9053-5
Furniture Design 3-8238-5575-1
Garden Design 3-8238-4524-1
Italian Interior Design 3-8238-5495-X
Kitchen Design 3-8238-4522-5
London Apartments 3-8238-5558-1
Los Angeles Houses 3-8238-5594-8
Miami Houses 3-8238-4545-4
New Scandinavian Design 3-8327-9052-7
Pool Design 3-8238-4531-4
Product Design 3-8238-5597-2
Rome Houses 3-8238-4564-0
San Francisco Houses 3-8238-4526-8
Ski Hotels 3-8238-4543-8
Spa & Wellness Hotels 3-8238-5595-6
Sport Design 3-8238-4562-4
Staircase Design 3-8238-5572-7
Sydney Houses 3-8238-4525-X
Tropical Houses 3-8238-4544-6
Wine & Design 3-8327-9137-X

Each volume:

12.5 x 18.5 cm, 5 x 7 in.
400 pages
c. 400 color illustrations